Economics and Social Conflict

Also by Carl D. Mildenberger

DER ETHICS OFFICER IN AMERIKANISCHEN UNTERNEHMEN – Vorbild für Europa? (*2007*)

Economics and Social Conflict

Evil Actions and Evil Social Institutions in Virtual Worlds

Carl D. Mildenberger

palgrave
macmillan

Softcover reprint of the hardcover 1st edition 2013 978-1-137-28188-3

First published 2013 by
PALGRAVE MACMILLAN

Palgrave Macmillan in the UK is an imprint of Macmillan Publishers Limited, registered in England, company number 785998, of Houndmills, Basingstoke, Hampshire RG21 6XS.

Palgrave Macmillan in the US is a division of St Martin's Press LLC, 175 Fifth Avenue, New York, NY 10010.

Palgrave Macmillan is the global academic imprint of the above companies and has companies and representatives throughout the world.

Palgrave® and Macmillan® are registered trademarks in the United States, the United Kingdom, Europe and other countries

ISBN 978-1-349-44838-8 ISBN 978-1-137-28189-0 (eBook)
DOI 10.1057/9781137281890

This book is printed on paper suitable for recycling and made from fully managed and sustained forest sources. Logging, pulping and manufacturing processes are expected to conform to the environmental regulations of the country of origin.

A catalogue record for this book is available from the British Library.

A catalog record for this book is available from the Library of Congress.

Transferred to Digital Printing in 2013

Contents

List of Tables

List of Figures

Acknowledgements

Many people played a part in the writing of this book and I am glad that I can finally thank them in a formal way.

There are three people who contributed to this book beyond everything one could reasonably expect: Dennis Wiebusch, who not only compensated for my lack of programming skills necessary for evaluating the huge amounts of data but also sacrificed his Sunday mornings to do so; Nicolas Evans, who corrected the drafts over and over again and never lost his sense of humor in the process; and Anna, my wife, whose knowledge was incorporated into this book: I have never been so happy that she too studied economics.

Chrysostomos Mantzavinos is best characterized in German terms: He was a true 'Doktorvater' – the best I could ever imagine. He managed to discipline my stray thoughts without ever claiming that he was right (he always was). Furthermore, many thanks to Jens Harbecke, who assumed the role of a secondary reviewer and thus showed more openness and enthusiasm than many others. Finally, I want to thank Frank Tolsdorf, who convinced economists and philosophers alike how valuable a research subject video games can be.

Nico Wiebusch introduced me to virtual worlds and confirmed my first vague assumptions about them. Marco-Antonio Meyer suggested considering *EVE Online* in particular. Eyjólfur Guðmundsson not only responded favorably to my request to do economic research in a world where he is simultaneously central bank governor and minister of economic affairs but also invited me to Iceland where I met such amazing people as Pétur Jóhannes Óskarsson who greatly supported me by procuring and evaluating the data I needed. Without these people there would have been no story to tell.

For the past several years, René Boucsein has been my most important antagonist for every intellectual discussion there is. With his ideas and criticisms he contributed to this book just like Florian Walch, David Holzer, and Lara Luttmer.

And then, there is my family. My parents not only supported this endeavor long before the first page was written but also throughout the writing of every single page of this book – and especially when there seemed to be nothing to write about from time to time. Anna, during all this time you not only lovingly told me when to start working but most importantly when to stop and to do something sensible instead, like going for a walk or having a beer.

The author and publishers wish to thank the following for permission to reproduce copyright material: John Wiley, for figures 1, 3, 4, and 5, from J. Hirshleifer, 'The Bioeconomic Causes of War', *Managerial and Decision Economics*, Vol. 19, 457–466, Copyright © 1998; John Dupre (Ed.), *The Latest on the Best: Essays on Evolution and Optimality*, fig. 14.5, p. 319; fig. 14.6, p. 320, © 1987 Massachusetts Institute of Technology, by permission of The MIT Press; Chicago University Press, for figures 4.1 (p. 57) and 4.2 (p. 62), from J. Buchanan, *The Limits of Liberty – Between Anarchy and Leviathan*, Copyright © 1975. Every effort has been made to trace rights holders, but if any have been inadvertently overlooked the author would be pleased to make the necessary arrangements at the first opportunity.

List of Abbreviations

AGR curve	Anger/Gratitude Response curve
Alt-char	Alternative character; the second, usually less powerful character of some EVE-players (cf. 'Char')
CCP	CCP Games; the developer of *EVE Online*
CEO	Chief Executive Officer; the most powerful player in a corporation in *EVE Online*
Char	Character; the EVE-specific name for the avatar you control in the game
CONCORD	Consolidated Cooperation and Relations Command; EVE's virtual police
Corp	Corporation; a formal association of players in EVE
CSM	Council of Stellar Management; a democratically elected group of players that represents the views of the player base in front of CCP Games
Dev	Developer; one of the programmers of *EVE Online*
EK	Erratic kill; a kill without obvious reason
EVE	*EVE Online*; a massively multiplayer online role-play game
FW	Factional warfare; war between the four empires in EVE (role-play aspect of the game)
GDP	gross domestic product
GM	Game master; an employee of CCP Games who solves in-game conflicts between players
GUP	gross user product; the virtual equivalent to the GDP
hisec	High security space; a comparably safe area in the virtual universe of *EVE Online*
ICK	Intra-corporation kill; a kill in which attacker and perpetrator are in the same corporation
ISK	InterStellarKredit; the currency of *EVE Online*
lowsec	Low security space; an area of medium security in the virtual universe of *EVE Online*
MMORPG	Massively multiplayer online role-play game
NPC	Non-player character; a computer-controlled avatar
nullsec	Null security space; the most unsafe area in *EVE Online*

PK	Player kill; a kill involving at least one humanly controlled avatar as attacker
PLEX	30 Day Pilot License Extension; bought from CCP Games and a method to buy ISK for EUR, but also an in-game item that can be traded on the market
PvP	Player vs. player; means that players are not competing with software created enemies but with human opponents
RMSE	Root mean squared error
RMT	Real money trading; the illegal act of exchanging in-game currency for real world currency
SD	standard deviation
SG	Suicide gank; a kamikaze-tactic in EVE

1
Introduction

Could it be that poor countries are not caught in a *poverty trap* hindering development but in a *violence trap*? This is the important suggestion of the recent World Development Report entitled 'Conflict, Security, and Development' (The World Bank, 2011). Wide evidence is cited that countries affected by violence incur huge economic costs and therefore progress significantly less. Although the causal relationship between poverty and violence is ambiguous, the message is very clear: 'Violence threatens development' (The World Bank, 2011, p. 51). Talking about the effects of violence, however, the authors do not refer to 'classic' political violence like inter-state and civil wars – their importance has declined over the past 25 years. The problem of the 21st century is 'repeated cycles of violence' (The World Bank, 2011, p. 2): a recurring mixture of local political conflicts, organized crime, high murder rates, and low-intensity conflicts. It is not only nation-states and other political organizations that are responsible for violence with serious economic effects but also *individuals* and *small random groups* of people.

Despite this publication highlighting the severe consequences of violence and conflict for economic performance, until today, economic research on these issues is *of rather conciliatory nature*, when looking at the individual and questioning his motivations to enter conflict. There are economic theories on why rational actors are opting to fight for goods in anarchy – but these are intended to highlight why formal institutions should be put in place to overcome conflict (Buchanan, 1975/2000), or why the state of nature will be overcome eventually (Hirshleifer, 1995); thus, not focusing on individual actions. There are also economic theories on why it might be rational to harm others out of strategic reasons – namely to avoid being exploited by others in the long run (for example, Schelling, 1960, 1978). And finally, there are economic theories of human beings possessing other-regarding preferences that claim – backed up by tremendous amounts of empirical evidence from bargaining games played in experimental economics – that people are sometimes willing to impair the income of others out of fairness considerations or because of conditional reciprocity (for example, Fehr & Schmidt, 1999; Rabin, 1993). To summarize these viewpoints: people might harm others (and in economics this mostly means that they either steal their goods or impair their income) because they profit from doing so either in the short run or in the long run, and sometimes because they want to punish them for 'unfair' behavior.

Given these economic explanations of violence, conflict, and the reasons behind harming other people, how can one say that they are 'of rather conciliatory nature'? One way to defend this claim is to look at what psychology says when considering antisocial behavior, for example its description of *sadism*. 'Sadism is the technical term for *deriving enjoyment from inflicting harm* or pain on others' (Baumeister & Vohs, 2005, p. 96; emphasis by author). Sadists do not commit violence or harm others out of some interest for profit, let alone fairness considerations – they harm others to harm them. Violence is an end in itself for sadists. Another approach is to look at philosophy and the concept of *evil*. Kant for example claims that everybody possesses the propensity to act in an evil way and reasons about human actions out of pure evil will (Kant, 1793/2009, pp. 27–34). According to him, the goal of such vicious actions is not to become rich but *to act evilly for the sake of evil*. Given the concepts of sadism and evil, only covering violence under the header of stealing or strategic behavior in economics may very well seem 'conciliatory'. Maybe economics has not yet considered all aspects of human conflict behavior and it is not just profit/interests of fairness considerations that cause people to harm others. Given the importance of violence for economic performance, *the purpose of this book is to find out whether the existing economic theories and the empirical evidence on harm done are enough to explain why humans sometimes harm each other.* More precisely, it will be argued that *economics should integrate the concepts of economically evil actions and evil social institutions* when trying to explain why people are willing to spend money only to impair other people's property. In fact, given the long intellectual history of the concepts of sadism and especially of evil, it is surprising not to see any significant impact of these concepts in economics. This is even more surprising as only recently the normatively opposed concepts of altruism, fairness, and reciprocity have been acclaimed in economics thanks to the efforts of experimental and behavioral economists (for example, Camerer, 2003; Fehr & Schmidt, 1999; Kagel & Roth, 1995).

1.1 Evil actions and evil institutions

In the narrow sense, an economically evil action will be defined as *an action that intentionally harms another person materially – without the actor benefitting materially from it*. Only observable, material (mostly monetary) payoffs generated by actions shall be considered when judging if they are economically evil. In the broad sense, three kinds of economically evil actions will be distinguished:

- if the perpetrator harms another person materially but obtains a positive material payoff himself, this will be called an *egoistic action*;
- if the perpetrator's payoff is zero, this is defined as a *wanton action*; and
- people harming others materially, only to lose money themselves from this action, will be said to commit *malicious actions*.

Evidence for all three kinds of economically evil actions will be presented. The goal is to show that such economically evil actions do not only *exist* but that they do so *to a relevant extent* given the economic consequences they cause. In this respect, the book wants to contribute to the evidence on human behavior deviating from the classic idea of economic man (for example, Camerer, 2003; Kagel & Roth, 1995). *This is the first minimal goal of this book: to provide additional evidence on people impairing other people's income*. It will be achieved by introducing a new environment for microeconomic research besides experimental games: human behavior in online computer games, namely in *massively multiplayer online role-play games* (MMORPG) (see below). This approach grants a new perspective on established findings.

This book, however, will not focus solely on the *actors* committing economically evil actions but will also have a look at the *circumstances and external factors* of these actions. Following up on the findings of psychological situationism (for example, Doris, 2002) and New Institutional Economics (for example, Mantzavinos, 2001), it will be argued that instigating circumstances that typically lie beyond human responsibility are an important cause of economically evil actions. More specifically, this book's concept of *evil social institutions* is intended to highlight this cause of evil actions. Whereas institutions are normally said to be normative social rules that shape human interaction in order to overcome the Hobbesian problem of social order (Mantzavinos, 2001, p. 83), *evil* social institutions are defined as institutions that actively *foster* social conflict and that emerged spontaneously in an invisible hand process or as the result of conscious deliberation. *The second minimal goal of this book is thus to provide further evidence that turning the attention towards social institutions is important for giving an encompassing picture of what drives human behavior* – in short, that *evil formal and informal institutions exist and matter.*

Beyond the two minimal goals of showing that *evil actions and evil rules exist and matter,* there are two more ambitious goals to be pursued in this book. Regarding evil actions, while there are economic theories able to explain harming, these established theories are not able to capture all aspects of the behavior to be presented in the empirical part of the book. Evil actions as defined in this book are a phenomenon in its own right not yet fully treated theoretically and empirically in economics. The rather conciliatory theories of harming in economics have to be adapted in order to integrate the new empirical evidence to be presented – *some people committing evil actions are motivated by what seems to be a 'taste for harming'.* Regarding evil rules, it will be claimed that this kind of social institution does not only exist and matter but that it is here to stay. *Although publicly known for fostering social conflict, some evil social institutions are able to persist in a society that generally possesses an adaptive institutional framework.* The theory that – in an evolutionary process – those rules not contributing to mitigation of the effects of social conflict will be replaced by more effective rules eventually (for example, North, 2005) might have to be adapted.

1.2 The research object: an 'MMORPG'

Even if there is no lack of empirical evidence on hatred, appropriation, confiscation, and wars all around the world, probably a part of the suggested underestimation of phenomena like sadism and evil in economics is due to the fact that empirical research on these concepts is rather complicated. Thinking of the ethical considerations arising when planning a laboratory experiment on people intentionally harming each other makes this point very clear. Given these concerns, a more suitable environment for conducting research on economically evil actions and evil social institutions in particular – but also for empirical research in the social sciences in general – are *virtual* environments, as provided for example by online computer games. Players join and leave these environments at will, and there is no supervisor telling them what to do. Massively multiplayer online role-play games are a 'new paradigm in computer gaming' (Yee, 2006, p. 313), the oldest ones only dating back to the 1990s. MMORPGs can be defined as computer games played online by thousands of concurrent users. They feature persistent virtual worlds existing independently of the individual player – typically themed as fantasy or science-fiction worlds – in which the players role-play their avatars. Not only do players identify with their avatar and try to advance her in game but also MMORPGs are inherently social games in which cooperating is essential for success and in which stable communities of players and distinct social institutions evolve.

The biggest advantage of MMORPGs compared to the real world is that, although they are complex, they are less complex than the real world. They are more *controllable* (because they are digital: everything you do is recorded), *smaller* (only thousands of inhabitants compared to around 100 million people for a medium-sized country), more *restricted* (they still feature less possible actions for the users than real life offers), and *younger* (typically less than ten years old) compared to real societies. MMORPGs allow for observing 100 percent of the players' actions and for huge, more representative samples with comparably low effort. *They are more complex, 'noisier' than laboratory experiments and yet stay manageable. They allow for doing fieldwork and for easier integration of social institutions into the examination* – both aspects being paramount when conducting research on human morality.

The virtual world of choice for this book will be the massively multiplayer online role-play game *EVE Online* (EVE), which was published by CCP Games in May 2003. The data basis of the empirical part is the server data of this science-fiction game. Around 66GB of data in the form of huge spreadsheets encompasses practically everything the 390,000 active players did in the month of January 2011. To my knowledge, this is the first time that *microeconomic research in virtual worlds has been conducted by analyzing the unmediated server data* instead of relying solely on personal playing experience, in-depth interviews with players and developers, or other qualitative data. The purpose of this book is therefore not only to provide new insights into human behavior but also to present a new method of doing research in the social sciences. *What* is found is as important as *how* it was found.

1.3 The structure of the book

The structure of this book is twofold, comprising a theoretical part (Chapters 2 to 4) and an empirical part (Chapters 5 to 9). Chapter 2 features two primers, one focusing on the existing philosophical literature on evil, the other one on the established psychological findings. The most important goal of this chapter is to clarify the conceptual roots of the terminology of evil actions and evil rules and to review the findings of two disciplines that have been examining evil substantially longer than economics. The distinction between moral evil (highlighting the actor's responsibility for the evil she commits) and natural evil (referring to external factors and the instigating circumstances for evil actions) will be of particular importance. Philosophical authors as diverse as Leibniz, Kant, and Arendt and opposing views on evil in psychology (virtue theory, situationism, evolutionary theories) will be presented.

Chapter 3 will then establish the genuinely economic foundations to talk about economically evil actions and evil social institutions. It starts by outlining how economically evil actions are defined in this book and why they are defined that way. This section is followed by reviews of the existing economic literature on phenomena related to evil as well as of some empirical evidence touching on the issue. Three different approaches able to explain why human beings sometimes are willing to harm other people – and to even spend money to achieve this – will be described. It will be argued that economists tend to underestimate the importance of evil actions, since they do not treat them as a phenomenon in its own right. The second half of Chapter 3 is devoted to the concept of evil social institutions. Their characteristics and how they could possibly have emerged will be set out.

In the following chapter, the focus shifts from examining the theoretical economic foundations of evil and will turn to the theoretical foundations of the research object: massively multiplayer online role-play games. To begin with, Chapter 4 extensively defines what an MMORPG is, as many readers may not be familiar with the research object. The second part of the chapter will highlight the advantages and limitations of doing research in virtual worlds and the third part will touch on the proper methodological approach to do so. Notably it will be asked whether human playing behavior is at all relevant for explaining behavior in economic contexts and whether the online behavior of players closely mirrors their offline behavior. Furthermore, the exact structure of the underlying data of this book is presented, followed by a discussion on whether the concepts of formal and informal institutions are applicable to virtual worlds at all. The line of argument in Chapter 4 is the first part of the effort to establish MMORPGs as a valid field of research in the social sciences; the second part being the practical example of such research given in the empirical part.

Chapter 5 is the first chapter of the empirical part. It features a short introduction to *EVE Online* (EVE). It will try to explain how it feels to play the game as well as delving more deeply into the microeconomic and macroeconomic aspects of this virtual world.

Chapter 6 is the first chapter in a series of three in which the server data granted by *CCP Games* – the developers of EVE – will be evaluated in depth. Like the two following chapters, it targets very precise phenomena in the game, namely piracy and ransoming, as examples of economically evil actions. Piracy and ransoming in EVE are examples for egoistic and wanton actions, respectively. The section on ransoming is accompanied by a discussion of the evil moral rule governing this behavior.

The second and third chapters in the series are Chapters 7 and 8. The subject of Chapter 7 is 'suicide ganks'. Suicide ganks are examples of malicious actions and the description of their effects is complemented by the overview of how the evil formal rule allowing for suicide ganking has emerged and persisted over the years. Chapter 8 treats wars in *EVE Online*. Without focusing too much on the evil action that war signifies, the evil formal rules allowing for war and other instigating circumstances of evil will be highlighted.

Chapter 9 presents the setup and findings of a simple experiment conducted in EVE. In an effort to replicate a dictator game as known from experimental economics, players of EVE were made to believe that they were accidentally endowed with a sum of money and kindly asked to give it back (NB: there is no possible way using in-game measures to force a player to give the money back). Although this experiment is not a perfect virtual analogy to laboratory dictator games, it addresses 'altruism' in EVE, that is the phenomenon which dictator games are typically said to measure.

The book ends in a *Conclusion*. The *Glossary of EVE terms* provides further material as to facilitate the understanding of the arguments of this book.

2
Introducing Moral Evil and Natural Evil

2.1 A philosophical primer

Philosophy is one of the disciplines that have been examining evil for hundreds of years. When looking for a human 'taste for harming' and for answers to the question in which terms to discuss evil, philosophy definitely has a say. It is however impossible to review all the relevant literature about evil in philosophy and adjacent sciences as numerous books have been written on this topic (e.g., Colpe & Schmidt-Biggemann, 1993; Neiman, 2004; Schulte, 1988). The only way to proceed is hence to pick the most prominent authors who *explicitly* thought about the notion of evil: Gottfried Wilhelm Leibniz, Immanuel Kant, and Hannah Arendt. Leibniz and Arendt are both authors that got confronted with a 'stereotypical' evil with respect to their time and thus illustrate well the changes the notion of evil undergoes in the course of the centuries. In addition, Kant has an important say in this context, being the most influential modern moral philosopher.

The main purpose of this primer is to show how the concepts of *moral evil* and *natural evil* emerged and developed in philosophical thought. This is important since later on, it will be argued that *economically evil actions* are an instance of moral evil, whereas *evil social institutions* are an example of natural evil.

2.1.1 Leibniz

Evil, originally, is often thought to be a theological rather than a philosophical problem. 'How could a good God create a world in which so many innocent people have to suffer?' is one of the traditional formulations of the *problem of evil*. Leibniz's immediate successors were confronted with the problem of evil after the earthquake of Lisbon in

1755. On November 1, 1755, the Great Lisbon Earthquake, followed by a tsunami and fires, devastated the Portuguese capital and killed between 10,000 and 100,000 people. For most of the contemporary witnesses it was clear that something evil had happened, and indeed the news of the earthquake troubled the thoughts of the authors of the upcoming Enlightenment all over Europe (Neiman, 2004, p. 23). In this context, Leibniz's undertaking was to show that comparable evil events are compatible with the goodness of God and that our world is in fact the best of all possible worlds. He coined the term *theodicy* for this project (Leibniz, 1710/1996). There are lots of logical and empirical aspects of the problem of evil (cf. Murray, 2008; Tooley, 2010); but Leibniz's definition of evil and his project to show that evil is a necessary part of the best of all possible worlds are interesting to set out in the light of this book.

To begin with, consider his distinction between three kinds of evil: *metaphysical evil, natural evil,* and *moral evil* (Leibniz, 1710/1996). The first refers to the finiteness of the substances from which our world is made; for example, whereas God created the matter from which all things are made, he did not create the forms as well. The latter are subordinate to the laws of reason and God was only able to choose the best-working combination of them. Natural evil refers to all the physical pain and sufferings a person has to tolerate in the course of her life, like for example being injured in the Great Lisbon Earthquake. The category of moral evil consists of all criminal and immoral actions humans are capable of, because of free will. The exact nature of criminal or immoral has to be judged against the background of Christian behavioral rules for Leibniz.

Leibniz would have thought of the Lisbon earthquake as natural evil. Nowadays, it sounds odd to use the term evil with respect to an earthquake; it might be called 'horrible', or a 'catastrophe', since the term evil currently first and foremost serves to qualify human actions, not natural disasters (Merriam-Webster, 2005). 'Sin' (that is moral evil) and physical suffering (that is natural evil) have become separate things. Not so for Leibniz. *For him, natural and moral evil are closely linked.* He even argues that there is a causal relationship tying them together and that natural evil only exists because of moral evil, for example because of the fall of man, that is the first moral evil ever committed (Leibniz, 1710/1996). There would be no natural evil such as earthquakes or diseases if there had not been any moral evil prior to it. If his readers do not see that moral evil and natural evil are actually linked, this is only because they have not yet figured out the exact underlying mechanism – but the progress of sciences will eventually prove this link to everybody, says Leibniz. The link is so obvious for Leibniz that he does not bother to further explain his reasoning (Neiman, 2004).

Leibniz seems to be very lenient when judging evil. Suffering itself is necessary for an even greater good (read: It all makes sense), since we live in the best of all possible worlds (Leibniz, 1710/1996). God was able to choose from a plethora of possible worlds and chose the best one following the rules of reason. Humans miss the big picture of it all. Everything and every coincidence in this world is linked. If possessing the divine calculus, it could be proven that other worlds are possible but less desirable; however, only God is capable of intellectually managing the complexity of other possible worlds with myriad other things and coincidences. Leibniz actually thought of the differential calculus that he developed simultaneously to Newton to be a step in the right direction: It enables the determination of *optima* mathematically. Moral evil and natural evil cause harm and Leibniz acknowledges that; but at least they are theoretically understandable. An even worse world would be one in which there is no rational link between moral and natural evil and in which God decides in arbitrary acts how to punish misdeeds. It is a question of *justice* that natural evil exists and that there is a causal link: Those who live a modest and faithful life will be rewarded with less painful experiences. What Leibniz calls evil is rather comparable to the radical cure of a benevolent doctor: It is very unpleasant but every alternative would be even worse (Neiman, 2004, p. 79). And if every evil action is inevitably followed by a punishment, one could assess evil rather as a pedagogic warning than as real ill. Economists, who may be inclined to qualify Leibniz's idea of a causal link between the different evils and its necessity for an optimal world as 'metaphysical gibberish' and 'outdated ideology', should not be too rash in their judgment. Adam Smith's way of linking morally questionable actions (the egoism of the butcher) to a greater good (that is greater social welfare) by the mechanism of the 'invisible hand' (1776/1999, p. 32) is just too closely related.

2.1.2 Kant

As in his epistemological reasoning, Kant turns towards the individual in his thinking about evil, too. Following Rousseau, he reduces the role of a punishing God, places the responsibility for evil on the shoulders of humans, and *is more often concerned with moral evil than with natural evil* (Neiman, 2004, pp. 73–113).

According to Kant (1788/1974, 1793/2009) the moral law is a fact known to everybody. Whenever facing a morally challenging situation (e.g., 'Should I lie to my boss?') it is clear what ought to be done. Kant defines that we act *morally* if we act out of pure respect for the objective moral law and if we choose subjective maxims, that is the rules that guide human actions, autonomously and accordingly (Kant, 1788/1974). To see if the maxims fulfill the criterion of complying with the moral law, one has to check them using the categorical imperative. The imperative is a 'compass' (Kant, 1788/1974, p. 31) that facilitates distinguishing between what is good and what is evil. In this context, Kant defines *moral evil* as the reason for the deviation of an individual's maxims from the moral law (Kant, 1793/2009, p. 31). Kant thus proposes a formal definition of evil compared to Leibniz's material one. An evil person, then, is somebody aware of the moral law who nevertheless chooses maxims that deviate from it (Kant, 1793/2009, p. 35). In the end, all the individual deviations from the moral law lead to a world that is no longer the best of all possible worlds. Evil, therefore, should be actively fought.

With everybody knowing the moral law and having the categorical imperative to check maxims, the question remains why humans behave in evil ways sometimes. Kant terms the reason why one may deviate from the moral law 'radical evil' (Kant, 1793/2009, p. 35) and says that it is a part of everybody. He explains that whereas humans have the *disposition* to act in a good way, they also have the *propensity* to act in an evil way (1793/2009, pp. 27–34); he distinguishes between the two concepts saying that a disposition is something 'original' (a constituting part of human nature) whereas a propensity is 'contingent' (Kant, 1793/2009, p. 30) in the sense that human beings, in principle, are conceivable without having this propensity.

For him, there are three theoretical levels of corruption of humans' natural and original disposition to the good (or the self-chosen maxims, respectively); these correspond to the reasons why they behave in an evil way. First, one may do something evil because of the *frailty* of human nature. If one only respects the moral law when *setting* maxims, but is too weak and always succumbs to self-love in the situations in which one should *act* according to them, frailty is the reason of evil. The second level of corruption is *impureness*: People may do something evil because the maxim that guides their behavior is not purely motivated by the moral law but rather is a *mixture* between respect of the law and self-love. Such actions may seem good at first glance (for example a merchant using correctly adjusted scales) but should not be judged as being good (because some merchants may do so out of the fear of losing customers, if they find out that he does not use correct scales). The maxim of the merchant to 'Always use correctly adjusted scales!' is corrupted by impureness in this case, because it is not his only goal to abide by the moral law but also to retain customers and make profit. The third level is *viciousness*: To completely disregard the moral law in maxim-formation and to purely apply self-love or any other depraved motive as the guiding principle. Examples are actions out of pure evil will (Kant, 1793/2009, pp. 31–33).

Kant does not put it past man to really act out of pure evil will, that is he instantly rejects the most pure form of corruption of the maxims as a possibility for human beings. In the same way that he does not put it past man to always abide by the moral law or to have a perfect good will all the time (that is to be God with respect to moral issues), Kant does not put it past man to be the devil either (1793/2009, pp. 38–39). For him, people do not just reject the moral law in an act of rebellion. Because of man's innate disposition to the good, the law always imposes itself on him and he would always act morally if it were not for the other incentives (self-love, physical needs) that guide his behavior as well. Kant's conviction of man's fundamental goodness is so strong that he even deems him worthy of practicing an *imitatio Dei*. This is precisely what one does when testing maxims with the categorical imperative: Reasoning how desirable a world with autonomously chosen universal laws would be. Kant allows man to do what Leibniz reserves to God, that is to imagine and choose the best of all possible worlds. The individual bears a lot more responsibility for evil in Kant's eyes compared to Leibniz. Yet his 'radical evil' (1793/2009, p. 35) only refers to the propensity to lawless maxims of the free will, not to some inherent diabolical trait.

> The human being (even the best) is evil only because he reverses the moral order of the incentives in admitting them into his maxims: he does indeed admit the moral law into his maxims, alongside the law of self-love; but when he becomes aware that one cannot subsist alongside the other, but that one must be subordinated to the other as its supreme condition, he makes the incentive of self-love and its inclinations the condition of compliance with the moral law – whereas, on the contrary, the latter should be admitted into the universal maxim of the power of choice as the *supreme condition*

> of the gratification of the former and as the sole incentive. (Kant, 1793/2009, p. 40)

Humans are frail and they are dishonest and impure from time to time; thus they act in evil ways. Still, they try hard to do their best, according to Kant. Man's most serious vice is his self-love, that is the propensity to argue against the objective laws of duty (Kant, 1788/1974, p. 32) and the trial to make his own subjective reasons the objective reasons of will in general (Kant, 1788/1974, p. 194). Kant states very clearly that no reasonable being could ever act in an evil way for the pure sake of evil: He who does that is in contradiction with himself, in contradiction with his own reason, and consequently has to despise himself.

In the 'Critique of pure reason' Kant (1781/2000a, 1781/2000b) argues that traditional metaphysics was unable to solve many of the problems it posed, since an answer would have had to go beyond the frontiers of human knowledge. Whereas Leibniz postulated a causal link between moral evil and natural evil, and thus gave a meaning to evil in the big picture, *Kant radically denies this link. With Kant, the problem of evil becomes structurally insolvable because only humans have ends and intentions, but not nature.* Nature does not punish somebody with an earthquake in order to restore justice; it inflicts harm without any intention behind it. For Kant, unlike Leibniz, one cannot actually talk of natural *evil* but only of natural *ill*, since earthquakes lack an evil human will. Neiman (2004, p. 112) thinks that the biggest difference between Leibniz and Kant is that the former believes that human knowledge is principally limitless and that it is only a question of time until science finds the link between the different kinds of evil, whereas the latter sees ignorance concerning many important points as part of human nature. Man will never know the link between moral evil and natural evil. This does not hinder Kant in acknowledging the human desire that the two should be linked – that is that good behavior may be rewarded and bad behavior punished. In short, that there is justice. According to Kant (1788/1974), whenever somebody says 'this should not have happened' she does not only mean that something evil happened, for example an innocent suffering, but also that evil behavior and punishment should be linked and that one should be the reason for the other.

Kant takes away the hope of ever grasping the link between moral evil and natural evil. Rather peculiarly and unlike Leibniz he also thinks that this is a good thing after all. If the mechanism that links good behavior to rewards as well as evil behavior to punishment were known, this would have a devastating effect on human morality. All of a sudden, no action would be any longer motivated by the pure incentive to respect the law but always also by calculations of self-love. If man knew exactly the consequences of his actions, only some saints would act without coldly calculating their own advantage; there would be no longer any place for pure good will (Kant, 1788/1974). And with good will the possibility of morality also vanishes. The concept of human freedom presupposes constraints for Kant: To act freely is to act without perfect information about the future; the fact that one does not know if good intentions are rewarded is the condition for their existence (Kant, 1788/1974; Neiman, 2004). If there are any incentives that guide behavior except for the respect of the law, or if the consequences of actions are considered, they can never be judged morally good. One is acting in an evil way if one is acting weighing benefits and disadvantages (which implies that one knows them in advance). Calculations of personal profit are all that distinguish the good merchant using correctly adjusted scales from the evil merchant using correctly adjusted scales (Kant, 1788/1974, p. 23). Man believes that moral evil and natural evil should be linked, but this belief is not knowledge 'and, hail us! that it is not.' (Kant, 1972, p. 1083).

2.1.3 Arendt

For the scientific discourse about evil, the events that took place at Auschwitz played a comparable role for contemporary philosophy as the Great Lisbon Earthquake did for modern philosophy, although the former was a moral and the latter a natural evil in Leibniz's terms (Neiman, 2004). Philosophers struggled in their optimism and were unable to explain how incidents like these were compatible with any faith in the power of human reason or the reasonability of the world as a whole. Whereas Kant firmly believed that humans are not capable of being truly devilish, of committing evil out of a pure evil will, Arendt seems to be empirically confronted with precisely this situation. She writes:

> Yet, in their effort to prove that everything is possible, totalitarian regimes have discovered without knowing it that there are crimes which men can neither punish nor forgive. When the impossible was made possible it became the unpunishable, unforgivable absolute evil which could no longer be understood and explained by the evil motives of self-interest, greed, covetousness, resentment, lust for power, and cowardice. (Arendt, 1951/1973, p. 459)

Arendt shares Kant's opinion that humans are not devils. But what kind of consolation does this insight offer, when people commit such horrible crimes? This is precisely Arendt's question with respect to evil: She is not interested in talking about 'usual criminals' (1965/2007a, p. 23) that harm and kill because of self-interest or eagerness for power (that is offenders of the type Kant described); but she wants to know how seemingly ordinary people can act in morally outrageous ways. Because of her findings, Arendt rejects the Kantian notion of a radical evil in human nature: 'evil is always only extreme, but never radical, it does not possess either depth or a demonic nature' (Arendt, 1989, p. 78; author's translation). In the light of the crimes of World War II, Arendt qualifies evil as being *banal* (1963/2007b, p. 371).

Arendt defines evil as something of which one says that 'it should never have happened' (1965/2007a, p. 17). It is characteristic that evil often lies beyond the typical discussions of morality and ethics, because it creates a state of speechless horror that mutes all arguments. The biggest evil is such that has been committed by *nobody*, by human beings that refuse to be persons, and that consequently can neither be *punished* nor *forgiven* (Arendt, 1965/2007a, p. 101). Such evil is committed by ordinary men – not by sadists – that turned into perpetrators only because they did what they had been told to do. These ordinary men can be said to be *nobody*, because they are not 'persons' according to the definition of Arendt. The perpetrators refuse to be persons, because they refuse to think for themselves and are not able to remember what they did (1965/2007a, pp. 92–102). 'The biggest culprits are those that do not remember, because they have never given a thought to what they did, and without memory nothing can hold them back' (Arendt, 1965/2007a, p. 77). It is difficult to *punish* such evil – it seems as if it is rather the anonymous system these men served that is blameworthy. It is impossible to *forgive* such acts of evil, because you can only forgive a person but never a certain act or a set of institutions that led to the crime. For Arendt, it is the reluctance to think for oneself or to render a judgment, the indifference towards your own actions, that is responsible for the worst evils in history – there are no human motives (like Kantian self-love) or understandable incentives that lead there. It is not narcissists or sadists that are dangerous, but ordinary people that execute orders according to rules: 'Therein lies the horror of evil, and its banality at the same time' (Arendt, 1965/2007a, p. 150).

With the notion of the banality of evil, Arendt strongly contradicts the everyday perception that abidance by the generally accepted moral rules is enough to do no evil. According to her, such thinking goes back to religious traditions in which every deviation from supposedly God-given rules was a sin (Arendt, 1965/2007a, pp. 32–33). But Arendt is confronted with the *paradox that moral rules can actually foster evil behavior*: Whereas *not following* social rules might be bad, more and bigger evil has been done by people who *unconsciously followed* rules. *Maybe the overall problem with evil is not people consciously committing* moral evils *but rather non-persons abiding by rules*. Decisions have to be based on conscious cognitive processes in order not to fall prey to the banality of evil. *In this context, rules can be said to be a form of* natural evil. Not in the sense of Leibniz's *malum naturale* but in Kant's sense of something causing harm and yet external to human beings, something without proper ends or intentions, something they did not craft personally, something already there, something they are not actively responsible for.[1]

Arendt concedes two problems with her rule-critical position: First, it is very unlikely to make every member of society think and judge for himself. And only if that were possible could a society do completely without rules. Second, the exact same activity – the individual, conscious critique of established rules – makes good people better and evil people worse (Arendt, 1965/2007a, p. 90). In a constant state of critique, good people might be able to prevent a lot of banal evil from happening, because many everyday rules may prove to be imperfect on closer inspection. In that same state, however, bad people might be inclined to throw overboard even the last remaining decency and morality. This is especially true as Arendt does not share Kant's conviction that everybody has a well-functioning moral compass that reliably teaches right from wrong: 'nobody can claim any longer that moral things go without saying' (Arendt, 1965/2007a, p. 26). It is the very function of moral rules to provide a short cut to extensive thinking; if there is a rule guiding a certain action, you do not have to get creative yourself to solve a problem (Mantzavinos, 2001). With respect to evil, says Arendt, this benefit of rules has to be weighed very carefully against the potential moral pitfalls caused by rule-following behavior.

Arendt denounces the efforts taken from Socrates to Kant to doubt the inherent badness of man (Arendt, 1965/2007a, pp. 42–44). Until Nietzsche, nobody even speaks of the sin of *sadism*; it is lacking in the catalogues and lists of human perversions. She gives the telling example of Thomas Aquinas who speaks of the joy of those in paradise when watching the suffering of those burning in hell – he quickly states that they do not enjoy the pain of the damned as such but as a proof of divine justice (Aquinas, n.d., lib. 4, d. 50, q. 2, a. 4, qc. 3).

Arendt unmasks these overly optimistic ideas of human nature. There are human beings who do evil things out of pleasure, who do evil for the sake of evil (that is sadists), and there also are people who do evil things out of indifference. That Arendt judges the latter to be the greater danger – because real sadists are rare but the thoughtless exist in abundance – is her lesson from Auschwitz.

2.2 A psychological primer

Compared to philosophy, social psychology is a much younger discipline and so are its efforts to examine evil – yet there is a surprisingly analogous discussion about the nature of evil and the question of the predominance of moral or natural evil. The most important difference between the two disciplines is probably that social psychology chooses a much more positive approach to the phenomenon: Observable human behavior as opposed to normative questions.

Zimbardo defines evil as 'intentionally behaving, or causing others to act, in ways that demean, dehumanize, harm, destroy, or kill innocent people' (2005, p. 22). It is a behaviorally focused definition, in which motivations and intentions play a huge rule, and that stresses the negative outcomes for a third party. In a very similar way, Staub defines evil as 'intensely harmful actions, which are not commensurate with instigating conditions, and the persistence or repetition of such acts. A series of actions also can be evil when any one act causes limited harm, but with repetition, these cause great harm' (1999, p. 180). He stresses the role of the actor by clearly distinguishing it from the instigating circumstances (for example rules guiding behavior) and the fact that many small harms can also lead to an outcome qualifying as evil. Speaking from an evolutionary perspective, Duntley and Buss define evil as 'behavioral dispositions that result in a massive imposition of fitness costs on another individual or group' (2005, p. 104), but also state that intention plays an important role: 'It is not enough that some entity is costly to one's fitness. The entity must desire, or be perceived to desire, to inflict those costs' (2005, p. 112).

Very close to the notion of evil, sometimes used interchangeably, is the notion of *aggression*. Anderson and Carnagey (2005, p. 168) simply label the most extreme forms of aggression as evil. Lorenz (1963/1998) sees aggression as an inherent drive – that can be found in humans as well as in many other animals – that leads to violent conflict between two parties. For him, aggression is a cause of intentional harm-doing. Staub (2005) argues along the same lines and defines aggression as the motivation for harming others. He distinguishes between hostile aggression (desire to harm), instrumental aggression (aggression as a means to an end), and defensive aggression (self-protection from violence) (2005, p. 67).

What unifies all these definitions of evil and aggression is the *emphasis on intentional human actions that cause harm to other people.* Beyond this common ground, however, one of the main questions in social psychology is whether the term evil is sometimes used too loosely and too soon thus making evil something ordinary and mundane (Berkowitz, 1999; Miller, 2005). It is not clear whether one can extend the meaning of evil beyond acts like torture, genocide, or rape to the simple obedience of rules in conditions of hierarchical organization. Arendt's notion of the banality of evil was influential in this respect. Berkowitz (1999) pleads for recognition of different degrees of evil to solve such problems. Miller (2005) sees it as one of the characteristics of social psychology to somehow link the ideas of *evil* and *ordinary*, because the discipline focuses on the behavior of most people rather than on the actions of some truly sadistic or hateful people. Using the term evil in ordinary situations could prove to be a dangerous trivialization close to a theodicy; yet, on the other hand, it might be grossly negligent to reserve the term for the most outrageous crimes, because 'learning about why people break promises can tell us something about why people commit mass murder' (Baumeister, 1997, p. 9).

Two questions concerning evil are predominant in social psychology: (1) Who are the perpetrators? (2) What are the root causes for evil? These two questions will structure the rest of this chapter.

2.2.1 Who are the perpetrators?

Many social psychologists believe that internal dispositional factors play a determinant role for evil behavior (e.g., Berkowitz, 1999; Funder & Ozer, 1983; Newman, 2002; Sabini et al, 2001). These authors typically do not totally negate the influence of situational and environmental factors but see the actors' lacking moral traits and virtues as the dominant causes: Those who do evil *are* evil. On the other hand, situationist authors like Zimbardo criticize this 'rush to the dispositional' (2005, p. 23). He claims that the bias towards personal factors is due to individualistic societies, in which people are individually praised for their achievements as well as blamed for their misdeeds. The fact that the legal, medical, educational, and religious systems in Western societies all are founded on principles of individualism should not blur the scientific view, however (Zimbardo, 2005, p. 25). Situationists do not trace back evil and aggression to the psyches of disturbed people but highlight the effects of situational and ecological variables like time pressure or obedience, as well as stressing the potentially negative consequences of the interplay of circumstances and the heuristics built-in in human brains (Doris, 2002; Gigerenzer, 2008; Gigerenzer et al, 1999; Milgram, 1974; Sosa, 2009; Zimbardo, 2005). Miller states that there is 'considerable empirical evidence, that personal or dispositional factors are frequently very weak predictors of behavior, even though they are *erroneously* perceived to be the key determinant of individuals' behavior. Moreover, the lay observer frequently underestimates the impact of situational forces on behavior' (Miller, 2005, p. 2). Ross coined the term 'fundamental attribution error' (1977, p. 185) for this phenomenon. A good overview of the discussion between virtue theory and situationism can be found in Sosa (2009) and Doris (2002). Using the philosophical terms introduced above one can rephrase the discussion's central question as: 'Which type of evil plays the predominant role in the world around us: moral evil or natural evil?'

The ongoing discussion between the defenders of virtue theory and situationists is not the only reason why a clear view on the perpetrators may be blurred. Baumeister and Vohs (2005) wonder why there are many violent and harmful acts all over the world while hardly anyone sees himself as an evil perpetrator. Where does all the evil come from if there are no evil people around? They argue that the question should rather be rephrased to 'Why do some people do things that others will regard as evil?' (2005, p. 85) – since what they find is that the degree of distortion of a story about an evil act is almost identical for victims and perpetrators. Whereas the former try to convey the picture that something truly outrageous and outstandingly cruel happened to them, the latter downplay the importance of the event illegitimately and present themselves as ordinary people. For example, victims tend to intensely describe the background of a certain 'evil' act; all the events that lead to it as well as all of the consequences it had (that mostly extend to the present time, according to them). The perpetrators on the other hand typically only describe the event itself, do not see any serious consequences of their actions, and tend to tell happy endings:

> Whereas the victim would say something like 'After the episode, I could never trust my roommate again, and our friendship is mostly over,' the perpetrator stories would tend to end with 'After the episode, we made up and now we are even better friends than we were back then'. (Baumeister & Vohs, 2005, p. 87)

When it comes to the reason for evil behavior, victims emphasize the lack of a valid reason for aggression, whereas the perpetrators present their actions as legitimate or at least understandable (Baumeister & Vohs, 2005). Miller states that these diverse accounts – although uncomfortable for those who want to judge – are 'part of the very essence of good and evil, not something apart' (Miller, 2005, p. 5). In his opinion, it is a crucial challenge for social psychology to always emphasize the role of social perception when it comes to telling apart good and evil. Thus, evil might be a very subjective, cognitive category for social psychology as well, although it is defined more operationally than in philosophy.

One of the big problems for this position is that scientists must then take the morally dangerous step to identify with the perpetrator (Baumeister & Vohs, 2005, p. 86). One cannot simply adopt the perspective of the victim out of sympathy for his suffering. This is even more difficult as scientists struggling to understand evil are often reproached for condoning or even exonerating the acts of the perpetrators (Miller, 2005; Miller et al, 1999). Understanding evil always seems to have this aspect of making it less evil – this has been known since Leibniz's arguments in the 'Theodicy'.

2.2.2 What are the causes of evil?

Thinking of perpetrators as evil persons with evil intentions or as ordinary people in adverse circumstances obviously influences the process of the identification of the causes of evil. Three different approaches to identify the root causes of evil shall be presented here (virtue theory, situationism, and an evolutionary theory of evil) that closely mirror the hypothetical ideas of man discussed above.

Virtue theory

Virtue theory identifies individual dispositions and robust character traits as being the root of evil behavior. Independently of the discussion whether inherited instincts, drives, or learned behavioral patterns are the cause of the disposition to aggression (Bandura & Reich, 1990; Berkowitz, 1993; Duntley & Buss, 2005; Freud, 1930/1994; Lorenz, 1963/1998), defenders of virtue theory generally agree that the main influence factor for evil actions is a somewhat corrupted personality. Thus, *moral evil* is the predominant form of evil. The most infamous behavioral disposition with respect to evil is the disposition to sadistic behavior. Some people are suspected to actually enjoy hurting others – not because they materially benefit from it but because they like to do evil for the sake of evil. In fiction and in the accounts of victims there are many allusions to sadists. However, Baumeister (1997) and Baumeister and Vohs (2005) regard the widespread belief in sadists as a myth: 'sadism is a genuine cause of violence, albeit a relatively uncommon one' (Baumeister & Vohs, 2005, p. 96). Very close to a sadist is what Hare defines as a *psychopath*:

> Psychopaths are social predators who charm, manipulate, and ruthlessly plow their way through life, leaving a broad trail of broken hearts, shattered expectations, and empty wallets. Completely lacking in conscience and in feelings for others, they selfishly take what they want and do as they please, violating social norms and expectations without the slightest sense of guilt or regret. (Hare, 1999, p. xi)

What distinguishes Hare's psychopath from Baumeister's sadist is the fact that the latter not only uses violence as a means to an end but also as end in itself. Both dispositions seem to be very rare. Only one per cent of the general population or about 20 per cent of prison inmates qualify as psychopaths according to Hare's Psychopathy Checklist–Revised (Bodholdt et al, 2000; Hare, 1991).

Despite their rarity, two things about sadists and psychopaths are disconcerting. First, although they are few, Baumeister and Vohs (2005) emphasize that the evil committed by sadists goes beyond what other causes of evil produce with respect to cruelty. And Hare (1999) finds psychopaths to commit twice as many violent and aggressive acts as other criminals. They are a minority that nevertheless has a sizable impact on the number and effect of evil deeds committed. Second, Baumeister and Vohs (2005, p. 97) and Tangney and Stuewig (2005, p. 339) propose that not only sadistic or psychopathic traits, respectively, are pervasive and robust to change (evil persons stay evil), but also that ordinary people with an aversion to inflicting harm can develop sadistic traits by repeatedly carrying out evil actions (good persons can become evil). 'The first time one hurts or kills someone, one has a strong negative reaction, but as one continues to perform such acts, ... [they] gradually yield more and more pleasure. Certainly the scattered observations on sadism seem to fit such a pattern. Enjoyment of sadistic acts is mainly reported or admitted by people who have been at it for a relatively long time' (Baumeister & Vohs, 2005, p. 97).

Situationism

Situationists claim that the causes for evil actions are not primarily the perpetrators' dispositional factors but rather situational and ecological aspects. In order to make a prediction of how a certain person acts in a given situation, the best predictor is the behavior of *other persons* in the *same situation* – and not how the *same person* behaved in *other situations* (Doris, 2002). Situationists tend to doubt the existence of robust character traits and dispositions that determine individual behavior across different situations. They mainly do so because otherwise it would be difficult to explain evil deeds committed by seemingly ordinary persons in the laboratory and in the field. There are just not enough sadists around to commit all the evils of past and present, and studies in prisons show that very different people are capable of committing the same crime (Zimbardo, 2005, p. 24). Human personality, thought to be stable in virtue theory, thus seems to be more fragile. *Natural evil* seems to be the predominant form of evil.

Some of the best-known experiments in this area are Milgram's (1974) obedience experiments. Milgram was able to show that up to 90 per cent of the subjects, who acted as 'teacher' in a teacher-learner scenario, could be got to give electric shocks of 450 volts to seemingly incompetent 'learners' in an experiment – the main influence factors being an authoritarian supervisor and observed peers that did just the same. Although the subjects were informed of the potentially lethal consequences of their actions, the mild insistence of the supervisor and the role model of other people sufficed to cause this behavior. Ninety per cent of the subjects were capable of what seemed to them to be killing other people, if asked to do so. On the other hand, the compliance rates were lowest when peers were observed rejecting the orders of the supervisor or when the learner-victim seemingly enjoyed the act of being harmed, that is behaved like a masochist. Zimbardo comments:

> What is especially interesting to me about this ... are the data Milgram provides on the predictions of his outcome by 40 psychiatrists who were given the basic description of the classic experiment. Their average estimate of the percentage of U.S. citizens who would give the full 450 volts was fewer than 1%. Only sadists would engage in such sadistic behavior, they believed. In a sense, this is the comparison level for appreciating the enormity of Milgram's finding. These experts on human behavior were *totally* wrong because they ignored the situational determinants of behavior in the procedural

> description of the experiment and over relied on the dispositional perspective that comes from their professional training. Their error is a classic instance of the fundamental attribution error at work. (Zimbardo, 2005, p. 27)

The body of experimental evidence for situationism is huge (cf. Doris, 2002; Gigerenzer, 2008; Sosa, 2009; Zimbardo, 2005). To name just a few of the factors influencing human behavior in a potentially 'evil' direction:

- Acceptable justifications or rationales: Ideologies and stories are a good tool to justify aggressive actions, because they tend to emphasize the greater good achieved by acting evilly (Baumeister & Vohs, 2005; Milgram, 1974; Zimbardo, 2005). A related phenomenon, altering the vocabulary and semantics (from 'hurting people' to 'helping them learn'), also might foster evil behavior (Zimbardo, 2005). This is the mechanic that underlies many ideologies: People who are motivated by high-minded ideals are told that they are doing something good when objectively doing something bad to others (Baumeister & Vohs, 2005, pp. 93–95).
- Formal and informal rules: Whenever there is a written or verbal rule governing the situation and presenting the actions to be executed as correct, people tend to follow this rule (even if it has negative consequences for others) (Milgram, 1974; Zimbardo, 2005).
- Role-play: If the interacting parties have meaningful roles to play they tend to do whatever they think is associated with their role, for example punishing as a guard in a prison (Zimbardo, 1992).
- Gradual degradation: If people start with minor evils and small acts of harming and then gradually increase the amount of harm involved, and if the difference between the steps is hardly noticeable and behavior slowly changes from reasonable to unreasonable, then people tend to inflict harm without major qualms (Baumeister & Vohs, 2005; Milgram, 1974; Zimbardo, 2005). There even seems to be a self-reinforcing effect of violent behavior: It is experienced as increasingly pleasurable (Zimbardo, 2005, p. 32).
- Fast and frugal heuristics (Gigerenzer et al., 1999): If people are uncertain of how to act in a given situation, they often turn to heuristics to guide behavior. Gigerenzer (2008, p. 2) for example sees the social heuristic 'Don't break ranks' as one of the reasons why some German soldiers took part in massacres against the population in Poland,

although they even felt physically ill after committing the murders (Baumeister & Vohs, 2005, pp. 96–97). Although the heuristics applied are normatively neutral in nature, they may induce harmful actions if used in adverse circumstances.

- Deindividuation: 'Anything that makes a person feel anonymous, as if no one knows who he or she is, creates the potential for that person to act in evil ways – if the situation gives permission for violence' (Zimbardo, 2005, p. 29). If the responsibility for an evil action is further diffused in an anonymity condition – for example it is not an individual acting but a group deciding together what should be done – this raises the level of aggression even further (Bandura & Reich, 1990; Diener et al., 1976). If the victims are 'deindividuated', for example simply referred to by identifying numbers or called 'animals', this also raises aggression (Bandura et al., 1975). Environmental anonymity – the perception that in a certain area there is no clearly identifiable community that looks after what is going on in their territory – also fosters aggression (Zimbardo, 1976).

The basic conclusion drawn by situationists from these examples is that one should not jump to the dispositional too quickly. There might be situational and ecological reasons for evil behavior that lie beyond the pure responsibility of the human actors. Situationists demonstrate the ease with which ordinary men can be transformed into evil perpetrators 'by turning on or off one or another social situational variable' (Zimbardo, 2005, p. 22) that is external to the actor. *External situational variables without proper end or intention of their own (that is natural evils) incite human beings to commit evil.* Huggins et al. (2002) also give the very telling example of professional torturers trained to extract information from 'enemies of the state'. Whereas sadists are systematically selected out of the training program (they are ineffective because of their sadistic joy which blurs the focus of the extraction of information), all the evil the torturers commit rather can be explained by '(1) the training they were given to play this new role, (2) group camaraderie, (3) acceptance of the national security ideology, and (4) the belief in socialist-communists as enemies of their state' (Zimbardo, 2005, p. 44).

An evolutionary theory of evil

Looking for the reasons behind evil actions, Duntley and Buss (2005) present an evolutionary theory that focuses on the advantages of evil actions with respect to evolutionary struggle. They see humans as 'reproductive competitors with other humans to become ancestors' (Duntley & Buss, 2005, p. 105) and stress the fact that all humans are descendants of ancestors who successfully competed for resources (food, shelter, but also mates) and from which they may have inherited some competitive adaptations that see evil actions as useful means to the end of reproductive success. Although the process of natural selection is value-free, the term evil may be used to qualify 'behaviors or behavioral dispositions that result in a massive imposition of fitness costs on another individual or group' (Duntley & Buss, 2005, p. 104). Examples range from badmouthing rivals to killing enemies and a generally higher disposition to aggression. The reasons behind evil acts are then 'utility calculations' – evil turns out to be a very effective, evolutionarily rational means to reach one's ends.

Duntley and Buss argue that the co-evolution of evolutionary strategies that favor evil actions and of strategies that provide good counter-mechanisms to aggression is very likely. For example killing might feature the advantages of preventing the victim permanently from reproduction, of gaining access to the opponent's mate for sexual reproduction, of claiming his resources, and of weakening the opponent's kin because of the loss of protection. On the other hand, killing also is dangerous and a potentially costly strategy. The killer might suffer from revenge, retribution from the larger group, and a loss of reputation. Potential anti-homicide strategies might range from stranger anxiety to ethnocentrism, fleeing mechanisms, and mind-reading abilities to detect evil intentions (Duntley & Buss, 2005, pp. 108–109). The fact that killing is beneficial to reproductive fitness, thus, does not only lead to a larger number of offspring for the killers but also to the evolutionary success of those particularly adept in defending against evil deeds. An arms race between ever more effective aggressive strategies and defensive ones that increase the costs of killing begins.

Besides providing a reason why humans have the disposition to do evil things (it proves to be a valid evolutionary strategy), the evolutionary approach highlights another very important fact: Evil is only bad for the victim.

> From the victim's perspective, of course, being the target of a homicide renders the would-be killer evil. From the killer's perspective, however, eliminating a victim may represent a 'good', and the victim's anti-homicide strategies would thereby be *viewed as* evil. (Duntley & Buss, 2005, pp. 110–111; emphasis by author)

It is the individual perspective that makes a value-free action either 'good' or 'evil'; good and evil are in fact *cognitive categories*. Duntley and Buss propose that these categories may serve the important adaptive function of helping to avoid becoming a victim and that stereotyping others as evil serves to make judgments when uncertain (2005, pp. 111–113). Once this category exists, it can be exploited in various ways: Victims can exaggerate the potentially inflicted damage and thus motivate others to join the defending coalition (which decreases the costs of such a strategy, as a larger group makes defeat less likely). Perpetrators, on the other hand, could 'actively cultivate a reputation as evil ... and avoid being exploited by others' (Duntley & Buss, 2005, p. 115). In other terms, the antagonistic competition goes to another level with words as the new weapons. The evolutionary approach shows that doing evil could very well be a strategy for which the net benefits outweigh the net costs and that, consequently, is evolutionarily successful. Selection may favor the evolution of human adaptations for evil 'eventually making them fundamental components of human nature' (Duntley & Buss, 2005, p. 118).

2.3 Moral evil and natural evil, evil actions and evil rules

Across all the different accounts presented above one finding seems to be clear: The human potential for evil actions is a real one. Apart from that, the question is whether there are individuals who enjoy the act of doing evil as an end in itself ('diabolical sadists'), or whether humans possess frail characters and most of the time long for good but sometimes succumb to evil (if evil is an effective means to their ends). Are there evil persons with a 'taste for harming' or only evil actions caused by adverse circumstances? Leibniz, Kant, virtue theory, and the evolutionary theory of evil would probably stress the former cause of evil (*moral evil* is predominant), whereas Arendt and the situationists would highlight the importance of the latter (*natural evil* is predominant). This question of predominance will not be answered in this book. Bearing in mind the purpose of examining evil from an economic point of view – notably by highlighting the importance of economically evil actions and evil social institutions – it will be argued that *both kinds of evil are necessary to explain why there is evil.*

2.3.1 Why one should consider moral evil and natural evil

Looking back at the many definitions, causes and evaluations of evil, one can recognize an interesting historical movement: A shift away from Leibniz's *malum naturale* (nature intentionally harming us physically) is followed by a renaissance of a closely related type of evil in the theoretical discussion.

As Neiman (2004) and Schulte (1988) point out, the philosophers succeeding Leibniz who worked on the notion of evil, such as Rousseau or Kant, gave more and more responsibility for evil to man. For Kant, man even becomes the only source of evil in the world, since nature does not have any ends. All the harm caused by earthquakes or similar natural catastrophes, therefore, must not be called natural 'evil' in the strict sense, but rather natural 'ill' (1788/1974, p. 177). It is one of the consequences of Kant's theory of human autonomy and its link to morality that man is the only *root* of evil: The *radical* evil is the only evil there is, because man is the only being that can choose his maxims freely and thus the only being that can be held responsible for any harm caused. Who could blame nature – the realm of strict causality in Kant's eyes – for an earthquake? This shift away from the importance of natural evil is typical for modern thought in individualistic Western societies (Neiman, 2004). Unsurprisingly, psychology that became established as an independent science in the course of the 19th century mirrors this way of thinking. Virtue theory, that is the classical approach of moral psychology to the issue of evil, tends to see evil persons behind evil actions. The perpetrator is fully responsible for an evil action, because it is his lack of character and morality that led to it.

The problem with such individualistic, subjective theories of evil as for example the Kantian one is that they are incapable of explaining all kinds of evil (Schulte, 1988, p. 350). Arendt and the situationists, who rethought the notion of evil after what happened in World War II, highlight this shortcoming. The historical aspect is of utmost importance here, since Auschwitz was a main driver for theories and experiments concerning evil. 'How could something like Auschwitz happen?' was the question that troubled the minds of those thinking about evil.

> Auschwitz represents a kind of evil that is caused by man, that is no natural ill or purely natural event, and that, nevertheless, cannot be attributed to specific individuals, since it by far exceeds the sphere of individual causation and responsibility. (Schulte, 1988, p. 350; author's translation).

The Eichmann trial and Arendt's report have shown all of the problems that Auschwitz caused: A huge evil to be punished, the desperate search for culprits, and the inability to find an appropriate and satisfying sentence. The repeated plea of Eichmann himself and his defenders that he was just an unimportant part of a monstrous system and that he only executed orders left a taste of insufficiency and the feeling that the 'real' culprits got away unpunished. This is precisely what Arendt means when she says that the biggest evils can never be punished (1965/2007a, p. 101).

Arendt and the situationists recognized that the problem with punishing culprits probably lies in the fact that there are no clearly identifiable individuals that caused the harm. Arendt says the culprits are not 'persons' (1965/2007a, p. 92). Situationists would pinpoint the situational influence factors and the power of the circumstances (for example the effects of obedience to supervisors (Milgram, 1974)). The kind of evil that took place in Auschwitz seems to have a 'natural' component; *a kind of* natural evil *gets reintroduced into the discussion in the form of non-persons as actors or situational influencing factors affecting human decisions*. This new natural evil is not the same as Leibniz's *malum naturale*: It is not God that uses nature as a means to punish the moral evils human beings committed by causing physical suffering with the end of restoring justice. But 'natural evil', as used in this book from now on, is not identical to Arendt's idea of the *banality of evil* either, that is that ordinary people following rules are responsible for the biggest evils. And despite the focus on the external circumstances of actions, this natural evil has to be called an *evil* in the strict sense, not just an *ill* as Kant claims. The new evidence seems to contradict Kant's idea that there is no evil besides human evil since Auschwitz cannot be seriously judged as a 'purely natural event' (Schulte, 1988, p. 350) and yet 'exceeds by far the sphere of individual causation and responsibility' (ibid.). Yet again, this new natural evil stays closely related to Kant's natural ill with respect to the fact that situational influencing factors do not possess proper ends or intentions. This evil is 'natural' in the sense that something beyond individual human responsibility gets highlighted.

In this book, speaking of natural evil means to appeal to the idea that situational factors external to the human actors exist, mostly[2] *beyond individual responsibility, without proper ends or intentions, and that may lead to harm being caused to human beings*. It means that something like 'situational', 'systemic', or 'institutional' evil exists. To be clear: The agents that commit evil acts are still human; but the seemingly objective and value-free natural circumstances obviously determine the seemingly autonomous and normative actions of man to some extent.

Speaking of natural evil highlights the instigating circumstances of harm done. Speaking of moral evil highlights the individual actors doing harm. The distinction between moral evil and natural evil, thus, turns out to be still very useful today, as not only moral evil but also natural evil are important causes of evil. It will be shown that one has to look at both phenomena if one wants to examine evil in economics. *The preferred example of moral evil will be* actors committing economically evil actions (to be defined in Section 3.2), *whereas the preferred instances of natural evil are going to be* evil social institutions (to be explained in Section 3.3). This is the playing field on which one has to further examine whether people have a 'taste for harming' and whether it is interesting to explicitly consider this taste in economic reasoning.

2.3.2 Evaluating evil

It is not the goal of this book to evaluate evil. It does not want to follow Welner in developing an objective 'depravity scale' (1998, p. 4) for evil acts. However, presenting a book on evil from an economic perspective, one has to at least set out common criteria for evaluating evil, so as to enable the reader to judge the presented evidence from *EVE Online* more easily for himself.

Looking at the presented approaches in the two primers, one has to consider at least two separate aspects, if judging the 'badness' of a certain action: The *intention* behind the act and its *consequences*. In general, the evaluation of both aspects seems to be quite easy: The more diabolical the intention (that is the more the perpetrator is motivated by the goal to inflict harm and nothing else) and the more severe the consequences (that is the more harm is done), the worse the action. This is fairly common ground – that, as usual, gets shaky upon closer inspection.

Intentions

Concerning the evaluation of the *intention*, but without delving into the problems of what exactly constitutes a human action (e.g., Anscombe, 1957/2000; Davidson, 1980; Frankfurt, 1978; Wilson, 2009), one can say that whenever there is no clear intention to do harm, the evil consequences seem to be less accountable to the actor, which greatly alters the evaluation. If there is the impression that the perpetrator was the rather passive executor of a higher power's desires or had a respectable goal, one may tend to blame her less for what she did. If the situationists were right and if everybody knew that he was only one step away from becoming an offender himself, the judgments concerning the degree of evil might become less harsh.

Doris captures the point by saying that 'moral praise and blame look beyond the surface properties of actions to associated psychological states such as belief, desire, and motive' (2002, p. 129). According to him (2002, p. 133), the two sorts of powers that are relevant for making responsibility judgments are challenged by situationism. The 'powers of self-control' (ibid.) are challenged because for example the Milgram obedience experiments seem to show that people often act other than as they think best. Second, the 'powers of reflection' (ibid.) are challenged: If there are many things around that influence decisions but of which people are not aware, how could they make informed decisions? Humans' normative competence is put into question (Doris, 2002, pp. 136–146).

The higher lenience concerning evil if situational factors are involved is also reflected in many legal systems all around the world, for example in the principle of *nulla poena sine culpa* ('no punishment without guilt'). The same is true for the *mens rea* (the 'guilty mind') as one necessary element for guilt: If the perpetrator does not act purposefully (with a clear goal in mind) and knowingly (that is knowing that his actions will lead eventually to the desired consequence) in some way, this is often regarded as an extenuating circumstance which leads to diminished responsibility. The courts thus distinguish between different degrees of culpability (and of evil) on a day-to-day basis.

Agamben (1998/2003, pp. 18–19) highlights that it is precisely the *non-responsibility* that applies to natural evils that is the reason for much of the terror that Auschwitz caused. It is the 'impotentia iudicandi' (Levi, 1986/1993, p. 60) that makes things even worse. This is a paradox, since although it is not always an individual's fault, not completely his responsibility how things developed, he does not feel less guilty. Arendt (1965/2007a) points in the same direction, saying that precisely the fact that these extenuating circumstances are reflected in the legal order – and have become second nature to every judging layperson, too – make it so hard to punish evil. One can only punish persons, not situational factors – does this make natural evil a non-evil with respect to intentions?

Doris argues that situationist insights in no way make human responsibility impossible. On the contrary, situationism leads to even more responsibility in some cases (Doris, 2002, p. 153). One may not be fully responsible for being obedient as a subject in Milgram's experiment but everybody is responsible for carefully choosing which situations to expose himself to. The most important lesson of situationism is that circumstances matter – therefore, every individual aware of this issue is ethically responsible for not entering potentially compromising circumstances (Doris, 2002, p. 153). Somebody may be less responsible for his actions in a concrete situation – but nobody just gets into situations out of nothing.

This is an extremely demanding approach to responsibility, because it concerns future actions. The solution it proposes to the situation faced in Milgram's experiments is that the subjects should not have agreed to the rules guiding the experiment in the first place. No evil would have been committed, if no one participated given the rules the experimenters set beforehand. The problem is: It was basic rules that even seemed pretty reasonable beforehand that caused much of the trouble and justified blind compliance.

> 'Failure to respond must be treated as an error' was a Milgram rule for shock omissions.... But then what happens when the learner complains of a heart condition, wants to quit, then screams, followed by thud and silence? The learner's apparent inability to respond to the teacher's testing due to death or unconsciousness must be continually challenged by further shocks. (Zimbardo, 2005, p. 28)

The situationist approach to responsibility is so demanding, because suddenly one even has to question rules that turned out to be functional and useful a hundred times before – and this critical review has to be done in advance of all the situations one may enter. Nevertheless, this approach is very viable in order to truly acknowledge the existence of natural evil without allowing for too easy defenses alluding to 'superior orders' and the 'necessity to obey' in order to morally and legally excuse evil deeds.

Consequences

Concerning the evaluation of the *consequences* of an evil action, two things are important to note. First, it is not only the amount of harm the victim suffers from (irrespective of measurement standards) that solely determines the badness of an action, but also the positive consequences for the perpetrator. Ceteris paribus, the less to be gained from an evil action for the perpetrator, the more evil it seems to be if carried out (Duntley & Buss, 2005, p. 111). NB: It is not just the difference between the absolute value of the costs inflicted and the benefits gained that makes an action more or less bad. An action with little benefit to the perpetrator and little cost to the victim might be judged in much the same way as an action with proportionately higher benefits and costs. Instead, one has to judge benefits and costs separately from each other. All other things being equal, the higher the costs, the worse the action; the lower the benefits, the worse the action.

Second, although most of the cited authors think that evil necessarily includes harm inflicted to someone, not every human-inflicted harm qualifies as evil. You might think of physicians that need to inflict some harm (for example to cut the flesh of the patient) in order to cure. You could also think of sports (American football, for example) or business: It is perfectly fine to undercut the prices of your competitor and thus hurt his sales and inflict financial losses on his side. Discerning between legitimate competition (undercutting prices; merchants tilting scales in an environment where everybody does it) and illegitimate actions (dumping prices; merchants tilting scales in Germany, for example) is far from obvious, taking into account that the fine line of distinction is defined by the social institutions (for example the commercial law) governing this specific situation. Additionally, quite often one tends to accept evil in the short run, if it brings about a greater good in the long run. Think for example of Leibniz's argument that the *malum naturale* restores justice. The whole evaluation of the evil act then may change: An *evil 'tout court'* becomes a *'necessary' evil*.

This shows that every definition of evil that does not take into account the formal and informal institutions that govern a situation is incomplete. This leads to the peculiar situation that one has to consider social institutions not only as potential cause of evil actions (*evil* social institutions) but also as rules that discern between what is good and evil in the first place. There might be a social rule that allows for harming other people and another social rule stating that in this particular case it is acceptable to harm other people. When talking about evil, not only the consequences of the 'rules of the game' (which rules cause harm and which do not?) matter but also the *principium diiudicationis* (Schulte, 1988, p. 67) that helps to tell good from evil on a very general level (what is good and what is evil?). Such a principle – be it material as with Leibniz or formal as with Kant – may overrule the psychological definition that evil is intentional harming.

As briefly mentioned in the introduction, the standpoint of this book is that social institutions actively fostering social conflict instead of providing solutions to it and thus inducing harming are *defined* as being *evil* rules (cf. Section 3.3 for more details). But in the end, this is only a name that *does not imply any sort of evaluation from the author's part.* The (economic) *principium diiudicationis* applied to discern between 'good' and 'evil' shall be, if material harm is done. This will become clearer when defining what is 'economically evil' in the next chapter.

2.4 Conclusion of the primers

When examining evil from an economic perspective, one should build on the philosophical theories and empirical findings from social psychology. Moral evil was described as intentionally harming other people and natural evil as the existence of situational factors external to the human actors, mostly beyond individual responsibility, without proper ends or intentions that may lead to harm being caused to human beings. In what follows, the preferred example of a moral evil will be actors committing economically evil actions. The preferred example of a natural evil will be evil social institutions. The goal is not to show which actualization of evil is more important – after all, both represent views on the same phenomenon but from different perspectives rather than being two completely different things. *Both actualizations of evil* exist *and* matter – *when theoretically discussing evil in economic terms as well as when practically analyzing the economic performance of a society.*

3
Defining Evil in an Economic Way

3.1 Why economics?

It is interesting that philosophy and psychology talk about evil while economics does not. To my knowledge, there exists no single economic work that explicitly uses the concept of evil in order to describe or explain human behavior. This complete non-consideration of evil behavior by economists is, to say the least, surprising. Given the long intellectual history of the concepts of moral and natural evil, it is surprising that there is no significant impact of these concepts in economics. Even more so as only recently economists started to talk about the normatively opposed concepts of altruism, fairness, and reciprocity (for example, Camerer, 2003; Fehr & Schmidt, 1999; Kagel & Roth, 1995). And Lorenz (1963/1998) finds that, from a biological and evolutionary background, 'evil' in the form of aggression is indispensable for the evolution of close-knit groups, trust, and cooperation. He says that in nature, we do not find love or friendship without aggression, because the former evolved as an evolutionary countermeasure to the latter. So where is the idea of evil in economics?

There are three reasons for examining evil from an economic perspective. The first reason is *the self-expression of economics as a social science capable of explaining all kinds of human behavior.* 'Economic imperialism', as put forward prominently by such merited figures as Gary Becker (for example, 1962, 1968, 1973) and Jack Hirshleifer (for example, 2001a), is the idea that the tools and concepts of economic analysis can also be applied to aspects of human behavior that do not seem to have any connections to classic economic subjects like for example prices, wages, economic performance of a society, or poverty. Central to this idea is the conviction that the 'combined postulates of maximizing behavior, stable preferences and market equilibrium, applied relentlessly and unflinchingly, form the heart of the economic approach' (Becker, 1976, p. 4), and that an additional focus on the concept of economic efficiency has 'allowed economics to invade intellectual territory that previously was deemed to be outside the discipline's realm' (Lazear, 2000, p. 99). Economics possesses concepts that other social sciences ignore and its analytical categories are 'universal in applicability' (Hirshleifer, 2001a, p. 308). 'Even more important is our structured organization of these concepts into the distinct yet intertwined processes of optimization on the individual decision level and equilibrium on the social level of analysis' (ibid.). If this is what economics claims, then surely economists should be willing to have their say in the explanation of evil behavior. It is precisely this self-expression that already led economists to examine social phenomena like altruism, fairness, or reciprocity (for example, Camerer, 2003; Charness & Rabin, 2002; de Quervain et al., 2004; Fehr & Schmidt, 2006). If economics examines moral or prosocial behavior (in philosophical or psychological terms, respectively), and if economic man is still believed to be a reasonable approximation of average human behavior – then one cannot ignore the darker side of the deviations from this idea of man in order to bring things back into balance.

The second reason as to why the economic approach to evil matters is that economics seems to contradict the findings on evil in philosophy and psychology. Because the economic 'heartland is an intellectual territory carved off by two narrowing conceptions: (1) of man as rational, self-interested decision-maker, and (2) of social interaction as typified by market exchange' (Hirshleifer, 2001a, p. 307), economics should be particularly apt in explaining why the idea of people committing evil actions out of pure evil will – and often with the consequence of both sides being worse off – is a misconception of human behavior. That is, *an economic analysis of evil is interesting because evil behavior seemingly runs counter to some of the most fundamental ideas in economics.*

'Rationality is an *instrumental* concept' (Hirshleifer, 2001a, p. 321) and thus questions the idea of sadists going beyond an instrumental use of evil in their actions. *Self-interest* implies that we do not attach utility 'to the impact of events upon the bodies or psyches of other parties' (Hirshleifer, 2001a, p. 311). But how can it then be explained that at least some subjects in Milgram's obedience experiments refused to harm other people albeit their perceived costs of retreating from the experiment? *Market exchange* is praised in economics because of its efficiency, that is making everybody better off without leaving anybody worse off. If one accepts this form of appropriation as a dominant one then one should also be able to explain why conflict (for example harming others, murder, war, stealing from others instead of paying them) is less efficient and about to disappear in the long run.

The third and final reason was briefly referred to in the introduction. New empirical findings suggest that *violence plays an important role for explaining the economic performance of a society* (The World Bank, 2011). Therefore, economics should start to examine individuals doing harm in order to better understand how violent behavior can be accounted for and eventually avoided. After all, to overcome the state of nature and to even out imbalances in economic performance seems to be much more difficult than usually thought in neoclassical economics (Hirshleifer, 1995).

To summarize: economists are experts in describing all kinds of instrumental, self-interested behavior of individuals and efficient social interactions. One should consider the economic approach if one is having trouble with people supposedly having a 'taste for harming' potentially leading to negative social consequences.

3.2 Economically evil actions

3.2.1 Defining economically evil actions

Using Zimbardo's psychological definition of evil as a point of reference – 'intentionally behaving, or causing others to act, in ways that demean, dehumanize, harm, destroy, or kill innocent people' (2005, p. 22) – the working definition of economic evil shall be: *if someone intentionally harms another person materially – without benefitting materially from it – he commits an* economically evil *action*. The two most significant differences to Zimbardo's psychological definition are the double insertion of the word 'material' and the comparison of the harm done to the victim and the benefits generated for the offender. These adaptations to the psychological definition, that constitute the new *principium diiudicationis*, are necessary in order to achieve a genuinely *economic* definition of evil – and require further clarification.

Material harm done

Let a be the active part in a given situation and p the 'other person' that passively incurs whatever a does: a can harm p in many ways but the two most important are that he hurts p directly, that is that he hurts p physically or mentally, or that he hurts p indirectly by impairing his property (for example goods in his possession, resources, income, territory, capital stock). The former shall be called *personal harm* and the latter *material harm*. Material harm does not play a major role in social psychology but for an economic perspective on evil this aspect is the dominant one. This is not to say that personal harm (be it harm done to the body or the psyche) generally speaking cannot be treated in economical terms as well. But the purpose here is to elaborate a genuinely economic definition of evil, and it therefore pays off to start with concepts widely accepted in economics: harm done by stealing goods or lowering the income of another person. *Economic evil only considers material harm done.*

Material benefits generated

An analogous reasoning applies when turning to the potential benefits a perpetrator creates for himself by harming another person. *Economic evil only considers material benefits for the offender.* This part of the definition is probably more contestable. One has to elaborate on what *motivates* a person to commit an evil action – and not considering any immaterial aspects (notably: satisfaction of needs, emotions) seems to only tell half the story. However, the classic economic approach is a positive one that focuses on hard, observable facts. Feelings, intentions, and mental states do not belong to the standard mainstream concepts of economics; although there are efforts to model these economically and although the central role of utility (intangible, unobservable in nature and incomparable between persons) opens the rigid framework of prices, goods and production functions a little bit. Defining evil in a genuinely economic way, one should not be too rash to talk about drives and needs but stay in the typical boundaries of economic analysis. As Alfred Marshall puts it:

> ECONOMICS is a study of mankind in the ordinary business of life; it examines that part of individual and social action which is most closely connected with the attainment and with the use of the *material* requisites of well-being. (Marshall, 1890/2009, p. 1; emphasis by author)

It is true that the presented working definition of evil reduces self-interest to *material* self-interest. However, material self-interest is the innermost core of economic man. Economic man maximizes his utility according to his utility function – which in turn illustrates the utility generated by a bundle of material goods or bads. This is what every student of economics learns in the first week. It is a simple, parsimonious model. It provides an *economic principium diiudicationis* proper.

The comparison of the harm done and the benefits generated

The last element of the economic definition of evil is the juxtaposition of the costs and benefits of an evil action. As it stands now, the rational action of a utility-maximizer to do something that is in his best self-interest and yet harms another person is considered evil (with respect to the psychological definition of evil). But qualifying the stereotypical behavior of economics (egoistic utility-maximization) as evil right away is problematic – there would be a lot of evil around without anybody naming it. In short, this judgment seems too harsh, at least for economists, as this would mean falling back behind Adam Smith when classifying rational behavior as evil. Even if only considering egoistic behavior in constant-sum games (that is whenever one person gains something, another person loses the exact same amount), it would seem inappropriate to call this behavior economically evil. The danger of trivializing evil by doing so is a real one.

In order to get a more precise and appropriate picture of evil actions from an economic perspective, it shall be proposed to distinguish between three different cases, between *three different kinds of economic evil*. Whenever an action of *a* leads to a negative payoff for *p*, we can say that *a* harmed *p*; *a* harming *p* materially is a necessary and sufficient condition for an economically evil action. But in order to qualify these actions as more or less evil we have to consider *a*'s payoff from this specific harming action, too. There are three logical possibilities: either *a* gains while *p* loses, or *a*'s payoff stays the same while *p*'s is impaired, or *a* loses and *p* loses as well (see Table 3.1). Following Duntley and Buss (2005, p. 111), one might propose that the less *a* gains by harming *p*, the more we can qualify *a*'s action as evil.

This book will refer to all three scenarios under the heading of *economic evil*, because all three involve material harm done to another

Table 3.1 Payoff combinations from evil actions

	Material payoff *a*	**Material payoff *p***
Case 1	Positive	Negative
Case 2	Zero	Negative
Case 3	Negative	Negative

person and thus fulfill the necessary and sufficient condition of economic evil. However, this means using the term evil in a *broad sense*. In a *narrower sense*, only actions that lead to case-2 or case-3 scenarios shall be considered evil. That is, because according to the working definition (if somebody intentionally harms another person materially – without benefitting materially from it – he commits an economically evil action) there must also not be any material gain for the perpetrator. The parenthesis 'without benefitting materially from it' is what marks the difference between economic evil in the broad and in the narrow sense. Only case 2 and case 3 feature no material gain for the perpetrator. If no material gain can be obtained, one might suspect that a 'taste for harming', a truly evil intention, is the motivation of the action. The exact nature of this intention (maybe the pursuit of utility generated by immaterial rewards?) remains a black box for this book. It is only implied that there has to be something that motivates the evil action. Some examples might clarify this reasoning.

Examples

Case 1 sounds familiar. This is for example the payoff-structure of a merchant who uses manipulated scales in order to make his customers pay more. And it is the case known from many games, like for example nine men's morris or chess: if I am able to take one of your pieces out of the game, it is good for me and bad for you. Speaking on a more general level, this is the case in which harming another person has a *material instrumental* value: harming you is a means to my end. In some economic contexts behavior like this may be qualified as *evil* in the strict sense (for example the dishonest merchant), whereas in other contexts one is used to qualify this behavior rather as *competitive* (the merchant that undercuts the prices of another neighboring merchant, thus hurting the sales of the latter). Concerning the precise evaluation, it all comes down to the 'rules of the game' governing the situation. One cannot make a final judgment if such behavior is really to be considered evil, without also considering the institutional framework for this situation (cf. Section 2.3 on 'Evaluating evil'). Actions that are representative of case 1 shall be called *egoistic actions*. Such actions create win-lose situations.

The second case is less familiar. One may think of mindless or negligent actions: somebody harming other people because she did not pay attention. This example is not 100 percent to the point since evil actions are defined as intentional actions that should therefore involve a certain degree of consciousness. Actions driven by envy are a better example.

If you do not begrudge someone something (for example professional promotion) but you still have the power to withhold the reward from her (because you are the boss), you may sometimes be inclined to decide to the disadvantage of the other person – although your own income or status would not be affected. Another good example for a case-2 scenario might be that of Kitty Genovese. She was attacked in her apartment in New York but before being killed screamed 'Oh my God, he stabbed me! Help me!' many times and so loudly that many of her neighbors noticed it, as has been proven. Yet nobody intervened – probably due to the *bystander effect* and diffused responsibility (Aronson et al, 2008, pp. 29, 366). Kitty Genovese was killed, that is she had a negative payoff, due to the *inaction* of her neighbors. The failure to help, thus, can on occasions be tantamount to an act of harming (Miller, 2005, p. 6). A less drastic example is the almost proverbial old lady who wants to cross the street but does not dare to do it on her own. There is no material payoff involved in helping her – and this might be the reason why not everybody does so. However, it might also be the case that the people walking by are just too busy and do not even notice her distress (cf. Darley & Batson, 1973). Actions that lead to the second case's payoff combination shall be called *wanton actions* – in line with the juristic term of 'wanton negligence'.

One example for actions falling within the third case is lawsuits initiated out of revenge, which are not about *being right* or about being compensated materially, but about officially *being proven right*, about getting 'justice'. Still, they are costly to both sides and the compensation for the winner may not always cover the costs. Hirshleifer and Osborne (2001) furnish an exemplary economic analysis of such trials. You might do things because of your conviction that 'they ought to be done'. On the positive side, the actualization of such convictions, values, and principles may often lead you to ignore your individual material benefit for the sake of a favorable outcome for your counterpart (think of altruism, for example). However, as already described, high-minded ideals may also be perverted and exploited by ideologies and actually lead to negative payoffs for both sides. Altruism and revenge are strangely closely related in that they both may lead somebody to give up a material benefit in order to influence the benefits of other people. Actions that lead to material lose-lose situations shall be called *malicious actions*. Such actions do not have any *material instrumental* value – following Staub (2005, p. 67) and his distinction of different kinds of aggression, it is the desire to inflict pain at whatever cost that motivates the perpetrators. One rather has to emphasize the *hostile* value of malicious actions.

Material and immaterial payoffs reviewed

It is true that – giving examples for the second and third case – emotions/ states of mind were referred to as potential motivating factors for behavior. The envy of the boss, the fear of Kitty Genovese's neighbors or the feelings of revenge are important aspects in explaining the final outcome. In fact, it is difficult to find a perfect example for behavior that leads to these types of payoff combinations when only considering material aspects. One might argue that the boss does not withhold the advancement because he profits *materially* from it but because he profits *mentally* from it: he satisfies his feeling of envy. So what looks like a lose-lose situation from the purely material perspective may turn out to be a win-lose situation when all facets are considered.

But this way of arguing is not an infringement of the principle to only consider material payoffs for defining economic evil. *The definition of economic evil remains untouched by invoking immaterial benefits as motivating factors.* The decision to ignore immaterial payoffs when defining economic evil does not require leaving the more general framework of utility-analysis or contradicting the idea that every conscious action features an intention. Thanks to the reasons mentioned above, it is appropriate to focus on observable material gains and losses in an economic analysis – even if one agrees to the idea that satisfying needs (for example longing for revenge) raises utility as well.

Summary

The absence of a material gain is a defining characteristic of economic evil in the narrow sense, because it is the very absence of a material gain that tells something about the intention of the actor. If you harm another person without benefitting materially from it, then the very desire to harm the other person must be an important motivation. And there is no better example of an action that is evil to the core than intentionally harming another person because of the very desire to harm him. The intention to harm and the harm done are enough to qualify an action as evil from a *psychological* perspective (cf. Zimbardo's definition). Talking about *material harm* done, which is not motivated by a *material gain*, defines *economic* evil. *If somebody intentionally harms another person materially – without benefitting materially from it – he commits an economically evil action in the narrow sense.*

There are three degrees of economically evil actions in the *broad sense*: all involve harming another person. More precisely, an action is *egoistic* if the material payoff of the perpetrator is positive, whereas that of the victim is negative. It is *wanton* if the material payoff of the perpetrator stays unchanged and only that of the victim declines. An action is *malicious* if both persons lose materially due to it. Only the last two should be called evil in the *narrow sense* when talking from an economic perspective. Only the last two fulfill the necessary condition of no material gain for the perpetrator. And only of the last two can one say that they imply an economically evil intention and point to the existence of a 'taste for harming' (Figure 3.1).

This 'taste for harming' stays a black box – this is why it will only be used in quotation marks throughout the book. It serves to explain why people spend money to impair other people's income although they do not gain materially from it; it is related to the psychological idea of sadism and to the philosophical idea of people doing evil for evil's sake. Besides this suggested 'taste for harming', there are still other causes for evil actions, notably evil rules (cf. Section 3.3) and causes already discussed in the economic literature (for example fairness considerations). The concept of a 'taste for harming' is intended to distance itself from these latter causes of harming known to economics, which will be set out in the following section.

3.2.2 Theories of harming in neoclassical economics

An overview of the economic literature on phenomena related to evil reveals that fighting, harming other people for strategic reasons (notably

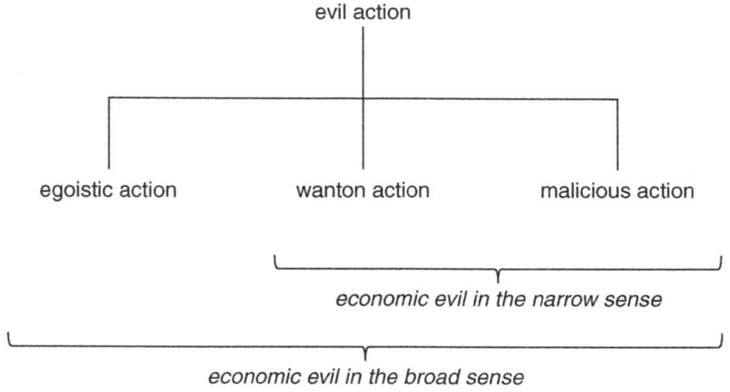

Figure 3.1 Different kinds of economically evil actions

for reputation building), or people accepting a lower income themselves only to impair the income of another person (conditional behavior in bargaining games), have gained some attention in economics. What the approaches have in common is that they try to explain why people are impairing other people's income. However, it is not economically evil actions as a phenomenon in its own right that these contributions discuss.

Models of anarchy and conflict: maximizing self-interest by fighting

Since the very beginnings of economics as an independent discipline, and notably since Adam Smith, a lot of economists talk about selfish actions and their consequences for the overall welfare of society – always eager to demonstrate that one should not condemn economic man for being selfish. *Selfish*, in this case, means not being interested in the payoffs of other persons but only striving to maximize their own income. The most prominent effort not only to talk about selfish competitive behavior but also about the darker side of truly harmful behavior (fighting in the literal sense) has been made by those authors writing about anarchy and conflict theory (for example, Buchanan, 1975/2000; Frank, 1988; Hirshleifer, 2001b; Schelling, 1960; Stringham, 2005; Tullock, 1972, 1974). Every economist at some point talks about selfish actions, because selfish people represent the underlying economic idea of man – but those talking about fighting in a state of nature come closer to touching on the issue of evil.

Consider for example Buchanan's (1975/2000) famous analysis of anarchy and his claim that in a state of nature every individual basically has to choose between two strategies for making a living: to produce oneself the goods one needs or to steal them from others. He takes the example of two persons (*A* and *B*) who live on an island where there are no laws, no property rights (obviously no enforcing agencies) and on which consequently every individual has a 'right' to everything. Each person is characterized by an individual utility function, an individual production function that determines on a general level the relationship between inputs and outputs, and a specific environmental setting. It is important for Buchanan that *A* and *B* differ with respect to their preferences, production capacities and environmental setting. Both persons are thought to be rational, self-interested utility-maximizers.

The utility of *A* (and that of *B* analogically) is solely determined by the individually available amount of a private, storable good *x*. The only way for a person to affect *x* in the natural state is to invest effort (*e*, a bad). This effort can be of three kinds: *A* can invest effort in producing *x* directly (production effort), *A* can invest effort to try to take from the amount of *x B* has stored (predation effort), or *A* invests effort in securing its own supplies of *x* from *B*'s attacks (defense effort). The input-output relation of all three activities is determined by the production function. One can summarize the model saying that in order to maximize her utility in an anarchic natural state each person can either spend her time producing *x* herself or taking *x* from others – and since everybody has the latter possibility, securing one's own supplies becomes necessary.

Buchanan (1975/2000, p. 74) stresses the fact that in an anarchic natural state defined this way, there is no reason for believing that people would limit themselves only to production – leaving predation and defense aside. To oversimplify: if there is one person who is very adept at producing (an 'intelligent' person) and another who is very adept at depredating (a 'strong' person), it may be more rational for the strong person to constantly rob the intelligent, rather than investing any effort in producing himself. After all, since there are no property rights and no sanctions for doing so, why should the strong person restrain himself from these actions? The outcome shown in Figure 3.2, which is the actual interaction sequence to be expected according to Buchanan then might emerge as a simple result of the utility-maximization of two persons exploiting their respective comparative advantages.

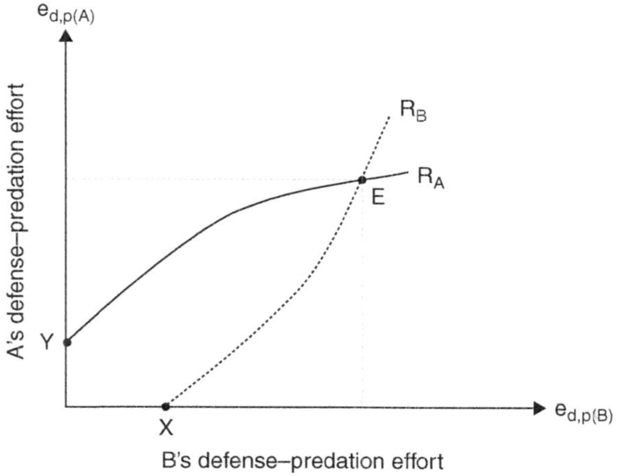

Figure 3.2 Defense and predation effort in anarchy (cf. Buchanan, 1975/2000, p. 75)

The ridge lines R_A and R_B indicate the optimal level of (combined) defense-predation effort for *A* and *B* in reaction to every level of defense-predation effort by the other person. As shown by the points *X* and *Y*, which are not identical with the origin that represents the no-conflict solution, each person has an incentive to initiate conflict. The behavioral equilibrium in this purely anarchistic setting is attained at *E*. Since both reaction functions intersect at this point, neither *A* nor *B* has an incentive to change his defense-predation effort; and all the time not consumed by these two activities will be devoted to actually producing the private good. The Nash equilibrium *E* describes the outcome that could be expected in a genuinely anarchistic order; it is the *anarchistic equilibrium*. The associated values x_A and x_B for this level and distribution of efforts characterize what Buchanan calls the 'natural distribution' (p. 75). This natural distribution prevails in the anarchistic equilibrium.

Buchanan's model of fighting in anarchy can be regarded as typical way of approaching phenomena related to evil actions the economic way. First, it is considered *natural* (sic!) that self-interested people also consider violent actions as appropriate means. Second, Buchanan only talks about *material* harm done – both persons steal goods from each other. In addition, the payoff from these acts of stealing is strictly measured *in material terms*, too. There is not a single word about aggressive thoughts or feelings of revenge in the whole text. Buchanan's thought experiment shows how conflict is approached in economic terms: two rational utility-maximizers look for their advantage and accept stealing from the opponent as valid strategy as long as there is no law in place that forbids stealing and thus diminishes their material payoff by the amount of the punishment to be paid. Even if there was a law in place, both persons might continue to steal, if this was a more profitable strategy than not to steal. It is important to note that, presenting this model of fighting in anarchy, Buchanan actually argues for the necessity of the establishment of social institutions ending the conflict. He is convinced that, if a society is generally able to establish enforceable institutions, fighting will end eventually – just as Hirshleifer talks in a related model about 'Anarchy and Its Breakdown' (1995).

Hirshleifer (2001b) probably offers the most encompassing examination of conflict. He summarizes the recurring themes and assumptions made in the field of the economic theory of conflict that examines 'the second major way of making a living' (Hirshleifer, 2001b, p. 1) besides production and trade, namely predation and conflict, as follows:

- The way of conflict is not less economic in the sense that it also features the problem of scarcity and allows for rational decision makers with preferences to make strategic choices. The concepts known from mainstream economics are applicable in the theory of conflict.
- In analogy to the technology of production there exists a technology of struggle. The most important difference between the two technologies is that the latter generally allows for violence (though conflict may not always be violent). 'Contest Success Functions' (2001b, p. 16) describe how inputs in the form of fighting efforts relate to outcomes in the form of victory and defeat.
- '*The way of production and exchange* enlarges the social total of wealth. *The way of predation and conflict* merely redistributes that total' (2001b, p. 2). Conflict is a constant-sum game – no mutual gains are possible.

According to Hirshleifer, economics does not have too negative an idea of man. To the contrary, as most economists focus on the analysis of production and mutual exchange as well as cooperation, the economic idea of man might actually be too positive: 'Mainline economics has been so concerned to convey the important though partial truth about the possible beneficence of self-interest as to almost forget there is still the dark side' (Hirshleifer, 2001b, p. 7). Hirshleifer acknowledges the dark side of human behavior and models it economically. He distinguishes between three sources of conflict: *opportunities, perceptions,* and *preferences.* Talking about what many people regard as a prototypical evil – war – let us consider *opportunities* first.

Taking purely self-interested, rational parties who only care about the maximization of their material income, one can 'safely predict that decision-makers will lean in the direction of conflict or lean in the direction of cooperative production and exchange, whichever is more profitable on the margin' (Hirshleifer, 2001b, p. 27). One can then represent the decision between peace and war by Figure 3.3.

Consider the left hand side first. With the income of the two parties *i* and *j* on the axes, let *QQ* be the upper frontier of the general opportunity set. Furthermore, let *P* be the expected income-distribution in the conflict case. Since *i* (*j*) only cares about her own, material income, she prefers everything to the east (north) of U_i (U_j) – which represents

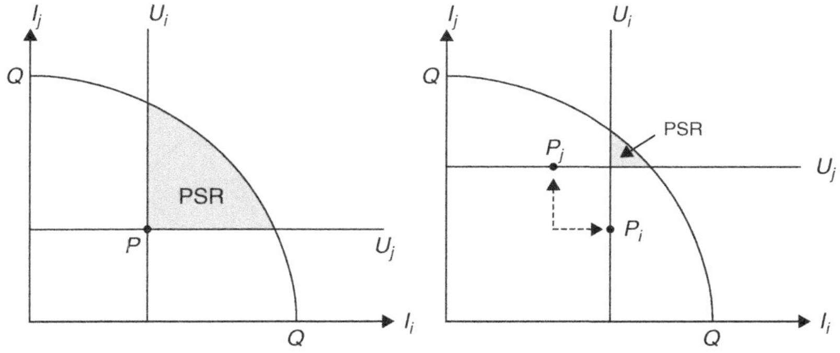

Figure 3.3 The opportunities of war and peace (cf. Hirshleifer, 2001c, p. 27)

her vertical (horizontal) indifference curve in the case of war. 'Since war is costly, under strictly materialist motivations *a Potential Settlement Region always exists* – assuming the parties correctly assess the opportunity set *QQ* and the outcome of war.... To that extent, peace always has the edge on war' (Hirshleifer, 2001c, p. 28). Furthermore, Hirshleifer assumes that the larger the Potential Settlement Region (PSR), due for example to a stronger degree of productive complementarity, the higher the chance of a peaceful agreement. The *perceptions* concerning the outcome of a war influence this picture as well – see the right hand side of Figure 3.3 for their effect. For instance, the more optimistic *i* is about the income attained in the conflict case, the more to the right lies her *perception point* P_i (that does not have to be identical to P_j), the more to the right lies U_i, the smaller the PSR gets (Hirshleifer, 2001c, pp. 30–31).

Finally, Hirshleifer drops the assumption that the parties are only motivated by their own material income, that is he alters the *preferences* of the interacting parties. He introduces other-regarding preferences. An interesting phenomenon is that there are actually two types of other-regarding preferences: *prosocial preferences* and *antisocial* ('evil') *preferences*. In both cases, the utility of a party is not any longer solely determined by her own income but also influenced by the income of the opposing party. The strange relation between evil (for example revenge) and good (for example altruism) from an economic viewpoint has already been noted: in both cases the actor gives up his own income in order to influence the benefits of others. Prosocial preferences describe the case in which a party is willing to sacrifice some income to enrich the other party (see Figure 3.4 to the left); antisocial preferences

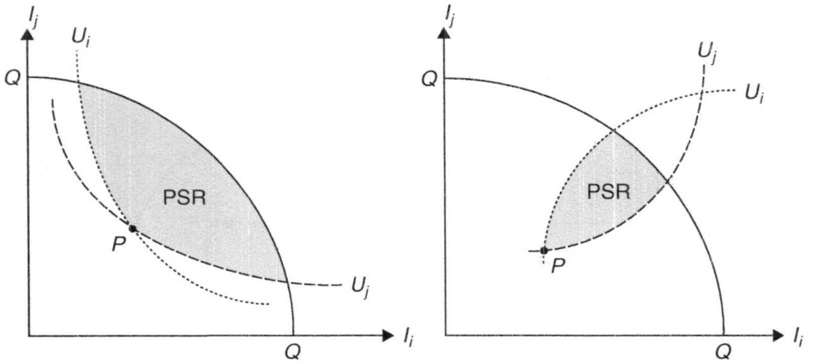

Figure 3.4 Other-regarding preferences (cf. Hirshleifer, 2001c, p. 31)

describe the case in which one party voluntarily sacrifices some income to harm the other party (see Figure 3.4 to the right).

Hirshleifer (2001c, p. 30) refers to the left hand side of Figure 3.4 as the *mutual benevolence case*. The indifference curves are not any longer vertical or horizontal lines, respectively, but take on their familiar convex form. Benevolent preferences enlarge the PSR. The right hand side of Figure 3.4 depicts *mutual malevolence*: the indifference curves have a positive slope and the PSR is reduced.

Models of fairness and emotions: conditional harming in bargaining situations

Hirshleifer's model of adjusted preferences silently passed the frontier between models explaining harming behavior by recurring only to material *self-interest* (typically models of conflict and fighting) and models that propose *other-regarding preferences* (models of conditional bargaining behavior). Fehr and Schmidt (1999) provide a comparable theory of adjusted preferences able to explain harming. However, in their model they do not talk about *general* benevolence and malevolence of the actor as Hirshleifer depicts it but rather about *outcome-specific* benevolence and malevolence. In their theory of fairness, people suffer utility losses from advantageous inequality when their own income (or the payoff from a bargaining game, respectively) lies above that of the competitor and utility losses from disadvantageous inequality when their own income lies below that of the competitor. In short: people feel *guilt* if they have more than others and experience *envy* if they have less (Fehr & Schmidt, 1999, pp. 822–824). For the two-player case, they propose a utility function of the form:

$$U_i(I) = I_i - \alpha_i \max\{I_j - I_i, 0\} - \beta_i \max\{I_i - I_j, 0\} \qquad (3.1)$$

where the second term measures the utility loss from disadvantageous inequality and the third term the loss from advantageous inequality (Fehr & Schmidt, 1999, p. 822). Thus, α measures envy and β measures guilt. They generally assume envy to diminish utility more heavily (that is $\alpha \geq \beta$) – the utility function obtains its maximum at $I_i = I_j$.

Envy can be the cause for somebody giving up own income only to impair the income of somebody else, too (negative payoffs for both parties). 'For example, if $\alpha_i = 4$, then player i is willing to give up one dollar if this reduces the payoff of his opponent by 1.25 dollars. We will see that observable behavior in bargaining and public good games suggests that there are at least some individuals with such high α_i's' (Fehr & Schmidt, 1999, p. 824). Fehr and Schmidt's model is one of *conditional* harming: if somebody has more than you, you might be inclined to spend some money to impair his income.

In fact, Hirshleifer (2001d) proposes his own theory about *conditional* malevolent actions. He then assumes action-dependent other-regarding preferences for an emotionally-affected second mover j that reacts to a purely self-interested first mover i. In order to depict j's emotional responses to i's choice of an income distribution from a given opportunity set QQ', he introduces the *Anger/Gratitude Response curve*:

> Second's responses to First's choice along QQ' are summarized diagrammatically by his Anger/Gratitude Response (AGR) curve. This curve might take on a number of possible shapes, subject to the restrictions that (1) increasing wealth empowers Second to spend more either on transferring income to or else withdrawing income from First, but (2) the more 'cooperative' is First's behavior (that is, the more her choice along QQ' approaches point J), the less is Second's anger and/or the greater is Second's gratitude – with the obvious implication for his willingness to confer benefit or injury upon the other. (Hirshleifer, 2001d, p. 210)

Figure 3.5 depicts an exemplary Anger/Gratitude Response curve.

QQ' represents the set of potential outcomes of a bargaining situation, with the income of i, the first mover, on the y-axis and the

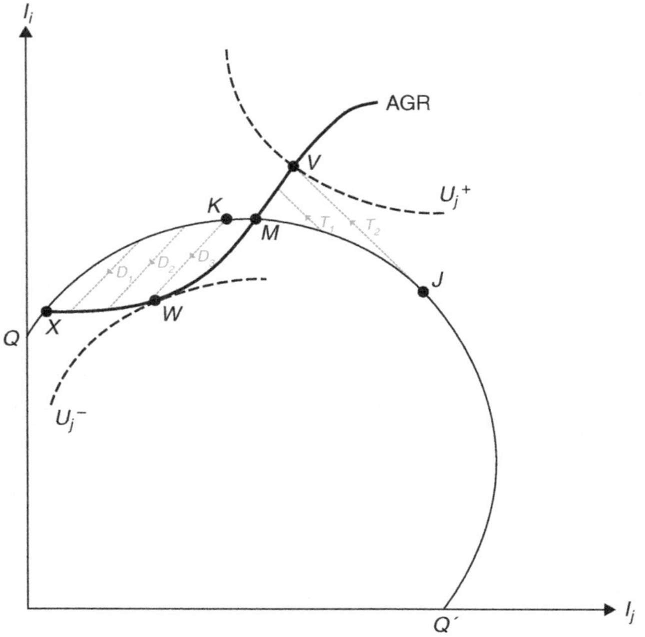

Figure 3.5 The Anger/Gratitude Response curve (cf. Hirshleifer, 2001d, p. 211)

income of *j*, the responder, on the x-axis: *i* is able to bring about every income combination on *QQ'*. In order to interpret Figure 3.5 one has to distinguish between three areas on *QQ'*: from *Q* to *X*, *j* just does not have enough income to retaliate against *i*'s very unfavorable choice of income-distribution. Between points *X* and *M* lies *j*'s 'effective anger region' (Hirshleifer, 2001d, p. 210). In this region, *j* possesses antisocial preferences (U_j^-) and chooses to spend some of his spare income to reduce *i*'s income. This is possible in Hirshleifer's model along the *deprivation lines* (D_1, D_2, and D_3) which allow for a 1:1 exchange of income between the players – one unit of own income given up causes a one-unit income loss for *i*. So, for example, if *i* proposes *K*, the final distribution reached is actually *W* due to *j*'s anger – which is the reason for a malevolent action on his part. The third region, finally, is from *M* onwards, where *j* possesses prosocial preferences (U_j+) and voluntarily gives up some income to further enrich *i*. He is able to do so along the *transfer lines* (T_1 and T_2), which obey the same mechanics as the deprivation lines. This is *j*'s 'effective gratitude region' (Hirshleifer, 2001d,

p. 210).[1] As we move from east to west, the second mover can increasingly afford to act out his malevolent feelings about the first mover but also becomes decreasingly inclined to do so, since his malevolent emotions are dependent on *i*'s actions.

The biggest difference between the models of Hirshleifer (2001d) and Fehr and Schmidt (1999) is that, while both rely on a reference distribution of income to explain harming, Fehr and Schmidt assume stable other-regarding preferences across different contexts. The feelings of envy and guilt are not a consequence of the behavior of the first mover but for example also apply to situations in which the reference income distribution is created randomly by a computer. Hirshleifer, on the other hand, assumes that the entire indifference curve map of the second mover changes with respect to the first mover's choice. Thus, it should be more suited to explain actions out of a feeling of revenge in a given situation, whereas Schmidt and Fehr's model rather applies to more calm, general and theoretical reflections about inequity, fairness, and justice. Both models have in common that they cover *conditional* harming of other people's income.

In general, one can classify models of other-regarding preferences and engendered actions (of which there are a lot) in two big categories: theories focusing on the *final payoffs* of the interacting subjects and theories focusing on the *behavior* of the subjects while bargaining. Each main category features two sub-categories.

Theories focusing on the final payoffs in experimental games ask the question which payoffs the playing subjects favor. Models of *unconditional altruism* constitute the first sub-category (for example, Andreoni & Miller, 2002; Hirshleifer, 2001c). Their main assumption is that people do not only care about their own payoff, but also about the payoffs of others. The second sub-category is constituted by theories of *conditional altruism* (for example, Bolton & Ockenfels, 2000; Fehr & Schmidt, 1999). Like in models of unconditional altruism, people care about the payoffs of others but always *with respect to their own gains* from the game. While subjects in models of unconditional altruism give to others independently of what they have themselves, subjects in fairness models always compare their payoffs to the payoffs of their counterparts. If they have more than their counterparts they feel 'guilt' and give something to them, if they have less than their counterparts, they feel 'envy' and would prefer a more equal allocation. In such theories, people generally favor more money and more equal allocations.

For theories focusing on behavior, the most important question is not 'What is my payoff and what is the payoff of my counterpart?' but rather: 'With whom shall I cooperate?'. These theories are also called theories of reciprocity, since subjects are typically thought to reason under which conditions they reciprocate kind behavior shown towards them. The first sub-category is models of *intention-based reciprocity* (for example, Charness & Rabin, 2002; Falk & Fischbacher, 2006; Hirshleifer, 2001d; Rabin, 1993). In such models people cooperate with people that *behaved fairly* towards them. It is thus necessary that some prior act of the counterpart can be identified as either kind or rude when making the decision to reciprocate or not. Rabin (1993) models these scenarios with the tools of psychological game theory. 'The same people who are altruistic toward deserving people are often indifferent to the plight of undeserving people, and motivated to hurt those whom they believe to have misbehaved' (Rabin, 1998, p. 21). Furthermore, Rabin explicitly models the role of intentions and motives: fairness is directly linked to intention since it is the latter that decides whether we perceive another person's given action as fair or unfair. 'When motivated by reciprocal altruism... people differentiate between those who take a generous action by choice and those who are forced to do so' (Rabin, 1998, p. 22). So our inclination to fairness varies with our interpretation of what the others' beliefs about the consequences of their actions were.

The second sub-category is theories of *type-based reciprocity* (Levine, 1998). In such theories, individuals cooperate with people whom they think to *be fair*. Unlike in models of intention-based reciprocity it is not prior, kind acts that qualify for reciprocating behavior, but rather the question of whether the counterparts are overall good or bad people. The key is not that they *behave* fairly but that they *are* of the fair type.

Reputation building: harming others strategically out of self-interest

Whereas the intensely discussed models of bargaining featuring envy and guilt (Fehr and Schmidt) as well as anger and gratitude (Hirshleifer) are able to explain why people harm their counterparts by *referring to individual utilities being influenced by the payoffs of others*, there is also a way of explaining this behavior *based on purely self-interested preferences*. Reputational considerations of strategically thinking actors with self-interested preferences then become the motivating factor for harming others.

Hirshleifer again provides a good example. Reasoning about the rationality of emotions that may encourage harming others, such as anger, he states: '*anger* tends to be... effective... in securing cooperation' (Hirshleifer, 2001d, p. 215). What Hirshleifer (2001d, pp. 211–213) emphasizes is the fact that emotions (and the actions they cause) might have a strategic value. If in a typical bargaining game a second mover can convince a first mover that he is very 'angry' and will harshly retaliate against any offer he perceives to be too low, this threat of behaving angrily may generate a higher material income for the second mover. Figure 3.6 illustrates this:

Figure 3.6 follows the exact same rules of construction as Figure 3.5 above: *QQ'* is the set of potential outcomes from a bargaining situation involving the first-mover *i* and the second-mover *j*. The incomes of the players are noted on the y-axis and x-axis, respectively. Compared to the AGR curve of Figure 3.5 (marked as dotted line), anger is now the dominant emotion of the second-mover *j* for his new AGR' curve: his effective anger region (that covered only a small part of *QQ'* in Figure 3.5) now stretches until *L*, that is even beyond *J* which used to be the efficient point. Any offer to the west of *L* will be retaliated by *j* along the deprivation lines, lowering the income of both players.

If the first mover *i* used to choose *J* on *QQ'* (and *V* was reached as final outcome due to the gratitude of *j* transferring income to *i*), *j* now only starts to transfer income to *i* if he is very well treated – the crossover point of the AGR' curve along *QQ'* lies far east. The optimal choice for *i*

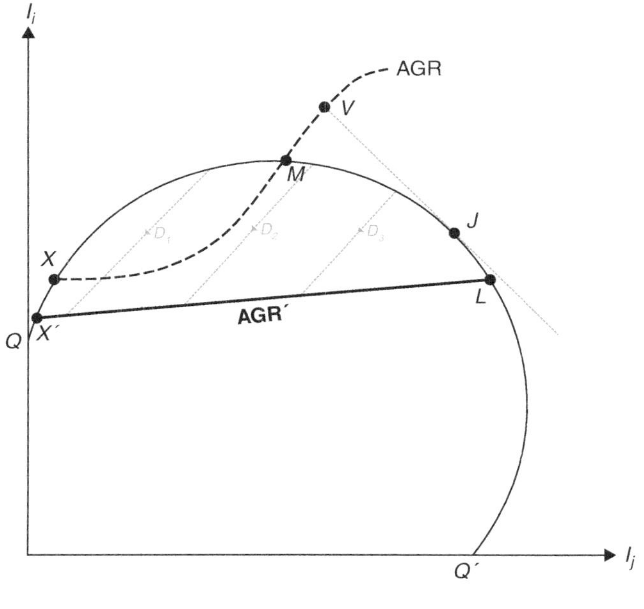

Figure 3.6 An alternative AGR curve (cf. Hirshleifer, 2001d, p. 212)

now is *L*, which leaves *j* with a lot more income than he used to have at *V*. Hirshleifer (2001d, p. 213) concludes that, if *j* can convince *i* that his AGR curve has a positive slope (that is with rising offers *j* is appeased) but only grows slowly (crossover point with *QQ'* far to the east), the threat of a harsh retaliation out of anger by *j* will lead to an excellent outcome for *j*. One way to convince *i*, that is to make the threat *credible*, could be to have opted against additional income for himself and his counterpart in the past (double negative payoff): *j*'s *reputation*, then, is a means to raising his material income.

NB: Hirshleifer does not in fact argue that *j* really possesses an AGR curve of the form of AGR', with a huge 'effective anger region'. Such an AGR' curve would still be an example of *other-regarding* preferences – be they of the antisocial kind. All that *j* tries to do is to convince *i* of having an AGR' curve, when in fact he is purely *self-interested*. In Figure 3.5, only *i* had self-interested preferences, whereas *j* had other-regarding preferences. In Figure 3.6, both players possess self-interested preferences but *j* tries to convince *i* of having antisocial other-regarding preferences to cash in on his bad reputation.

What Hirshleifer does is to rationalize emotions that potentially cause harm to others by assigning them, ex post, a strategic value. If you act angrily from time to time, this may actually increase your material income in the long run, due to others' fear of not appeasing you adequately. To voluntarily accept a lower income in order to hurt somebody else, therefore does not have to be the expression of conditional other-regarding preferences ('I am angry because he got too much'). It might just well be strategic behavior purely motivated by self-interested preferences and material gains in the long run. This line of attack of reducing emotions (and the harm they potentially cause) to strategic thoughts is very common to explain the rationality of harming other people without having to refer to other-regarding preferences in economic contexts. Hirshleifer's threat of being angry follows the exact same rules as Buchanan's (1975/2000, pp. 79–81) threat of the stronger person to fight in anarchy (cf. Section 3.3). Also in non-cooperative game theory credible threats and reputation effects play a dominant role, for example in entry deterrence games (Holler & Illing, 2006; Kreps & Wilson, 1982). Such arguments are often formed in order to explain why people spend money to harm others following a biological (evolutionary) logic. Schelling gives some examples of 'strategic' declarations made by predator and prey that could be made consciously or even through calculations:

> I'm harmless and I couldn't hurt you if I wanted to.
>
> I attack everyone who comes near me.

> I'll expose us both if you don't do what I ask....
>
> I'll destroy my property if you approach it.
>
> I will not fight for my property, so you don't have to kill me to get it....
>
> I hurt anyone who fails to help anyone who helps me. (Schelling, 1978, p. 230)

Also the psychological approach of an evolutionary theory to evil stresses this advantageous effect of an evil reputation that leads to being exploited by others less often (cf. Section 2.2). Empirical evidence shows that this strategy actually works. If in ultimatum games players are continuously paired with the same people, responders are able to build up a reputation of being a very 'tough' responder with high rejection rates. In several experiments (Andreoni & Miller, 1993; Engelmann & Fischbacher, 2002; Gächter & Falk, 2002; Seinen & Schram, 2006) both offers and rejection rates increased if there was a higher probability of being paired with the same subjects again and thus a reputation could be built up.

3.2.3 Empirical evidence on harming in neoclassical economics

The different theories of other-regarding preferences capable of explaining harming did not emerge by coincidence; most of them were provoked by findings in experimental economics that seemed to question the fundamental assumptions that economics made about human beings. The idea of testing the theoretical predictions of game theory with human subjects in laboratory environments has not only led to Nobel prizes but also to a huge body in literature on experimental games (for a good overview see Camerer, 2003; Fehr & Schmidt, 2006; Kagel & Roth, 1995). The key finding of this field of research could probably be stated as follows: there are many ways in which real people deviate from the game-theoretical predictions based on the idea of the rational maximization of material income. The discussion here will be limited to three particularly striking instances of behavior that are worth being considered from the perspective of economic evil.

Public good games[2] are often used in order to test for altruism – the more people are contributing from their own income to a public pot, the more altruistic they are according to the general assumption (Ledyard, 1995). Fehr and Gächter (2000) show with their experimental design that one can also draw conclusions on harming behavior from public good games – NB: without intending to do so or explicitly speaking of this perspective. In order to examine the well-known phenomena of declining contributions, unraveling cooperation, and increased free-riding in repeated public good games (Andreoni, 1988; Banks, Plott, & Porter, 1988; Brown-Kruse & Hummels, 1993; Camerer & Fehr, 2002; Isaac & Walker, 1987), Fehr and Gächter (2000) designed a two stage repeated public goods game: the first stage being a ten-period standard public goods game, but in the second stage allowing the players to assign punishment points to players who did not contribute enough in the first stage. Each player could assign up to ten punishment points that each lowered the punished player's income by 10 percent but also reduced the income of the punisher. Though the game-theoretic prediction is that no punishment occurs and that the contributions do not change – since both punishing and contributing is costly to the individual player – the subjects made intense use of this new possibility. In the second stage, Fehr and Gächter observed a massive increase in cooperation. In the last period of the game almost everybody contributed his whole endowment to the public pot although almost no punishment occurred. Those who did free ride in the first stages were punished and quickly changed their contribution behavior.

The behavior of those handing out punishment points is a clear example of people spending money to impair the income of others. Notice that Fehr and Gächter do not speak of harming or evil at all but rather of fairness and altruism. Due to the underlying mechanics of the public good game by Fehr and Gächter, harming another player's income has the consequence that the 'free rider' contributes more to the public pot which leads in turn to a higher income for the punisher in the long run. It is not clear whether the intention of the punishers was to harm the free rider out of some feeling of anger for not contributing enough, or rather to restore high levels of contribution from which they themselves benefit. Based on this evidence alone, one cannot distinguish between long-term strategic behavior motivated by material self-interest and behavior induced by other-regarding preferences.

This shortcoming can be overcome by turning to one-shot ultimatum games,[3] as these games cancel out the possibility of strategic punishing. Camerer summarizes the typical outcome of ultimatum games as follows: 'Modal and median offers are usually 40–50 percent and means are 30–40 percent. There are hardly any offers in the outlying categories of 0, 1–10, and the hyper-fair category 51–100. Offers of 40–50 percent are rarely rejected. Offers below 20 percent or so are rejected about half the time' (2003, p. 49). In general, the rejection rate declines as the size of the offers rises; and considering the results of a whole experimental group of people, 10 to 15 percent of offers in ultimatum games are typically declined (Camerer, 2003; Fehr & Schmidt, 1999; Hoffman et al, 1996; Hoffman et al, 1994).

Any single responder in one-shot ultimatum games that rejects an offer is willing to give up his own income in order to punish what he perceives as an unfair offer. If we call such behavior 'just' (because he might be motivated by fairness considerations; this is what economists typically do) or rather 'evil' (because he intentionally harms his counterpart) is a question of interpretation. Remember Leibniz's (1710/1996) argument for a causal link between *malum morale* (a low offer in this case) and *malum naturale* (the rejection by the responder with the consequence of foregone material income), because otherwise *justice* would be impossible. The words *evil* and *just* seem to be used frequently in the same breath. It is a fine line here that distinguishes high-minded ideals from evil behavior and every rejection fulfills the necessary condition of economic evil. Even more so as neither repetition of the game (List & Cherry, 2000; Roth & Erev, 1995; Slonim & Roth, 1998), nor raised stakes (Camerer, 2003; Hoffman et al., 1996; Slonim & Roth, 1998), nor cultural factors (Camerer & Fehr, 2002; Henrich & Smith, 2004; Henrich et al, 2001; Roth et al, 1991) are able to dramatically change the bargaining behavior. Section 3.2.4 will further elaborate on these interpretational issues.

Those still skeptical about the empirical relevance of harming behavior in economics should consider the evidence from third-party punishment games. It is the merit of Fehr and Fischbacher (2004) to have introduced this game:

> We studied third-party sanctions of violations of a distribution norm by adding a third player with a punishment option to a DG [dictator game; C.D.M.] played between Player A, the dictator, and Player B, the recipient.... Player A had an endowment of 100 points and could transfer 0, 10, 20, 30, 40, or 50 to Player B, who had no endowment. The third party, Player C, was endowed with 50 points, and had the option of punishing Player A after observing A's transfer to B. Player A's payoff was reduced by 3 points for every punishment point that Player C assigned to Player A. In principle, Player C could use up to 50 points (C's whole endowment) to punish A. At the end of the experiment, points were converted into real money at an exchange rate of 1 point = CHF 0.3. Player B could not affect the payoff of any other person in the game – he or she was just the passive recipient of A's transfer. (Fehr & Fischbacher, 2004, p. 66)

The game-theoretic prediction is that A allocates nothing to B – as in standard dictator games – and that C never punishes this seemingly unfair behavior – since each punishment point spent on punishing A is costly to C. The three most important outcomes of Fehr and Fischbacher's game are the following: first, normally player A was not punished if he gave more than half of his endowment to player B. Second, the less player A transferred, the more he was punished by player C. Third, although nearly all players A who transferred nothing to B were punished (severely) by players C, it still paid off not to allocate anything to players B: in this case, A received on average 14 punishment points which in turn reduced his income by 42 points and left him with 58 points. This means however, that his payoff is still larger in this case (on average) than if he transferred the presumably fair amount of 50 points (leaving him with 50 points and a 5 percent chance of being punished additionally). Third party punishment is typically weaker than second party punishment (Fehr & Fischbacher, 2004). On the other hand, Camerer and Fehr (2002) report that in a public goods games with supplementary third party punishment – there is an *uninvolved* punisher able to punish defection in the group trying to establish a public good – third party punishment is nearly as strong as second party punishment (measured in standard public good games with punishment as described above).

Overall, third-party punishment games show even more clearly than responder behavior in ultimatum games that people are willing to intentionally harm other people even if this implies giving up own income. Given that much prosocial behavior is observed in experimental economics (fairness, altruism and reciprocity), experimental games also provide empirical evidence for harming behavior in an economic context – if one looks at it from the perspective of evil.

Evidence on the role of emotions

Notably the theories of other-regarding preferences rely heavily on emotions to explain how harming behavior actually comes about. In fact, de Quervain et al. (2004) were able to show that emotions do play an important role for punishment behavior in economic games. They observed the brain activity of subjects who played a modified trust game[4] with punishment opportunity using Positron Emission Tomography (PET). Three different conditions were tested: in the 'costly' condition (C) the investor could assign up to 20 punishment points to the trustee, if the latter abused the former's trust. However, each punishment point cost 1 USD to the investor – and reduced the trustee's income by 2 USD.

In the 'free' condition (F), punishment was only costly to the trustee. In the 'symbolic' condition (S), the investor could assign punishment points to the trustee but these had only a symbolic value, that is there was no way for the investor to actually diminish the trustee's payoff.

De Quervain et al. suspected that effective punishment might be emotionally rewarding. This claim was supported by the data, as in both scenarios, the F-S and the C-S contrast, the dorsal striatum – an area for which there is strong evidence that it processes reward-related information – was strongly activated whenever effective punishment was possible and occurred. Since, in addition, the majority of the subjects punished as strongly as possible in the F condition and less severely in the C condition, one might argue that punishment is analogous to buying a good: 'Rational subjects buy the good [, that is punishment,] as long as the marginal costs are below the marginal benefits' (Fehr & Schmidt, 2006, p. 21). Thus, as already stated, one does not have to leave the framework set by utility analysis in order to rationalize why people give up money in order to harm others. While de Quervain et al. (2004) showed the relationship between the emotion of revenge and harming other people's income, Fliessbach et al. (2007) were able to reach similar results for the emotion of envy.

This evidence is especially interesting if taken together with the theory that moral sentiments are 'socially developed sentiments' (Mackie, 1985, p. 219). Humans may have learned to like to hurt other people; or, as Mantzavinos puts it: 'Once the long-lasting process of rule acquisition has taken place, both the cognitive and the motivational systems are formed in such a way that respect for the moral rules is secured' (2001, p. 117). NB: The only things that 'objectively' distinguish morally praiseworthy punishment from evil harming are ideological reasons.

However, in a critical article, Elster (1998) argues against the standard economic approach that emotions shape rewards in a simple cost-benefit-way that can be integrated into rational choice models with stable preferences. He argues for a 'dual role of the emotions' (Elster, 1998, p. 73), namely that they not only shape rewards but also choices. One should rather understand emotions as *temporary preferences*, too. '[T]he envy man is not made happy by carrying out his urge to destroy the envied object or its possessor.... Implementing the action tendency of envy makes the agent worse off' (Elster, 1998, p. 69). Looking back, he might want to have decided differently. According to Elster, you might be overreacting in a state of emotional arousal: 'While inducing action to alleviate the negative emotion of envy, it [that is envy] prevents us from thinking clearly about the consequences of such actions' (Elster, 1998, p. 69). Preferences for material self-interest are not only to be augmented with preferences for non-material benefits; they are temporarily put out of operation in a state of emotional arousal. This approach is able to explain some of the 'irrationality' associated with evil behavior and well in line with Baumeister and Vohs' (2005, pp. 98–99) argument that the *proximal cause* for evil is lacking self-control (which is typical of emotional states as well as alcohol intoxication, for example). 'Many events give rise to aggressive impulses, but self-control prevents people from acting on them. In a sense, self-control is the last defense against aggression' (Baumeister & Vohs, 2005, pp. 98–99). From an evolutionary perspective, this temporal change of preferences might not be a shortcoming of human nature but '"impulsivity" is actually a design feature ... that promotes ... tactical effectiveness' (Duntley & Buss, 2005, p. 118). If the proposer in an ultimatum does not consider a rejection of a low offer very likely and strategically calculates the size of his offer, he might be punished more effectively. The arguments and complications brought up by Elster against a too trivial modeling of emotions and the like in economics are just one reason why this book in general treats the non-material benefits of evil actions as a black box.

3.2.4 Conclusion on evil actions

The actions of people harming others materially without profiting materially from it have received some attention in economics – however not as an independent phenomenon in its own right and not under the header of economically evil actions assuming a 'taste for harming'.

From a theoretical standpoint, there are three approaches able to explain why human beings harm each other. First, following Buchanan (1975/2000) and Hirshleifer (1995, 2001c), one can state that people may harm each other if this increases their material payoff directly and in the short run. The best examples are fighting and conflict in general. The models of these authors might depict something that resembles an egoistic action, but one should not forget that Buchanan rather pursues the goal of normatively proving the necessity of rules and Hirshleifer is rather interested to show in general that conflict can be modeled with economic concepts. Both authors are not interested in describing evil actions of individuals per se but touch, in an all-embracing manner, on the general economic modeling of situations in which evil actions might occur (anarchy, war). Both authors are convinced that the establishment of enforceable institutions will put an end to fighting eventually.

Second, following Fehr and Schmidt (1999) and Hirshleifer (2001d), one can state that if humans possess other-regarding preferences, emotions like envy and anger may cause them to give up own income only to lower the income of their counterpart in a bargaining game, too. The condition for acting this way is that they think that either the outcome of the game played or the behavior of their counterpart was 'unfair' in some way. The final payoff combination in these cases might be the same as for a malicious action but the authors argue in the direction of a theory of altruism, fairness, and reciprocity rather than in the direction of viciousness and evil. Their main line of attack is that other-regarding preferences might induce actions that *positively* deviate from the idea of economic man. Interestingly, the wide evidence on people punishing in public goods games, rejecting offers in ultimatum games, and punishing in third party punishment games did not alter the fact that the treatment of this behavior has only been marginal and in a conciliatory fashion.

Third, one may follow Hirshleifer (2001d), Schelling (1960), and others in highlighting that reputation-building measures may lead people to give up income only to harm others. The goal of increasing one's own payoffs in the long run backs up their arguments. This line of reasoning also comes close to explaining evil actions. Still, the authors are focusing on the potential strategic value of emotions in evolutionary categories rather than talking about economically evil actions of individuals out of a 'taste for harming'.

Overall, the approaches cited may be *able to explain some forms of economic evil* but they were *not intentionally designed for this purpose.* Nobody reasoned about a 'taste for harming' with the goal of committing evil for evil's sake. *It is one goal of this book to explicitly name impairing other people's income for what it is (an economically evil action) and to show that these actions matter in economic contexts and are phenomena in their own right, since they have relevant consequences for the economic performance of a society.* By researching economic actors in a new, different environment (the MMORPG *EVE Online*), new empirical evidence on these issues will be gained. It will turn out that the established economic theories are not able to account for all the behavioral evidence found in EVE, for example for what seems to be the actors' 'taste for harming'. One must not restrict the examination of evil actions to *conditional* evil that still has an *instrumental* value – as the theories and experiments cited do. One has to examine *unconditional, unprecedented, hostile evil* of the type that sadists commit, or the subjects in Milgram's obedience experiments, in economics, too. In addition to the research on altruism and fairness with economic means, it is interesting also to research viciousness, cruelty and ruthlessness in an investigation of its own right.

If the literature does not explicitly refer to the unifying concept of evil as for example psychology does but rather uses scattered terms like envy, anger, or malevolence in different contexts, this might be due to a lack of awareness that these different actualizations of evil human behavior have something in common – notably the desire to harm another person. That economics does not yet consider the existence of a 'taste for harming' is one reason for the supposed underestimation of the importance of evil in the domain of economics. Maybe economics is too concerned with proving that humans are actually better than the predictions of economic man to see that there are also negative deviations from this model of behavior. The sheer lack of empirical opportunities to examine harming behavior in detail has already been proposed as another potential reason for the *conciliatory nature of economic interpretations of harming behavior.*

There might also be a third reason that has something to do with the *principium diiudicationis* applied to define what evil is in the first place. It is astonishing that one encounters phenomena closely related to evil actions in economic theories about fairness and reciprocity as well as in bargaining games said to measure altruism. This is a surprising finding about the theories of other-regarding preferences: the general evaluation of those behaviors that deviate from the selfish predictions of economic man is quite positive. People *harm* others – but for the sake of *fairness.* The emphasis lies in conditional altruism and voluntary contributing to public goods. It might be a subtle distinction, *a question of tone rather than content,* but most of the authors present a positive interpretation of their findings: humans are not as bad as economic man predicts. This book's general line of attack should make everybody skeptical about the prevailing optimism. The philosophical and psychological findings showed that the concepts of fairness and justice are often too easily applied in explaining malicious actions. And other-regarding preferences can be split up into prosocial and antisocial preferences. Both good and evil behavior is closely related from an economic viewpoint since both present deviations from the parsimonious economic idea of man: material self-interest.

Maybe there are also historical reasons for this oversight. Foucault states that in former times the relationship between committed moral evil (for example defection in bargaining games) and the (bodily) punishment was one of symmetry and that the judges as well as the perpetrators were quite aware that the punishment in itself constituted another evil; evil was doubled by the punishment, so to speak, and this was common knowledge (Foucault, 1975/1995, pp. 55–57). In the course of the centuries punishments became milder and started to aim at resocialization rather than retribution and expiation (ibid.). The comparably mild punishments of today's courts may foster the hidden role harm plays in every punishment – also in punishment in public good games or third party punishment games. Thus, one should be careful in underestimating the importance of evil.

In this book, the *principium diiudicationis* of material harm done is used to qualify actions and institutions as being evil. What used to be 'just punishment' might now turn out to be a 'malicious action'. To be clear: considering public good games and ultimatum games primarily means talking about monetary payoffs in a given strategic situation. All that exists is raw data of human behavior. To reinterpret these payoffs from representing 'just' actions to 'evil' actions is, to say the least, problematic. It is an interpretative bias to refer to these payoffs as signifying 'fairness' – *just as it would be an interpretative bias to immediately call it 'economic evil'.* The reader should be advised that the interpretation of actions as 'just' or 'evil' is far from going without saying. A change of tone – from speaking of fairness to speaking of evil – might nevertheless be advisable; especially if one accepts the idea that the role of evil in economics is an underestimated one and that looking at material payoffs is a good way of starting to evaluate things. Overall, these phenomena are far more complex than paying a certain amount of money in a given situation. All these notions are interpretations that only make sense in a concrete social context with rules guiding and defining the behavior of the community members. It was mentioned that due to social rules governing interactions, not every harm inflicted is qualified as being evil – sometimes this may be appropriate, sometimes not. That is the very reason why this book did not examine laboratory games but conducts field work in EVE: simply because there are no good or evil actions per se and because it matters what the relevant community defines as being evil. Rules define what is evil and what is good. Let us now turn to defining evil social institutions.

3.3 Evil social institutions

The effects of acceptable justifications, rationales, ideologies, or changed semantics and vocabulary on human behavior were responsible for reconsidering the idea of the existence of *natural evil* in this book. In addition, human behavior is often governed by conscious or unconscious rules or heuristics (Gigerenzer, 2008; Gigerenzer et al., 1999; Mantzavinos, 2001). If the rule holds that you should act in a particular way, then you will probably do so, partly ignoring the evil consequences of your actions. This is the first reason for speaking of rules if one wants to examine economic evil.

The second reason is that the concept of evil itself is always rule-bound. The general principle distinguishing good from evil is as important as the rules of the game that concretely tell people to harm or not to harm in a specific context. Going back to the example of the merchant using incorrectly adjusted scales and thus materially harming his clients by charging too much, one could judge this behavior as economically evil according to the definition presented – it is an egoistic action. But does not the picture change if every merchant that is part of the community manipulates his scales? If everybody manipulates scales, could you really say that doing so as well is an egoistic action – or should not you rather judge the merchant's behavior as *competitive*, since he would not be able to offer competitive prices with correctly adjusted scales in such a corrupted environment and thus would have to close his store fairly quickly? Some communities might be very strict in controlling manipulated scales (and consequent punishment); others might be inclined to be more lenient with respect to this issue. After all, how evil is it to tilt the weights of a scale a little bit into a favorable direction, if everybody does it and, consequently, everybody (including the customer) expects it?

'Evil' social rules may be an important cause of evil actions, because they are an instance of natural evil. Furthermore, rules in general play an important role in defining what evil is for a given community in the first place. In this section, *the focus will be on the former type of rules, that is on rules that induce people to commit evil actions*. After having examined evil *actions* (moral evil) from an economic perspective, the next step is examining the *rule* aspect of an economic definition of evil (natural evil). *Evil social institutions* will be defined, and it will be argued whether such rules are likely to exist and persist from a theoretical point of view. In order to do so, the findings of New Institutional Economics (NIE), more precisely the cognitive version of it, will guide the way (for example, Denzau & North, 1994; Mantzavinos, 2001; Mantzavinos et al, 2004; North, 1990, 2005). Most notably Mantzavinos's (2001) approach will be used in order to better understand how rules concerning evil could evolve and change as well as how they are adopted and enforced.

3.3.1 Individuals and institutions

Buchanan's (1975/2000) already cited account of fighting in anarchic conditions gives a good impression of the adverse economic consequences following from two self-interested people meeting in the natural state. In the absence of rules, individuals will almost necessarily not only start to produce goods but also to steal from others and thereby exercise positive amounts of depredation effort. However, Buchanan is convinced that this negative status quo will be overcome eventually by constitutional and post-constitutional contracting. The underlying assumptions of this reasoning are that, first, social conflict (most prominently, fighting) is a wasteful activity that only redistributes wealth – if not even a destructive activity that lowers the capital stock of an economic community – and that, therefore, everybody would be better off without social conflict. Second, social utility could rise even further by focusing all efforts on productive actions and, subsequently, by profiting from the gains from trade that arise from the division of labor and exchange processes (for example, Buchanan, 1975/2000, p. 39). Yet, although Buchanan is convinced that social institutions will evolve eventually he is not so much interested in describing how they actually emerge but rather in explaining why they are necessary in general.

This changes with NIE. Without leaving the mindset of mainstream neoclassical economics in this aspect, Mantzavinos (2001, p. 13) sees striving to increase individual utility as the main motivation of human beings. The social problems brought about when such individuals meet are precisely the point when institutions enter the picture. 'Institutions are normative social rules, that is, the rules of the game in a society, enforced either through law or through other mechanisms of social control that shape human interactions' (Mantzavinos, 2001, p. 83). Institutions exist, because they provide solutions to social conflicts; their existence is 'the first step toward overcoming the Hobbesian problem of social order' (ibid.). If there is a rule in place that forbids any kind of fighting and if it is enforced by a powerful State that administers severe punishments whenever somebody transgresses it, fighting becomes unprofitable for the individual – and the social conflict less severe.

'Institutions emerge either deliberately or spontaneously, that is, either as a product of collective action or as a product of a spontaneous process of social interaction' (Mantzavinos, 2001, p. 90). The sovereign or any other decision-maker can put institutions into place, if she is conscious of the existence of a social problem (that is any problem concerning more than one person) and tries to enact a solution. Since overcoming social conflicts is thought to always be beneficial to the interacting parties, one can also rely on a spontaneous, evolutionary process of the emergence of institutions. Sooner or later the people stuck in a situation of social conflict will find a way to end fighting and start cooperating instead. The agents do not have to be aware that their problem-solving activities function as a role model for other agents with the same problem (Mantzavinos, 2001, p. 92). If, however, they figure out a good solution the chances are high that other agents imitating this successful strategy adopt it too. All institutional evolution and change, be it deliberate or spontaneous, can thus be traced back to a learning process by individuals.

Once a certain institution has been established and spreads throughout a community, another reason for the existence of institutions becomes obvious; it has to do with the *cognitive* architecture of humans and complements the *motivational* reason of rule-existence (that rules provide solutions to social problems).

> Because of the restriction of their cognitive capacity, all individuals mobilize their energies only when a new problem arises and follow routines when they classify the problem situation as a familiar one. This distinction is rooted in their limited computational capacity and is a means to free their minds from unnecessary operations in order to deal adequately with the problem situations arising in their environment.... Because of the perceived complexity of the social environment, people adopt – consciously or unconsciously – *rules* as solutions to social problems rather than deciding each time anew how to act and react to the setting where coordination with other individuals is needed. (Mantzavinos, 2001, p. 87)

Because humans' limited minds are overwhelmed by the complexity of the social environment, they use rules to guide their behavior in order to facilitate interaction. This is the cognitive reason for the existence of rules – it is closely connected to one important function of social rules, namely that they stabilize expectations about the behavior of others we meet (Mantzavinos, 2001, p. 89). Rules reduce uncertainty about how one should behave and how others will behave in a given situation. In line with the reasons for the existence of rules and their function, Mantzavinos (2001, pp. 38–42) distinguishes between two kinds of human behavior: rule-following behavior and choice behavior. Whenever somebody perceives a problem he encounters as a new one, he will enter a process of deliberate choice that determines his action.

On the other hand, 'if the current problem is identified as a familiar one...then the appropriate solution in the form of a [already learned] rule will be applied automatically' (2001, p. 35). The individual member of a community acquires already established rules in the process of socialization – you learn the most important rules as you are brought up in a community.

3.3.2 Moral rules as solutions to evil actions

The most important kind of institutions with respect to evil are *moral rules*. The function of moral rules, according to Mantzavinos (2001, p. 106), is to induce cooperative behavior in a situation where it seems to be in the best self-interest not to cooperate. He illustrates moral behavior with cooperation in a prisoner's dilemma with an exit option: mutual cooperation would be the Pareto-optimal outcome, while defection is the individually rational strategy, and there always is the possibility not to play at all. Since the defection of player A always induces a lower material payoff for player B irrespective of his own choice, it can be qualified as an economically evil action – and moral rules act as a mechanism to prevent such actions.

Belonging to the class of informal rules (that is rules that do not refer to the State as the enforcement agency), moral rules rely on the individual agents as controller and emerge spontaneously in an invisible hand process (Mantzavinos, 2001, pp. 84–85, 108). Nobody can force one of the prisoners to cooperate; *only I can force myself to abide by a moral rule*. Unlike Kant, Mantzavinos does not speak of the intentions of the prisoners – all that counts is the outcome, the actual observable behavior. The impossibility of enforcing a moral rule in Mantzavinos's example is not due to the Kantian requirement of an autonomous good will to incite the action, but solely due to the fact that nobody can force a prisoner to cooperate in a standard prisoner's dilemma since this is against his material self-interest and no sanctions are around that could alter this picture. For Mantzavinos, you abide by a moral rule every time that you choose not to opt for an individually rational outcome that is not Pareto-optimal, and instead opt for a Pareto-optimal outcome whose establishment is uncertain since it also depends on the choice of another person that faces the same incentives as you do. For Mantzavinos, all that counts is the outcome; for Kant, all that counts is the intention.

Although moral rules sometimes serve the purpose of preventing evil actions, they are unable to do so perfectly. Firstly, Mantzavinos stresses the fact that it is typical for moral rules not to be respected by everybody in a population: 'The empirical phenomenon to be explained is the *existence* of moral rules in a society that are followed by *part* of the population' (Mantzavinos, 2001, p. 106). Whereas Kant refers to the frailty of our character or the impureness of our maxims as the reasons for immoral behavior, Mantzavinos sees the *conditional nature* of moral rules as the reason for this phenomenon: one is willing to cooperate in situations that resemble prisoner's dilemmas, only on the condition that the counterpart also cooperates (2001, p. 109). Those unfortunate individuals that continually interact with transgressors of the rule will never learn them. That is, *even in a society with established moral rules evil actions still happen as not everybody has adopted them.*

Secondly, even if everybody abided by moral rules, evil actions might still take place. Until now, those who do *not* abide by moral rules have seemed to be the blameworthy ones; those not following moral rules are acting immorally, maybe even evilly. But remember Arendt's (1965/2007a) rule-critical position (Section 2.1). For her, it seems as if abiding by moral rules does not always lead to mutual gains. She argues that it is often not enough to passively obey the given rules if you do not want to fall prey to the banality of evil. One has to consciously think for oneself – that is one has to be a 'person' (Arendt, 1965/2007a, pp. 92–102) – in order to prevent such evil from happening. Whereas rule-following seems to be the appropriate behavior in *normal* conditions, *exceptional* conditions force people to challenge all the rules they normally abide by in order to commit no evil. The conscious cognitive process of looking for a solution then becomes the key to moral behavior. In other words, moral rules may actually foster more (banally) evil behavior. Gigerenzer (2008) argues in much the same direction when pointing out the dangers of mindlessly acting according to the built-in heuristics of human brains. Arguing in line with Kant, Schulte (1988, p. 350) states that pure legality (understood as abiding by generally accepted rules) can be morally radical evil. Rule-following alone is not enough to achieve morality, since 'the problem of the formation of the State, hard as it may sound, is not insoluble, even for a race of devils' (Kant, 1795/2010, p. 25). Even if humans were devils, they could establish an institutional matrix that ends the most extreme forms of social conflicts. *Pure rule-following will never be enough to prevent evil.* Arendt and all the other authors arguing against blind rule-following propose that natural evil exists. These warnings can easily be reconciled with the NIE approach by Mantzavinos, though, who himself stresses the underlying cognitive processes that lead to the formation of institutions. The human tragedy would then be that people too often perceive given problems as old ones (and act according to already established rules) instead of consciously deliberating about what to do – and thus minimizing the danger of falling prey to the banality of evil. The limited human cognitive abilities along with the failure to discern normal conditions from exceptional conditions, old problems from new problems, then would cause a lot of evil. Mantzavinos accounts for this case stating that '*interpretation and classification errors* are far from impossible' (2001, p. 40).

Beside these two known reasons for the existence of evil actions in the face of established moral rules (people who do not abide by moral rules and people who follow rules but unconsciously misapply them), this book suggests a new, third reason as to why economic evil potentially takes place: the existence of *evil* social institutions alongside other social rules. Evil rules that directly advise harming represent a different form of natural evil compared to interpretation errors or banal evil. *Economic evil may happen because people abide by evil social institutions.*

3.3.3 Evil rules and their emergence

An evil moral rule *can be conceptualized as the negative mirror image of a moral rule: it does not tell you to* cooperate *even if this may diminish your material income but instead to* defect, *again, even if this may diminish your material income.* Such an evil rule is one that advises everybody to cause harm to the opposing party (irrespective of their own payoff from that action).[5] *An* evil social institution *in general, then, simply is a rule that fosters social conflict instead of providing solutions.* It is a rule that can also be described as not solving the Hobbesian problem of social conflict but instead intensifying the struggle in the natural state.

Suggesting the existence of evil social institutions, the most urgent question is how they could potentially emerge in the first place and persist in the long run. This question is especially hard to answer for evil *informal* institutions. *Evil formal institutions could simply be put in place and kept in force by a powerful sovereign – at least for some time.* But how about evil moral rules, given that it was stated that informal institutions evolve in a spontaneous invisible hand process, because people learn that it is mutually advantageous to abide by them since they end social conflict? Keeping up the assumption that conflict is at best a constant-sum game whereas cooperation leads to mutual gains, every evil rule that might emerge should be eliminated over time, since it does not survive the evolutionary trilogy of variation, selection, and retention. This general reasoning explaining the existence of institutions does not, however, fully apply to the situations in which moral rules in particular arise. Moral rules 'are characterized primarily by the fact that they require a kind of behavior that, while socially beneficial, seems to be – at least prima facie – contrary to the interests of the individuals themselves' (Mantzavinos, 2001, p. 106). But in morally significant situations that resemble a prisoner's dilemma, people learn many things: not only that mutual cooperation is advantageous, but also that defection is even better if the other cooperates, and that defection is always the better strategy in one-shot interactions. *This is a very ambiguous learning environment.* It might be too optimistic an assumption that only moral rules develop in such scenarios.

Three reasons for the potential emergence of evil rules

Mantzavinos himself acknowledges that not every person that finds herself in a prisoner's dilemma learns to abide by a moral rule. This is due to the conditional nature of moral rules: 'the emergence of moral rules is the outcome of a learning process *on the part of the individuals who follow those rules*' (Mantzavinos, 2001, p. 109; emphasis by C.D.M.) But the other part of the population has the same cognitive need for institutions to structure complex social interactions. Why not follow the evil rule to always defect in prisoner's dilemmas and to opt for short-term self-interest then? To always choose conflict is not a mutually beneficial choice but it is a simple rule that structures social interactions very clearly. Irrespective of the question whether aggression and conflict are behaviors that are evolutionarily speaking prior to cooperation (Lorenz, 1963/1998), one cannot deny the potential of evil rules to address the cognitive need for behavioral guidance very effectively.

As a second reason for the emergence of evil rules beside this cognitive one, the underlying motivational reasons may favor the establishment of evil rules, too. It is a *dominant strategy* to defect in one-shot prisoner's dilemmas – so it is very likely that some individuals learn to abide by a rule advising this strategy. But given that one-shot interactions are not a typical scenario for the environment in which social rules most likely developed, that is in small groups of people living together, this short-term strategic dominance might be not enough to account for the emergence of evil rules. The very reason why moral rules emerge eventually is that cooperation is mutually beneficial in the long run, in repeated prisoner's dilemmas. However, even if this assumption holds, there might be other strategies that are even more beneficial in the long run than pure cooperation, at least to one party. Buchanan (1975/2000) shows in his model of anarchy that already the uncritical assumption that the two persons interacting in a prisoner's dilemma differ with respect to their ability to produce, depredate and defend themselves can challenge the long-term advantages of mutual cooperation. To be clear: Buchanan's model cannot be used directly for explaining the development of evil rules. In contrast to Mantzavinos, Buchanan is not interested in describing how social institutions actually emerged. Nevertheless, the assumptions of his model (a prisoner's dilemma adapted for interactions in the natural state) seem to be close enough to reality to at least challenge Mantzavinos's argument for the straightforward emergence of moral rules and moral rules only, as it highlights the ambiguous incentive structure of repeated prisoner's dilemmas.

As already outlined in Section 3.2.2, if there is one person who is very adept at producing (an 'intelligent' person) and another who is very adept at depredating (a 'strong' person), it may be more rational for the strong person to constantly rob the intelligent one rather than investing any effort in producing himself. Figure 3.7 further clarifies the consequences of the comparative advantages. In this figure, A lives in a superior environmental setting or is just better at producing x compared to B. This is reflected in the flatter curve of his production function P_A. In the case depicted, A can even secure some goods without any effort at all. B on the other hand faces a much steeper curve P_B – symbolizing his relative inefficiency in producing the private good. The *direct-production position* in which everybody only consumes what he produces himself (the same as represented by the origin in Figure 3.2) is attained when A attains point E_A and B attains point E_B. These points represent the situation in which the most favorable indifference curves (I_A and I_B, respectively) are tangent to the production curves.

However, the curves P_A and P_B represent only the non-conflict scenario, in which the only possible activity is production. If conflict is allowed, as it is the case in anarchy, different curves emerge as B may well find that his most productive expenditure of effort lies in predation (Buchanan, 1975/2000). If A does not respond to the newly introduced predation activities from B's side – an assumption Buchanan makes – then the new production curves may look like P_B' and P_A' and the new equilibrium position is reached at E_A' and E_B'. Buchanan (1975/2000, p. 82) states that since he assumed no responsive action undertaken by A, A's actual production function is not changed, but he is producing a portion of his goods for B.

The new equilibrium is not identical to the anarchistic equilibrium E in Figure 3.2, since in E also A invests a positive amount of effort in defense and predation. Figure 3.7 simply illustrates the fact that

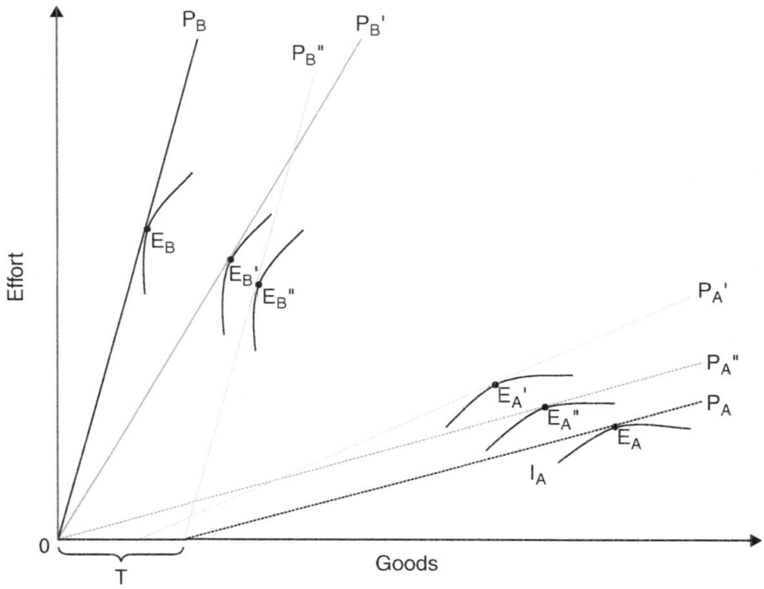

Figure 3.7 Utility-maximization with predation vs. no predation allowed (cf. Buchanan, 1975/2000, p. 81)

the stronger person would never agree to a constitutional contract assigning property rights based on the distribution of goods in the direct-production position. Even if there was a mutually agreed upon and *individually rational* (since it allows for gains from trade) constitutional contract, the stronger person would always have an incentive to break it and just usurp a share of the goods the intelligent person has produced. In this case, *stability* is the property lacking for making such a contract self-enforcing. The benefits of mutual disarmament, property rights and potential gains from trade that can only be reached through a constitutional contract might just be not big enough to be a valid incentive for the stronger person.

In the setting depicted by Figure 3.7, however, another way of achieving the basis for a constitutional contract exists. *A* might get *B*'s agreement to install property rights by offering him a transfer of goods (the amount *T*) if he abstains from fighting. The new equilibrium E_A''/E_B'' that lies on the new production curves P_A'' and P_B'', respectively, is a Pareto-improvement compared to the conflict case. Such a transfer is precisely what Buchanan thinks of when stating that contractual agreements in anarchy must include 'something beyond limits to behavior' (Buchanan, 1975/2000, p. 82). The interesting point about the equilibrium in E_A''/E_B'' is that it is a non-conflict equilibrium: because the stronger person decided to fight, he reached a situation that is superior to the direct-production position (E_A'/E_B'). On the other hand, if he now abstains from fighting, he gains even more compared to the starting position (E_A''/E_B''). The optimal solution for the stronger person in this example clearly is not to fight – but this optimal solution can only be reached by fighting in the first place (or at least threatening to fight the intelligent person and thus motivating the transfer payment).

The reason behind the reflections of the stronger person is that in the natural state 'the direct-production position ... may or may not be Pareto-superior to the natural equilibrium at E' (Buchanan, 1975/2000, p. 79). In other words, in many cases the direct-production position (mutual cooperation in a prisoner's dilemma) is only better for the weaker, the intelligent person, whereas the stronger person profits from moving to the anarchistic equilibrium by saving a larger share of the produced goods. The predominance that has been given to the direct-production position in theoretical considerations about how property rights and trade emerges stems from the (implicit and unjustified) assumption of equality among men (Buchanan, 1975/2000). The new option, that is even more profitable for *B* than constant cooperation over a long time, is (the threat of) defection in the first period.

Going back to Mantzavinos's line of argument, this profitability could very well have been learned by some individuals over time and have become a social rule. Notice that in Buchanan's model, the evil action of the strong person is beneficial to him *in the short run and in the long run*. In the short run, conflict is beneficial to the strong person precisely for the same reason as it is beneficial to defect in a one-shot prisoner's dilemma. In the long run, conflict is beneficial since it alters the initial distribution that functions as point of reference for exchange that may succeed anarchy. In the long run, even the strong decides to cooperate in Buchanan's scenario. But only after an initial act of violence – that is very rational since it significantly alters the bargaining position for everything that follows. The first prisoner's dilemma played, thus, is different from the ones that follow, since it conveys information about the strength of the interacting parties. In this context, *choosing conflict must not always be Pareto-inferior.* Evil rules are a potential outcome of this incentive structure.

The third and final reason why evil rules may have emerged spontaneously considers that prisoner's dilemmas are not the only scenarios in which such rules might develop. There are other environments for social interaction in which it may prove to be *socially beneficial to act maliciously.* That is, although both the perpetrator and the victim of the malicious act lose materially from it, the overall community may profit from this kind of behavior in the long run. One example that has already been mentioned above shall suffice here: the evolutionary theory of evil argues that an arms race between ever more effective killers and ever more effective defenders against evil is highly likely to have happened (Duntley & Buss, 2005). The deterrent effects of a suicidal counter-attack of the victim, that seriously wounds (or even kills) the perpetrator, may very well be beneficial for the remaining kin of the victim. Such an attack is a clear sign that aggression against this specific kin does not pay off and has long-term reputational effects (Schelling, 1978). Thus, at least for extreme situations of existential threat spontaneous evolution may very well bring about evil rules that advise the victim to commit malicious actions.

Summary

To opt for conflict in social interactions is a simple, widespread rule effectively addressing the cognitive needs of human beings. Furthermore, in some prisoner's dilemmas conflict is not necessarily Pareto-inferior in the short run and in the long run, and in yet other situations, conflict might even prove socially beneficial. These are the three reasons why evil rules might have emerged spontaneously in an invisible hand process just like moral rules. The ambiguous learning situation of prisoner's dilemmas and related social interaction scenarios might not only have led to the development of moral rules but also to the rise of evil rules. Evil social institutions then are an additional cause for evil actions to take place in the light of established social rules beside the known causes of people generally not abiding by the latter and people misapplying learned rules to new environments.

The discussion concerning the existence and emergence of evil social institutions in the preceding section may seem to be highly theoretical; however, by examining the evidence from *EVE Online*, it will be found that evil informal rules can in fact emerge following the mechanics set out in this chapter.

3.3.4 Evil rules as social institutions

'Learning about something' means making a rule out of a payoff scenario: IF such-and-such, THEN so-and-so (Mantzavinos, 2001, pp. 22–34). It is appropriate to call a social institution an *evil rule* if it does not diminish the degree of social conflict but rather increases it and if it advises someone to harm the opposing party no matter what his own payoff may look like. Such an evil rule nevertheless belongs to the class of *moral rules*, since it is informal and first-party enforced. In the same manner that nobody can force you to cooperate in a prisoner's dilemma (because it is against your material self-interest), nobody can force you to launch a suicidal attack against an aggressor (because, again, it impairs your material payoff). That is why evil rules are also first-party enforced. This classification of 'good' and 'evil' under the same heading of 'moral' might be surprising at first but follows Mantzavinos's approach in that it classifies social institutions according to their enforcement agency (2001, pp. 84–85). It is just another example of the close relationship between good and evil in economic terms. Just as with the case of other-regarding preferences that can be split into prosocial and anti-social preferences, moral rules can also be split into *good moral rules* (fostering cooperation through first-party enforcement) and *evil moral rules* (fostering harming through first-party enforcement).

It is not evident, however, whether evil rules as defined here even fulfill the requirements to be an *institution* in the first place. Remember that the raison d'être of institutions is that they provide solutions to the problem of social order (Mantzavinos, 2001, p. 83) – which seemingly contrasts with the characteristic of evil rules to incite conflict. *In a certain sense, however, evil rules also put an end to social conflict.* The rule that conflicts of interest generally should be solved by fighting (with the winner gaining the right to decide on the matter) is indeed a rule able to guide behavior and end conflict in the long run – just that few would consider it to be a very good rule. It may be very effective, though, and lead to what Hirshleifer considers a 'vertical social contract' (1995, p. 48).

> It is useful to distinguish *vertical* from *horizontal* social contracts. The vertical alternative, Thomas Hobbes' version, would be represented by arrangements such as hierarchical dominance in the biological realm or dictatorship on the human level. (1995, pp. 48–49)

If in a given situation there exist increasing returns to fighting effort – 'at the extreme, this may imply a "natural monopoly" in fighting activity;

that is, the struggling is likely to end up with all the resources under one party's control' (Hirshleifer, 1995, pp. 48–49) – such vertical social contracts are very likely to arise. Hirshleifer states that most often technological innovations initiate such developments and cites evidence on the rising importance of naval conflict and social organization in ancient Greece as well as the political consequences of the invention of the cannon (1995, pp. 44–46). One may not acclaim such scenarios, but nevertheless they are able to appease social conflict for some time. Therefore, evil rules are a valid example of social institutions, too.

4
Massively Multiplayer Online Role-Play Games as a Field of Research

Economics may lack a good research access to evil. Theories of fighting in economics, for example, are mainly theories of anarchy in the natural state (Buchanan, 1975/2000; Hirshleifer, 1995; Stringham, 2005; Tullock, 1972, 1974). But the obvious problem with the natural state is that it originally is a philosophical *thought experiment* which everybody acknowledges has never really existed that way (Hobbes, 1651/1998; Locke, 1690/1988). This is not intended as criticism – but it is an inherent problem of the idea of a natural state that it can be observed almost nowhere in its pure form. And a related problem exists for experiments: ethical considerations might forbid conducting experiments explicitly designed to incite people to harm each other.

The serious lack of empirical evidence on evil is one particular reason to introduce MMORPGs as a new field of research for economics. These computer games feature the whole spectrum of human behavior concerning evil: fighting, war, anarchy, the natural state, alliances, killing, lying, cheating, punishing, harming, badmouthing, anger, envy, revenge. Turning to MMORPGs means gaining the possibility of testing existing theories of conflict and predation as well as a huge new pool for empirical observations. MMORPGs are a great tool to enlarge economic knowledge of evil.

4.1 What is an 'MMORPG'?

The precise definition of an MMORPG is typically discussed in the academic literature focusing on the design of computer games. Unfortunately, and probably due to the relative recentness of this type of game – Yee talks of a 'new paradigm in computer gaming' (2006, p. 313) and the first MMORPGs were only released in the early 1990s – there is no standard definition of MMORPGs yet. However, most authors agree with the following criteria for classifying a computer game as an MMORPG (Egenfeldt-Nielsen, Smith, & Tosca, 2008; Kolo & Baur, 2004; Salen & Zimmerman, 2004; Tulathimutte, 2010; Yee, 2006): *MMORPGs are computer games played online by significantly more than two players at the same time and feature a persistent world; the main goal of the players is to advance their role-played avatar.* This definition however needs further clarifications.

That MMORPGs are played *online* is quite clear: only with the rise in broadband Internet connections in industrialized countries have MMORPGs had their breakthrough. Before the Internet era, several computers were connected locally in order to play together. But physical meeting is no longer possible with thousands of concurrent users for medium-sized MMORPGs. MMORPGs are called *massively multiplayer* games as they are played by significantly more than two users at the same time. While classic videogames were typically designed for one player or two competing players, MMORPGs are designed for several thousand concurrent users. The most successful MMORPG at the time is *Blizzard Entertainment*'s 'World of Warcraft' with more than 11 million registered users (MMO Data, 2010a). Many other successful MMORPGs have between 100,000 and 1.5 million registered users (MMO Data, 2010b). Not all of the registered users are playing at the same time but that several thousand users inhabit the same virtual world simultaneously is quite common.

The greatest revolution of MMORPGs compared to other video games is that they feature *persistent worlds*. Although this criterion does not have its own letter in the widely used acronym, it is the single most important distinction criterion. MMORPGs are the first games that really feature virtual *worlds*. In classical computer games the world in which you play only exists while you play. If you play a racing game for example, the virtual courses on which the race takes place do not exist if you do not play. Nothing changes in this virtual world when you are not playing and it always looks the same every time you play the game. A persistent virtual world on the other hand is a world independent of the single user. Things happen while you are not logged in, and maybe the next time you play you face a somehow different environment. Even if nobody is online, even if nobody plays the game, the programmed physical processes of the virtual world go on; for example the weather changes. The changes in the world are the same for all the players of the MMORPG, and if one of the fellow players fells a particular virtual tree while you are offline, you are no longer able to do the same when you go back online. Nowadays, the virtual worlds of MMORPGs are graphical environments which come to life in rich 2D or 3D graphics.

The fourth defining criterion of MMORPGs is that players *role-play avatars*. 'Avatar' or 'character' is the name for the virtual representation of the player. It is the virtual person whose actions the player controls over the human-computer interface, that is with mouse-clicks and keyboard-commands. Typically, what the avatar does is observed from a third-person perspective; but also first-person perspectives are common. Avatars are a new type of computer game alter ego: unlike prior ones (like Mario in *Nintendo*'s 'Super Mario Brothers' or Lara Croft in 'Tomb Raider') they can be richly customized. Avatars in MMORPGs can typically be male or female, have different hairstyles, be tall or small, have different races (Caucasian, Asian, dwarf (!), troll (!), extraterrestrial (!), and so on), practice different professions and so on; the avatar's looks and actions are the player's choice alone. The game designers' goal is that players identify with their avatar, that is that they *role-play* it. You typically start your experiences in the virtual world with a weak and poor level 1 avatar, and as you fulfill *quests* – that is tasks given to you by other, computer-generated avatars controlled by the game software itself – you gain experience and resources. The most important goal in MMORPGs is typically to level up to the maximum achievable level, to gain more resources, better equipment and abilities or in brief: to *advance* (although also non-leveling MMORPGs exist).

One might argue that advancing the character is not much to do since one reaches for example the maximum level in 'World of Warcraft' normally within about 30 to 50 days of play. But this is characteristic for MMORPGs. It is the player who decides what to do with his avatar: explore the virtual world, socialize with other users, gain experience and level up, or something else. Originally, the designers thought of this lack of clear goals to be a shortcoming: they started to think about what all the avatars should do and, in an effort of central planning, organized community events – that ended up being disastrous (Morningstar & Farmer, 1991). The new freedom curiously did not lead to boredom but rather to a situation in which the players themselves think about what could possibly be done in the game. Besides, the virtual worlds are so huge and complex (and continuously enlarged with updates and add-ons) that there is normally always a new place to go to, a new quest to engage in, or new equipment to be gained even at the maximum level. The motive of keeping up with competitors, to be the most powerful, most experienced, richest or most special character seems to be a strong and lasting motivation also in the virtual world. In the end, it is competition that drives the actions of MMORPG-players; competition for virtual social status and virtual resources.

The designers of MMORPGs stress the social aspects of the games: nearly every MMORPG has a 'guild', 'clan', or 'corporation'system. Guild, clan and corporation are the names for permanent associations of players of a game that like to adventure together or to fight against other guilds and corporations. Furthermore, avatars in MMORPGs – unlike other computer game alter egos – are designed for social interaction. You can easily contact other users via text-based- or voice-chat, you can add them on your *friends list* so you get informed whenever they are online. The social aspects are also the single most important factor when it comes to the success of a game. Most players only bind themselves to one MMORPG – getting to know a game, leveling up, and raising one's online status are quite time-consuming tasks. Additionally, some users prefer to play together with their friends from real life. The network effects of MMORPGs, therefore, are very important. If one MMORPG becomes standard, nearly all new users will choose to join this particular game, too.

It is therefore a logical consequence of this social side of MMORPGs and of the fact that they are massively multiplayer games in persistent virtual worlds that communities evolve around them. The players of MMORPGs typically not only play the game but also 'live' it to certain extent; they live the events and the fictitious history of their world. Each big game has its own community of players and subscribers do not only spend time with the game actually playing but also doing *meta-gaming*. They read all the news concerning their game, participate in forum discussions with other users outside of the game, visit fan fests organized by the publishers, and so on.

Most MMORPGs, unlike other video games, are not purchased at a certain point in time for around 50 US dollars (USD), but users have subscriptions to them. Besides the costs of buying a copy of the game in the store, you also have to pay a monthly subscription fee of typically 10 to 25 USD in order to be allowed to continue to play.

To summarize: MMORPGs can be defined as computer games played online by thousands of concurrent users at the same time. They feature persistent virtual worlds – typically themed as fantasy or science-fiction worlds – in which the players role-play and advance their richly customizable avatars. Not only do players identify with their avatars, but also MMORPGs are inherently social games. In the virtual world, gamers join 'guilds' or 'corporations' and the success of MMORPGs is attributable to the existence of stable communities of players whose central interest is the game.

4.2 Doing research in MMORPGs

Using an MMORPG for data collection on human behavior requires some introducing remarks as to why such games could be appropriate providers for valid data and as to how this data is going to be collected. Social scientists typically know laboratory experiments and know field work – but generally do not know and have never carried out research in MMORPGs. The purpose of Section 4.2 is to compensate for this lack of common knowledge from a research perspective. MMORPGs need a special approach in order to be of use for research in the social sciences and it must be noted that there are also many criticisms concerning the value of research in them.

First, Section 4.2.1 will give a general answer to the question as to why anybody should do research in MMORPGs. What are the advantages of doing do? Section 4.2.2 will then look into the most pertinent criticisms of research in MMORPGs, notably the question of the validity of the findings and whether player behavior in computer games has anything to do with real, everyday human behavior. Section 4.3, finally, will shed some light on the methodology suitable for approaching MMORPGs and for collecting data.

In what follows, it might be a small problem from time to time that *EVE Online*, that is the MMORPG of choice for this book, has not been exhaustively introduced yet. The choice was made to first discuss some limitations of the research object before actually introducing it, that is to conclude the theoretical part before jumping to empirical evidence. Those who prefer to first get a good impression of the research object might directly switch to Chapter 5 before delving into the theoretical foundations of research in MMORPGs.

4.2.1 Advantages of doing research in MMORPGs

There are many *subject specific reasons* why – for this book – it is advantageous to conduct research in MMORPGs. Most important is the fact that this allows for observing people doing evil things without, as an experimenter, having to force or at least incentivize them to do so. By looking at EVE, one can examine evil without causing more evil through the research itself. There are, however also very *general considerations* why research in MMORPGs is promising. Castronova goes as far as calling these games the 'Petri-dish of the social sciences' (2008). He argues that whereas for example biologists study cells, economists and social scientists in general are concerned with how societies work. Biologists can easily grow and manipulate different cultures and experiment with them without too many ethical considerations. Social scientists on the other hand cannot just grow a society and test how it reacts to the spreading of an infectious disease or how it could better react to a hurricane devastating large areas of coastland. Social scientists cannot really experiment with their research object because of ethical considerations and the huge consequences these experiments would have on the participating subjects. Unless they turn to virtual worlds and societies, one might add. The most telling example in this line of argument is probably that of the spread of a virtual infectious disease in the MMORPG 'World of Warcraft'. Many avatars contracted a virtual disease that was intended to only infect high-level avatars in a certain, clearly delimited region. But somehow the disease spread beyond the intended boundaries and attacked low-level avatars as well – that soon died afterwards, not without acting as incubators themselves. Many medical journals in the real world reacted to this event and tried to learn lessons for real life from this virtual plague (Balicer, 2005; Lofgren & Fefferman, 2007).

From a certain perspective, the purpose of this book – namely to examine evil actions from an economic point of view – is nothing more than *a cannily chosen example to demonstrate how one could do behavioral research in the social sciences using MMORPGs*. This book demonstrates *the power of this approach, especially for subjects that are normally not as easily accessible to empirical observation*. This book's aim goes beyond microeconomic research in virtual worlds with the sole urge of producing final results. *How* these results came about is almost as important.

General considerations concerning the advantages of doing research in MMORPGs

The biggest advantage of MMORPGs compared to the real world is that, albeit they are undoubtedly complex, they are less complex than the real world. They are more *controllable* (because they are digital: everything you do is recorded), *smaller* (only half a million inhabitants for a typical MMORPG compared to around 70 million people for a medium-sized country), more *restricted* (they still feature less possible actions for the users than real life offers), and *younger* (typically less than ten years old) compared to real societies.

MMORPGs are more *controllable* since in their digital environment every single action of each user can be monitored. If a group of players fights together, earns a reward, and splits this reward among the members (a situation quite close to an experimental public goods game), one can easily observe who invested how much time in fighting, how large the reward was, and who received how much of the public pot. The computer automatically gathers this data. Everything a user does can potentially be monitored and the exact sequence of his actions can be determined. In addition, this data is much easier to evaluate than classic observational data. All sorts of statistical methods are much easier to apply and data is gathered incredibly fast. Large sample sizes are administered quickly and with less effort than in classical field work – and yet it is still *field work*, since all the interactions are embedded in the day-to-day life of the avatars and since contemporary games have several millions of registered users.

MMORPGs are *smaller* and more *restricted* than real life: they feature enough possible actions to let social institutions evolve, but still have less disturbing variables than the real world. And MMORPGs, even if some of them possess a genuine culture, are quite *young*. The average age of current MMORPGs is about four to five years. These time spans – in which a true history, distinct institutions, and so on emerged – are manageable ones. All the debates about which institutions are the right ones to govern the virtual world are recent and still recorded (text-based) in Internet forums. Using MMORPGs, one can retrace the making of a culture and its specific institutions from the very beginning. All of the important contemporary witnesses are still alive.

MMORPGs allow for raising complexity compared to laboratory experiments while at the same time keeping the controllability high. MMORPGs are vast but handy, possess their own culture and are still manageable. Last but not least, although the population of these games certainly does not mirror that of real world societies with respect to many demographic factors, they prove to be a lot more diverse than the stereotypical research with undergraduate students (cf. Section 4.2.2.2 on the demographics of MMORPGs).

Doing research on morality: the advantages of MMORPGs

Additional and more specific arguments for doing research in MMORPGs apply if the scope of research is narrowed down. Online computer games are particularly useful, when conducting research on *human morality*. The status quo in empirical research on moral behavior in economics is that empirical evidence from experimental laboratory games is used in order to describe, explain, and predict moral behavior in everyday life: cooperation, altruism, fairness, reciprocity (Camerer, 2003). But there are two problems with this approach. First: can human morality, that reveals itself in everyday interactions in a 'noisy' environment, really be captured and described in an abstract laboratory environment? Can lab behavior be used as a basis for constructing general theories of everyday human morality? And second: are preferences really the only 'rules' that influence human behavior? Can 'good' and 'evil' behavior even be defined without turning to the rules that govern interactions, that is, without turning to institutions? MMORPGs provide solutions for both problems.

Concerning the first problem: giving away more money than rationally expected to a fellow player of a lab game is not automatically moral. Not to defect in a public goods game with punishment opportunities is not automatically to be called cooperation. Morality is more complex than just following the behavioral rules set by our preferences and is always situated within a 'noisy' environment with all kinds of social influence factors intervening. Morality is a social phenomenon – highly influenced by the complexity and vagueness of real world day-to-day interactions. *All the undertones and subtleties of moral interactions in the real world* – that laboratory experiments try to eliminate as effectively as possible – *are not disturbing but rather paramount for research on morality*. Of course, experimental economics is well aware of the fact that everyday life differs from lab behavior and that it influences the outcomes of the simple bargaining games because for example rules and norms are imported to the laboratory environment (Camerer & Fehr, 2002; Fehr & Fischbacher, 2004; Henrich & Smith, 2004; Henrich et al., 2001). It is generally accepted that lab games do not measure the 'real-life' values of their variables, and that they examine a rather poor and isolated version of morality. What is gained is control – but at what price?

MMORPGs allow for studying non-laboratory, socially embedded interactions in an environment that is much more controllable than the real world. It is socially embedded behavior stemming from a *virtual* world but it is nevertheless *socially embedded* moral behavior. The virtual world is not the real world – but at least it is a *world* – and thus captures the 'noise' typical of social interactions. This noise, this social embeddedness in everyday situations, is crucial if one wants to say something about human morality. And MMORPGs allow for keeping up the noise while listening more precisely due to the fact that everything is recorded in real time, yet can be examined with more time and considering all the aspects that are appropriate.

Concerning the second problem: it is not only other rules besides preferences that influence behavior but also goodness/evilness cannot even be defined without resorting to institutions. MMORPGs are one of the best places to thoroughly examine how the institutions governing the social interactions in a society – be it virtual – emerge, are enforced, and change. MMORPGs possess their own history and culture transmitted by the community of players. Where so many people gather in one place it is obvious that they need formal and informal institutions for coordination. As stated above, these rules (and the discussions that surround them) are readily accessible for MMORPGs. EVE mirrors the development of a society from the very beginning (with only a few thousand players) to a community with almost 400,000 members nowadays. You can literally watch how institutions emerge and change, how the complex structures of social organization evolve – within the time span of less than ten years – just like cells in a Petri dish in an incubator.

Doing research on evil: the advantages of MMORPGs

Narrowing down the focus even further, from doing research in the *social sciences* via research on *human morality* to research on *evil behavior* specifically, some very fundamental principles apply. EVE allows for doing research on many different facets of evil behavior. It is a closed society in which one can potentially find all aspects of evil besides physical aggression. It would be completely out of the question to conduct all the different *experiments* necessary for gaining such a rich impression of human evil behavior. Considering the ethical implications of research on evil behavior, probably not even a single experiment with paid subjects should be carried out. Thus the advantage is that EVE is – after all – a game. Everybody who plays EVE does so voluntarily. It is only because people voluntarily join and leave this dark and harsh environment that empirical research on evil behavior like revenge, murder, and war can be conducted without ethical concerns.

It is already a major finding that should not go unnoticed that so many people are ready to spend their time in an environment in which so many evil rules developed and lots of evil actions occur. Proposing to do research in an MMORPG should not blur the view for the circumstances of these findings. Do people have a 'taste for harming'? At least they like to play games that further evil behavior.

4.2.2 Limitations of doing research in MMORPGs

The most common criticism of doing behavioral research in MMORPGs is that the actions of players might not have any relevance or relatedness to real-life human behavior whatsoever. Firstly, this criticism tacitly implies that you cannot (or maybe should not) conduct *purely descriptive* research of MMORPGs – which, of course, you can and should. There is nothing wrong or 'unscientific' about describing games and player behavior. Even if the task of this book were 'only' to describe EVE and the actions of the players within it, it should be done. Despite the sometimes depreciative view of them, computer games are nowadays an important cultural phenomenon that is still growing as the pioneering generations in this field get older and new generations of players are born. As of today, the gaming industry makes more money than Hollywood film productions (Yi, 2004) and the release of blockbuster games with millions of players is becoming more and more common. The academic research of computer games as a cultural phenomenon in its own right is legitimate and important.

But taking this beyond mere description of computer games, the question becomes whether you can in fact learn something about real-life human behavior from looking at actions in computer games. Are the behavior, actions, and decisions of players – as well as the institutions guiding their actions – comparable to the behavior of people acting and deciding in real life and the social institutions of real-life societies? Can you infer real world predictions from virtual behavioral evidence?

These are very difficult questions far from having a precise answer at the moment. For the case of MMORPGs – compared to studying *virtual worlds* in general – these questions even have a *twofold structure*: is not EVE just a *game*, that is all fun and play? And is not EVE, furthermore, just a *computer* game, that is not even a 'real' game played with material pieces or dice? Game studies and ludology are very young disciplines. The question of the connectivity of online and offline behavior is a very young field of research in psychology. Therefore, the whole complex of questions is a very dynamic and ongoing field of research at the moment – there are no final answers yet. But there are valid theoretical and empirical reasons for *doubting that* (1) *games and playing in general are irrelevant when trying to examine and predict economic behavior in general and that* (2) *behavior in virtual worlds has no connection to real world behavior whatsoever.* Instead, it will be argued that (1) *games* are good environments to conduct valid research for *economic behavior in general* (Section 4.2.2.1) and that (2) *online* behavior is related to *offline* behavior (Section 4.2.2.2). Computer games are not a perfect mirror of offline economic behavior and you cannot easily predict real world decisions on the basis of evidence from virtual worlds; there is absolutely no doubt about this. Still, claiming that behavior in MMORPGs has no predictive power for real world economics is a weak claim.

Overall, this Section 4.2.2 may appear too comprehensive since it does not add directly to the goal of providing evidence for economically evil actions and evil social institutions. However, this section is *paramount for the interpretation* of the data found in EVE later on. There are important criticisms of drawing *any* conclusion whatsoever from the data presented in the empirical part and to properly understand the limitations of doing research is key when examining data from a new research environment. The goal of convincing the skeptic reader – who has never done research on games in general or who has never visited a virtual world himself – that MMORPGs tell a lot about real life justifies the pages to follow

Games and economic activities

The most influencing definition of *playing*, that is the activity associated to games, comes from Huizinga (1955). According to him, playing is

> a free activity standing quite consciously outside 'ordinary' life as being 'not serious', but at the same time absorbing the player intensely and utterly. It is an activity connected with no material interest, and no profit can be gained by it. It proceeds within its own proper boundaries of time and space according to fixed rules and in an orderly manner. It promotes the formation of social groupings which tend to surround themselves with secrecy and to stress their difference from the common world by disguise or other means. (Huizinga, 1955, p. 13)

Games are not serious, as ordinary life is, as they are not about material interest or profit. However, Huizinga argues that one should rather emphasize the things that games and economics have in common, since 'law and order, commerce and profit, craft and art, poetry, wisdom, and science. All are rooted in the primeval soil of play' (1955, p. 5). That is to say, although ludic life and economic life are typically separated domains nowadays, you can find in economics something that is archetypical for games, namely the *contest for something*.

Not all types of contest, of which economic competition out of profit-interest is just one instance, are play in the strict sense. The '"non-seriousness", the ludic factor proper' (Huizinga, 1955, p. 30) is what distinguishes them from each other. Yet, games absorb the players 'intensely and utterly'. Everybody who ever watched children play games can testify to how serious players can take games.

> For us, the opposite of play is *earnest*, also used in the more special sense of *work*; ... The significance of 'earnest' is defined by and exhausted in the negation of 'play' – earnest is simply 'not playing' and nothing more. The significance of 'play', on the other hand, is by no means defined or exhausted by calling it 'non-earnest', or 'not serious'. Play is a thing by itself. The play-concept as such is of a higher order than is seriousness. For seriousness seeks to exclude play, whereas play can very well include seriousness. (Huizinga, 1955, pp. 44–45)

Thus, the frontier that separates playing and 'serious' economic behavior is a blurred line. Who would doubt this in the light of the most recent widely acknowledged changes to the ideal of *homo economicus* – which originated from the field of *game* theory and, more precisely, from subjects *playing* bargaining games in laboratory conditions?

Juul's (2003, 2005) more recent definition of what a game is helps to grasp the similarities and differences even more clearly. His explicit goal is also to account for the particularities of computer games, which is also very useful in the light of this book. Juul (2003, p. 35) lists six features of games: (1) Games are rule-based. (2) Games have variable, quantifiable outcomes. (3) Different values are assigned to the different potential outcomes, some being positive and some being negative. (4) The player invests effort in order to influence the outcome. (5) Players are attached to the outcomes of the game in the sense that a player will be the winner and 'happy' if a positive outcome happens, and loser and 'unhappy' if a negative outcome happens. (6) The same game can be played with or without real-life consequences. In his opinion, only games which possess all six features are to be called games in the strict sense.

According to Juul, economic activities are not playing because of the sixth criterion: economic life – like for example traffic, professional sport or war, too – always has real-life consequences. Whereas you can decide for every game you play, if it shall have real-life consequences (for example by betting money on the outcome), you cannot do the same for economic life. Games in the strict sense have 'negotiable consequences' (Juul, 2003, p. 38). That is, even if most economic activities fulfill all the other five criteria– which is also very meaningful with respect to the relationship of games and economic life – they do not constitute playing.

However, one could also doubt that economic activities fulfill the third criterion of being a game, the *valorization of the outcome*. He says that simulations, unlike games in the strict sense, do not possess *explicit* goals (Juul, 2003, p. 39). Think of a flight simulator for example. Most would agree that the goal is to somehow start the engine of the plane, lift off from the ground, fly a little bit, and then to land safely again. But only because many do precisely this when 'playing' the simulation, one should not forget that nobody explicitly told them to do so, says Juul. You could also drive the airplane on the ground without lifting off and look at the nice virtual landscape. Simulations do not possess explicit goals but rather try to *mirror reality* as perfectly as possible – this is why they are borderline cases in Juul's eyes. Now, economic activities do not *mirror* reality, they *are* reality. Even if most people think that the goal of working or producing or trading is to make profit, nobody explicitly tells you so. Your job could be your vocation at the same time. NGOs are in many aspects similar to ordinary corporations but they do not aim for profit but rather for some idealistic goal. That is, much economic activity does not fulfill the criterion of valorization of the outcome either.

The astonishing thing now is that *EVE seems to violate the exact same criteria for being a game in the strict sense as economic activities do: the presence of negotiable consequences and the valorization of the outcome.* Nobody in EVE tells you what to do, what EVE is all about, or what you have to do in order to 'win' EVE. It is not you who win EVE – 'EVE wins you' (CCP Prism X*, 2008),[1] as one of the lead developers puts it. All MMORPGs alter the concepts of variable outcomes as well as the valorization of outcomes, because the player 'never reaches a final outcome but only a temporary one when logging out... [and because the games are] not describing some possible outcome as better than others' (Juul, 2003, p. 42). Furthermore, computer games generally allow for much *more complex rules* than standard games, since the players themselves are not responsible for upholding the rules. More complex rules, in turn, lead to a playing experience that simulates reality more closely. EVE is probably best understood as an MMORPG with an economic *simulation* at its core – and as such it violates the criterion of valorization of the outcome.

Concerning the criterion of *negotiable consequences* and comparing EVE to real-life armed conflict one has to admit that actions in EVE are always *harmless* (Juul, 2003, p. 38). On the other hand, comparing EVE to nine men's morris, one also has to acknowledge that EVE is always played for money. Every virtual asteroid mined is added to your virtual wealth and every ship lost in a fight is subtracted. Since you can sell your virtual wealth to fellow players for real money using the exchange rate between virtual and real world currency (cf. Section 5.2.2), all of your actions do have real-life financial consequences.

EVE is a borderline case for a game. It violates the exact same criteria for being a game as does economic activity. In the end, it does not matter what precisely EVE *is* – but it should be clear by now that the criticism of EVE being 'just a game without relevance for human economic behavior' is illegitimate.

Online and offline behavior

Who plays MMORPGs? Why do people play these games? Are people not generally behaving differently in the anonymity of a computer game than in real life? How does real life influence online decisions? There are a lot of psychosocial implications when using behavioral data from MMORPGs.

Not all potential questions regarding the differences between online and offline behavior can be considered at this moment. This is mainly due to the substantial lack of literature on this issue in psychology, sociology, economics, and many other social sciences. In general, the literature concerning virtual worlds is very *recent* (that is the findings might prove to be wrong after further research is done), mostly *theoretical* (there is not much empirical work on MMORPGs yet), *unstructured* (many different scholars try to say something about the importance of virtual worlds for their respective discipline), and highly *controversial* for nearly any subject touched. This situation is a logical consequence of the fact that these are pioneering efforts.

This section will give a short, mostly descriptive overview of the relevant findings until now. In general, it will follow Lehdonvirta (2010) who argues against the dichotomous approach in studying virtual worlds. You cannot simply regard virtual worlds *either as completely distinct* from real life *or as perfect mirror images* of daily reality. Virtual worlds feature many things known from offline reality but also possess a lot of particularities.

Demographics

The social cliché of a gamer is probably a male teenager with pale skin, few social contacts and low self-esteem, though typically of more than average intelligence. It is wrong in its absoluteness as are all clichés – but has a grain of truth. A representative study showed that 24 percent of Germans older than 14 years play computer games (SOFOGA, 2010a). Although the highest proportion of gamers can be found for the group of the 14 to 17 year old, also 26 percent of all adults (older than 18 years) play computer games. The typical gamer is male and often well-educated (SOFOGA, 2010b). While 30 percent of men play computer games, only 19 percent of women do. The highest proportion of gamers can be found for those having passed the German *Abitur*, that is the general qualification for university entrance. Gaming typically is not an isolated activity, age being the most important influencing factor for this issue. While 93 percent of all players aged 14 to 17 regularly engage in multiplayer games, only 13 percent of players aged 65 and older do so (SOFOGA, 2010c).

The data from the SOFOGA project is representative *for Germany* and *all types of computer games*. For *MMORPGs* more specifically, Yee (2006) has gathered data of more than 30,000 MMORPG-players over a three-year period. Comparable results to those presented in the following can be gained from studies of Griffiths et al (2004) and Meredith et al (2009). Yee (2006) finds that the majority of MMORPG-players are male (85.4 percent) and on average 26.57 years old (*SD* = 9.19). However, only about 25 percent of players are teenagers. The biggest share of MMORPG-players, irrespective of gender, is full-time employed (cf. Table 4.1).

The average MMORPG-player spends 22.71 hours per week (*SD* = 14.98) playing his favorite game (Yee, 2006, p. 19). Around 8 to 9 percent of respondents spend even more than 40 hours a week playing. More than 60 percent of the respondents had already experienced more than 10 hours of permanent play. These numbers are almost not correlated with age. Castronova (2003) reports that 22 percent of the users of the game 'Everquest' whom he interviewed expressed the wish to spend all

Table 4.1 Occupational distribution by gender

	Full-time student	Part-time student or work	Full-time employed	Unemployed	Home maker	Retired
Male (*n* = 2383)	23.9%	12.8%	50.9%	10.1%	1.5%	0.7%
Female (*n* = 438)	12.8%	11.4%	48%	12.1%	13.3%	2.5%

Source: Yee (2006, p. 18).

their time online and that 40 percent said that they would indeed live online and quit their regular jobs, if there only were a sufficient wage available online. These findings underline how important these games are to the individual player.

Player typology and motivation for play

Bartle (1996, 2004) developed the *Bartle Test of Gamer Psychology* that classifies players of MMORPGs according to their playing preferences. He distinguishes between four characteristic types: *achievers, explorers, socializers,* and *killers*. Achievers play the game in order to have the most powerful avatar and equipment; they go to extremes in order to acquire unique items – not because they gain an immediate advantage from this but because of the prestige of having it. Explorers like to know everything about the virtual world: they want to see all the places and know every detail about the fictitious history. Socializers do not care so much about the game itself but rather use the game in order to connect or keep in touch with new friends and old acquaintances. Killers are motivated by the direct competition with other human players: fighting against computer-generated enemies does not thrill them; overthrowing other human players in battle and demonstrating their skills is their main goal. Current empirical data for the Bartle Test taken from a sample of 522,290 MMORPG-players who have taken the test since 1996 states that about 39 percent of players are explorers, 28 percent killers, 19 percent achievers and 14 percent socializers *(gamerDNA,* 2008*)*.

Bartle also lists some characteristic statements for each type (Table 4.2). The biggest merit of Bartle's taxonomy is that it is intuitively appealing for everybody who ever played an MMORPG. Every player can cite an incident when he ran into an achiever, explorer, socializer, or killer from his own gaming experience.

Concerning motivation for play, Yee (2006, p. 21) is able to identify five factors that all describe primary motivations for playing MMORPGs (Yee, 2006, p. 22):

1. *relationship*: desire to interact with others and willingness for meaningful relationships that transcend to real life
2. *manipulation*: inclination to manipulate other users for own goals, for example through deceiving, scamming, and taunting.
3. *immersion*: enjoyment of the role-play aspect of MMORPGs and to be 'someone else'
4. *escapism*: the extent to which the virtual world is used in order to avoid, forget, or escape the real world.
5. *achievement*: the desire to become powerful in the virtual world.

Table 4.2 Typical statements of achievers, explorers, socializers, killers

Killers	**Achievers**
• 'Ha!' • 'Coward!' • 'Die!' • 'Die! Die! Die!'	• 'I'm busy' • 'Sure, I'll help you. What do I get?' • 'So how do YOU kill the dragon, then?' • 'Only 4211 points to go!'
Socializers	**Explorers**
• 'Hi!' • 'Yeah, well, I'm having trouble with my boyfriend.' • 'What happened? I missed it, I was talking.' • 'Really? Oh no! Gee, that's terrible! Are you sure? Awful, just awful!'	• 'Hmm ...' • 'You mean you *don't know* the shortest route from <obscure room 1> to <obscure room 2>?' • 'I haven't tried that one. What's it do?' • 'Why is it that if you carry the uranium you get radiation sickness, and if you put it in a bag you still get it, but if you put it in a bag and drop it then wait 20 seconds and pick it up again, you don't?'

Source: Bartle (1996).

Similar studies by Griffiths et al (2004) and Schultheiss (2007) support these results. Wang et al. (2008) emphasize the role of intrinsic motivation and passion for online gaming.

Online identity

Two opposite views concerning online identity, in this context mainly understood as the behavioral mannerisms and singularities of a person, are widely held (Messinger et al., 2008, p. 4). Online identity starkly differs from offline identity (Lehdonvirta (2010) calls this the 'schizophrenic' view) or online identity is closely linked to offline identity (the 'mirror' view).

The 'schizophrenic' view

Defenders of the 'schizophrenic' view emphasize the freedom that the players experience online: to be whatever they want to be online, for example to be the bad guy and do things you would never do in real life. In this light, McKenna and Bargh (2000, p. 57) identify four major differences between online and offline identity/social interactions: greater anonymity, reduced importance of physical appearance and physical distance, as well as a greater control of time and pace of interactions. The most important online/offline difference with respect to potential evil actions is the increased *anonymity*. If you think that your actions go unnoticed by others or that they are not accountable to you because you do not use your real name, or because you think your actions are submerged in the hundreds of actions of other people, it may cause a feeling of deindividuation (McKenna & Bargh, 2000; Zimbardo, 2005). Deindividuation in turn may foster

> a weakened ability for an individual to regulate his or her own behavior, reduced ability to engage in rational, long-term planning, and a tendency to react to immediate cues or based largely on his or her current emotional state. Furthermore, an individual will be less likely to care what others think of his or her behavior and may even have a reduced awareness of what others have said or done. These effects can culminate in impulsive and disinhibited behaviors. (McKenna & Bargh, 2000, p. 61)

Indeed, McKenna and Bargh cite a broad base of evidence on more angry, blunt, aggressive, offensive, and hostile behavior online. On the other hand, they stress that anonymity and deindividuation do not themselves present negative phenomena – they only lead to a decrease in the importance of individual standards and to an increase in the importance of local group norms. Depending on the group norms, deindividuation may prove to be a positive phenomenon (cf. L. L. Downing & Johnson, 1979). Under conditions of anonymity, people might also be more open and talk about how they truly feel or think (McKenna & Bargh, 2000, p. 62). McKenna and Bargh suggest that intimacy and closeness between two people might develop more quickly this way.

It is important to take into account this positive effect of anonymity that may also promote the building of new peer-groups online that are unrelated from those in real life. And it needs to be stressed that in MMORPGs there are typically few one-shot interactions but rather repeated interactions that lead to relationship formation. *People are anonymous in Internet interactions with respect to their offline life but not at all with respect to their online identity.* The guild/clan/corporation system clearly fosters this establishment of new acquaintances and new peer-groups. Additionally, the fact that in MMORPGs people face more than pure text messages when interacting – namely they see a lovingly customized avatar – may further reduce the feeling of deindividuation on both sides (Messinger et al., 2008).

Enlightening in this respect is the virtual reprise of Milgram's obedience experiments by Slater et al. (2006). Instead of the original human learner, Slater et al. used an avatar as receiver of the electric shocks. The subjects of the study who, just like in the real experiment, were told to act as a teacher and to punish every failed attempt could observe the reactions of this computer programmed person on a screen. Slater et al. describe the situation faced by the subjects as follows:

> The Learner had a quite realistic face, with eye movements and facial expressions; she visibly breathed, spoke, and appeared to respond with pain to the 'electric shocks'. Not only that but she seemed to be aware of the presence of the participant by gazing at him or her, and also of the experimenter – even answering him back at one point ('I don't want to continue – don't listen to him!'). Finally, of course, the electric shocks and resulting expressions of discomfort were clearly caused by the actions of the participants. (Slater et al., 2006)

The aim of the study was to test whether immersive virtual environments were valid environments for conducting such powerful social-psychological studies as the Milgram obedience experiments. Discussing a wide range of quantifiable (for example the skin conductance level) and non-quantifiable criteria (the participants behavior as observed by the experimenters), Slater et al. find:

> The main conclusion of our study is that humans tend to respond realistically at subjective, physiological, and behavioural levels in interaction with virtual characters notwithstanding their cognitive certainty that they are not real. The specific conclusion of this study is that within the context of the particular experimental conditions described participants became stressed as a result of giving 'electric shocks' to the virtual Learner. It could even be said that many showed care for the well-being of the virtual Learner – demonstrated, for example, by their delay in administering the shocks after her failure to answer towards the end of the experiment....
>
> People tend to respond to virtual environments as if the objects and events depicted are real, in spite of low fidelity representations and certain knowledge that the events taking place are within a virtual reality. (Slater et al., 2006)

Although Slater et al. state clearly that it was not the intention of the study to test obedience or the frequency of evil actions in a virtual environment, they still advance some thoughts about this issue. They argue that although knowing that they were not inflicting pain on a real person the abidance by the experimenters' instructions caused discomfort to the participant – and still they went on complying. Most of the subjects continued until the end of the experiment, some withdrew, and generally the level of stress was higher when they were able to see the avatar than when they were only interacting by text chat. To the question whether this behavior could be called 'obedience' in the strict sense, Slater et al. (2006) respond: 'whether participants complied because of "obedience to authority" or politeness, or respect for expertise does not really matter. The fact is that they continued to carry out a task that they found to be unpleasant, when there was no reason for them to do so' (Slater et al., 2006). The findings of Slater et al. seem to strengthen the view that people are not generally behaving *more* evilly online: if they feel as discomforted when 'harming' a computer-generated avatar as when thinking they are harming a human being, this discomfort might prevent some evil from happening.

From these questions of anonymity and evil behavior, let us get back to the question of the supposed small connectivity between online and offline identity more generally. Allison et al. describe the clinical case of an MMORPG-addict who 'could put on a new identity like a new suit of clothes, becoming someone who walked on water, healed others, and cast lightning bolts, in stark contrast to his daily experience of himself as inadequate' (Allison et al, 2006, p. 381). And Messinger et al. examined a sample of players of 'Second Life' and find that 'compared to real-world behavior, respondents indicate that their virtual-world behavior is more outgoing and risk-taking and less thoughtful/more superficial. Finally, people with avatars more attractive than their real selves state that they are more outgoing, extroverted, risk-taking, and loud than their real selves' (Messinger et al., 2008). However, the actual relationship between ('improved') online self-representation and online behavior may be even more complex. Yee and Bailenson (2007) find that not only people who consciously *design* a more attractive avatar are more outgoing and extroverted but also people who are just *assigned* a more attractive one. In particular, people who got assigned a more attractive avatar (as measured by Western beauty ideals) were more intimate with respect to self-disclosure and interpersonal distance, and people with taller avatars behaved more confidently in negotiation tasks (Yee & Bailenson, 2007, p. 271).

The 'mirror' view

Defenders of the 'mirror' view often claim that 'an avatar is the virtual reflection of a person, the person's virtual body through which they express their identity in the virtual world' (Lehdonvirta, 2010). There simply is no such thing as a specific online identity. Lehdonvirta (2010) argues that most things done online have a direct relation to real life: players discuss things from their everyday life, school, work, family and TV shows online. In addition, one should assume that people cannot just turn off their principles and values acquired in real life when going online. Aas et al (2010) let their subjects fill out two personality questionnaires checking for the traits of extroversion, friendliness, conscientiousness, neuroticism, and development: one for themselves and one for their avatar at an interval of seven months. They conclude that 'results show no difference for any of the five subscales... suggesting that users of virtual realities do not create a "virtual" personality for their avatar' (Aas et al., 2010). Actually, users might not only take some of their identity and behavior online, where it is reproduced virtually, but also take back offline some of the things they did and experienced online (S. Downing, 2009; Messinger et al., 2008, p. 5). Yee (2006) for example presents evidence that MMORPGs are a good place to acquire leadership skills of which players can make use in their everyday lives.

A strong identification with the avatar has to grow, as Bartle (2004) suggests. He describes four stages of identification with the avatar. First, players consider the avatar as a strange 'puppet' before they begin to actually play. In the second stage, they see it as a 'representative in the virtual world'. In the third stage they perceive it as 'extension' of their self, while in the last stage of this progress, they 'become' the avatar. 'The player *is* the character. You're not role-playing as a being, you *are* that being; you're not assuming an identity, you are that identity; you're not projecting a self, you are that self' (Bartle, 2004, pp. 155–56). Aupers (2007) finds evidence for this categorization and the progress from stage to stage. He cites players with the following statement: 'When I talk with other people in the game about places we've been or fights we had, I never say my character was there. I say: "I was there". It's just you in that world' (Aupers, 2007, p. 5). Or also: 'It becomes a bit "you" because – I think – you invest a lot of time in it' (ibid.).

It also seems as if behavioral regularities known from the real world transfer to online environments. Yee et al. (2007) find, for example, that if two male avatars are interacting online, they choose a larger interpersonal distance and make less eye contact than female-female dyads. As the interpersonal distance grows, also male-male dyads choose to make more eye contact. These behavioral regularities are well-known from real-world observational studies. Bailenson and Yee (2005) find that also the *chameleon effect* – that people who imitate nonverbal gestures of their counterpart appear more likeable – transfers to avatars.

Real-world physical appearance of the gamers is also found to exert an influence on its virtual counterpart, too. It is known that many players try to make their avatar look similar to their real-life appearance. Bessière et al (2007) find that 'World of Warcraft' players often take their own physical appearance as a starting point but try to design an online self closer to their ideal self. Messinger et al. (2008) find the same to be true for 'Second Life'.

Summary

To quote Bargh et al (2002, p. 34): 'The idea that people possess multiple senses of self, or personas, is not a new one in psychology and sociology.' In this respect, all the conflicting evidence concerning online and offline identity should not be overestimated. Furthermore, circumstances significantly influence behavior. Overall, there is *little inducement to think that the behavior observed in MMORPGs has no relationship whatsoever with behavior one could expect in the real world.*

Relationship formation and social dynamics

It is widely acknowledged that relationships formed online can be as meaningful and deep as offline ones (Lehdonvirta, 2010; McKenna & Bargh, 2000; Walther, 1996; Yee, 2009). Yee (2006) finds that 22.9 percent of male players and even 32 percent of female players have told their online friends things they never told real-life friends. Furthermore, about 40 percent of male players and more than half of female MMORPG-players stated that the quality of their online friendships were comparable or better than their offline friends. Hussain and Griffiths (2008, p. 47) find that one in five gamers prefers socializing online and that particularly male players find it easier to converse online. Many players also start real-life friendships or even romantic relationships with people they first met online (Cole & Griffiths, 2007; Kolo & Baur, 2004; Yee, 2006, 2009). Cole and Griffiths (2007, p. 575) conclude their study of social interactions in MMORPGs saying that 'MMORPGs were found to be highly socially interactive environments providing the opportunity to create strong friendships and emotional relationships. The study demonstrated that the social interactions in online gaming form a considerable element in the enjoyment of playing. The study showed MMORPGs can be extremely social games, with high percentages of gamers making life-long friends and partners.'

This overwhelming empirical evidence seriously questions opinions saying that online interactions are cold and lack trust, and that online gaming necessarily leads to social isolation. Furthermore, it stresses once again the fact that offline and online actions are highly intermingled. Especially since the connection between online and offline relationships is a two-way connection. Not only that gamers frequently start to physically meet and date people they first met online but also that they often take their real-life relationships online. Offline friends, family members or business acquaintances decide together to join a specific MMORPG or to change games (Kolo & Baur, 2004; Lehdonvirta, 2010). Already established offline friendships are used for ensuring trust and decreasing risk of cooperating with complete strangers online (Lin et al, 2003). The simple and supposedly clear distinction between online and offline environments thus cannot be upheld in this context, either.

Maybe more interesting than the sheer finding that online social relationships can be as meaningful and deep as offline ones, are the reasons behind this. McKenna and Bargh (2000) find that the important 'gating features' (2000, p. 57) of physical appearance and physical distance lose their importance online. Yee (2009) identifies a whole class of factors facilitating online relationship formation compared to real life that stem from the fact that MMORPGs are *designed* environments in many aspects. He argues for example that the people playing a specific MMORPG are *pre-selected* with respect to which kind of playing they favor: out of the huge range of different computer games, the players choose to play an MMORPG with all its characteristic features (for example social in nature, slow in pace), and in addition choose to play a fantasy MMORPG instead of a science fiction one. Furthermore, the *social architecture* of MMORPGs, that is the conscious design of its institutions (the 'rules of the game') has an outstanding importance (Yee, 2009):

- *The necessity of grouping*: Most MMORPGs require players to work together. The most common mechanism is that, as players advance, it becomes harder to defeat the computer-generated adversaries or to fulfill the received quests on your own. However, MMORPGs differ with respect to their 'soloability' (Yee, 2009), that is the possibility to play the game without the help of others. EVE is a game with a very low soloability, since the positive effects of division of labor kick in quickly. The lower the soloability and the higher the necessity of grouping to successfully play the game, the more prone the MMORPG is to create relationships.
- *The costs of altruism*: Yee cites evidence for a wide spread of altruism in 'Everquest'. Because of the high interdependence of the avatars, a culture of seeking and providing assistance has been established. 'A

five second spell at minimal cost to the provider can save another player an hour of painful and dangerous [work]' (Yee, 2009). He cites a player that, in his opinion, articulates the different nature of online and offline altruism as well as the consequences for the community:

> I find people's altruism extraordinary. In RL [real life], much altruism is met with suspicion...'if you're trying to help me, you must want something'. Or it's dangerous to be altruistic, like picking up hitchhikers, or intervening if there is a crime in progress. But in virtual worlds, I find an outlet. I get a lot of satisfaction from performing random acts of altruism. And I'm always touched when people do the same with me. I think it taps into people's need to be needed. But I also just like making people happy...so a lot of it is about an outlet for generosity. (Yee, 2009)

Yee concludes that the social architecture of 'Everquest' removes the ambiguity and danger of real-life altruism while at the same time providing the players with powerful ways and lots of opportunities to help each other.

- *Crises, trust, and honor*: Many MMORPGs regularly put players into situations of crisis, in which collaboration becomes essential to group survival. It is these situations in which a social reputation is formed: Are you trustworthy and honorable or rather dishonest and coward? Players take these examples of online behavior as a valid clue for offline behavior and meticulously remember how they were treated and what they observed, since they are highly emotionally invested in their characters (Yee, 2006). 'If anything, [Everquest] is a sustained exercise in team-building and trust with strangers and friends' (Yee, 2009).

In his discussion about the effects of the social architecture of an MMORPG on the formation of online relationships, Yee highlights the fact that the former is the outcome of social engineering by the developers of the game. 'Nothing is intrinsic or immutable..., not even death. Death ... can be defined and coded in many ways. Once defined however, the ["rules of the game"]...shape the social fabric of the community – the amount of social contact, the necessity of collaborating with others, the formation of trust, and the potential for altruism' (Yee, 2009).

This is to say that what counts in evaluating interactions from MMORPGs is not to stress the fact that one is dealing with *virtual* interactions here but that – in analogy to real life – the established institutions shape the behavior of the community. One should not be preoccupied with identifying all the potential differences between offline and online behavior but rather conduct a thorough analysis of the institutions in place in virtual worlds in order to be able to judge online behavior.

Conclusion: Does EVE mirror the real world?

Looking at it from an economic viewpoint, virtual economies cannot be fully detached from real world economies anyway. Lastowka and Hunter (2004) argue there will soon be legal trials in the real world about who owns virtual things: to date, the avatars and virtual goods that the players control or possess, respectively, are the property of the developer of the game. This, however, seems to be problematic, for example in the case in which the developer wants to stop providing the game: thousands of hours of 'work' by the players then would be gone. The whole legal concept of property might need an overhaul in the light of virtual worlds (Humphreys, 2009; Lastowka & Hunter, 2004). The most important indicator for the connection between virtual and real economy is real money trading, that is the purchase and sale of virtual in-game items for real money for example on *eBay*: some argue that it should be forbidden in order to prevent richer players from getting an 'unfair' advantage, others argue that unless it is officially allowed, those with more time available will have an advantage (Lehdonvirta, 2010). But if Chinese farmers start to mine virtual gold instead of tilling their real fields and if some MMORPGs have higher GDPs than Eastern European countries (Castronova, 2003), and if the different demand characteristics of Japanese and North American players lead to daily fluctuations of the price of virtual goods (Nash & Schneyer, 2004), how can we deny that there already is a substantial relationship between the virtual and the real economy?

After all, the presumed ditch between virtual worlds and the real world is neither too deep nor too wide to completely exclude the possibility of drawing conclusions for offline behavior based on online empirical evidence. *Games are not identical to serious economic life. Virtual worlds do not perfectly mirror real world economies. Thus, one has to be careful when interpreting the data gathered online and even more so if one wants to use it for predictions of offline behavior. But both games and virtual worlds do have a lot of things in common with everyday economic activities in the real world. EVE is not (just) a game and online behavior is a good predictor for real-life behavior.* The demographics of computer games in general and MMORPGs in particular show that the cliché of the teenage gamer is not true and that the players are highly devoted to what they do online. Players are not 'strange people' – and the evidence on the motivations, identities, and relationship formation of gamers shows that they do not 'behave strangely' either. The motivations for playing are social and competitive ones. There is no clear evidence that gamers really construct a second identity for what they do online. Online relationships are meaningful and feature high levels of trust. It is out of the question to simply disqualify the players and the games they play as not worthy of scientific attention.

Last but not least – and without establishing a thorough philosophical argument here – one should not forget that the reasons for distinguishing two different worlds (one online and one offline) are very weak: in the case of MMORPGs real persons make real decisions and commit real actions (mouse clicks and keyboard commands) which possess real consequences. People spend big shares of their daily time on playing MMORPGs, they pay money for it, they make money playing these games and they even are beaten up in real life because other users do not like how they behaved online (Klink, 2009). Or to follow Lastowka and Hunter: of course, virtual worlds are 'artificial, fictitious, imaginary, intangible, and invented' (Lastowka & Hunter, 2004, p. 7) – but where is the difference from laws, myths, many cultural achievements, or the willingness for 'paying an extra dollar or two for a certain logo printed on a T-shirt' (Lastowka & Hunter, 2004, p. 10)? The world may be virtual – but the behavior and the people are real.

4.3 Methodology

There are many different ways of conducting research in and around video games and, even more fundamentally, many ways of approaching video games in the first place. Comparing different studies on computer games across disciplines, the game scholars Egenfeldt-Nielsen et al (2008, p. 8) conclude that the initial approach is mostly influenced by the academic discipline of the researcher: art students are interested in the aesthetics of video games, communication scholars tend to analyze the interactions of players, and philosophers tend to question what a game actually is and how different games can be distinguished. Following Egenfeldt-Nielsen, Smith, and Tosca, at least four different units of analysis should come into play for an encompassing analysis of a game: the *game*, the *player*, *culture*, and *ontology*. The first notion refers to comparative analysis of different games and to learning about their structure, their rules, their graphical representation, the fictional story, their respective virtual world and so on. When focusing on *players*, 'the activity of playing games is more important than the games themselves' (2008, p. 10). Psychologists try to find out how players experience games and sociologists explore games as a social space. The notion of *culture* refers to everything around games: how they are seen by society in comparison to other media, for example. *Ontological* research, finally, studies the philosophical foundations of games and play.

The approach chosen in this book clearly stresses the second unit of analysis – the player – as far as the examination of economically *evil actions* goes. With respect to the examination of *evil rules*, the first unit of analysis – the game – gains importance. This unit of analysis also matters in the general description when explaining to the reader what type of game we are dealing with (cf. Chapter 5).[2]

4.3.1 Examining evil actions in computer games

Even within the presented framework, within the game research dimension of the *player*, and within the discipline of economics, there are different ways to study games. Some people take standard experimental economics games online and thus play ultimatum and dictator games in a virtual environment – mainly with the benefits of smaller costs and a more diverse sample of people (for example, Atlas, 2008; Chesney et al, 2007). Other economists describe economic relationships in virtual worlds and try to identify macroeconomic performance figures in order to compare the economic performance of virtual worlds to those of the real world (for example, Castronova, 2001, 2003, 2008; Guðmundsson, 2007, 2011). Yet others try to identify basic economic concepts and to apply theories in virtual environments – showing that they also make sense online (for example, J. H. Smith, 2006a, 2006b).

The works just cited rely either on first-person observation, that is on actually playing the game, on surveys conducted in the respective Internet forums for the games (with questionnaires for example), or on in-depth interviews with the players or developers. These ways of finding out what is happening in a specific game, however, have their shortcomings. Most notably, the subjective perspective of the researcher (she cannot be anywhere in the virtual world, she cannot experience everything herself that belongs to the game, and she cannot talk to a representative of every 'school' of playing the game) and the typically small sample size for the qualitative research. 'My free, improvised play had not helped me to discover essential parts of the game. In failing to discover the main quest, I failed as a model player, in spite of my great enjoyment in the game' (Aarseth, 2003, p. 5) This is how Aarseth, an experienced game scholar and player, expresses his sudden feeling of surprise when realizing the shortcomings of a first-person approach to games.

This book's approach differs strongly from the ways economists have researched games up until now. Instead of basing the research on personal playing experience and on the subjective impressions of others, the data underlying the empirical part on economically evil actions will be the computer-created server logs of player interactions. *Putting forward a new approach, this book directly examines the unmediated server data on human interactions for microeconomic purposes, that is to trace the behavior of individual players.*

This approach promises more valid results, especially when speaking about evil actions often involves exaggerations from the people involved (cf. Section 2.2). The computer-generated server logs of what people did are as objective as it gets when recording human behavior, since you do not have to rely on personal experience or the stories told by the people involved. Furthermore, *the logs theoretically encompass what all (!) players did and potentially everything (!) they did*, apart from the things they did offline simultaneously to playing EVE (drinking, thinking, calling someone, and so on).[3] The tables presented in Section 4.3.1 expose precisely which data was made available by CCP Games as the basis for the research in this book.

Because the goal is to conduct microeconomic research and not comparative game studies, this approach with all its benefits is possible. Here the benefits of doing research in MMORPGs outlined above will unfold their full potential. Using the opportunity of looking at the unmediated data of what about 400,000 people did in a given period is a very powerful approach.

4.3.2 Examining evil rules in computer games

When putting the player interactions into a bigger context and trying to understand why they acted that way, it is indispensable to also consider the *game* unit of analysis. In order to classify the findings on evil actions, this book will always come back to describing the game and its rules. The thorough examination of the evil social institutions in EVE also requires heavy referral to this unit of analysis.

Here the book will be closer to the traditional approaches of game studies used in economics and notably follow Aarseth's counsel: 'In gathering information about the game, we should use as many sources as possible. Playing is essential, but should be combined with other sources if at all possible' (2003, p. 7). A wide range of sources like other players' reports, reviews, forum discussions in the official EVE-forums, the official EVE wiki, game documentation and interviews with game developers will be utilized. The protocols of the meetings of the Council of Stellar Management (CSM) (a group of players democratically elected by the whole player base to represent their views to CCP Games) and CCP Games will also be referred to extensively. *Dev blogs*, that is short texts written by the developers in order to announce new developments in *EVE Online* to the player base (including the discussions they generate in the community), will be a preferred source, too. These blogs represent the most official and direct communication between developers and players. Even a small variant of a classic bargaining game, the adapted version of a dictator game, will be conducted (cf. Chapter 9).

4.3.3 Structure of the server data

All in all, CCP Games made available 15 files from the server logs for *EVE Online* containing different bits of information, mostly for the period of January 2011. Taken together, the size of these files amounts to more than 66 gigabytes of data. Considering that a typical A4 page full of text has around five kilobytes, the equivalent of these 66 gigabytes are around 13,000,000 pages of plain text. In the following, it will be briefly outlined which kind of information can be retrieved from each of the 15 files.

killsJan2011.csv This is one of the two central files for the empirical part. Basically, it lists all kills, that is all ships that were destroyed by players in EVE in January 2011; a number just above 500,000. For each kill the following attributes are listed:

Summarizing this data, you can tell from this file who killed whom, where and when, with which ship, and what items were destroyed and dropped (that is can be picked up by other players) during the attack. NB: This file lists all ships flown by players that were destroyed – either by NPCs or by players – but not all the NPC ships that got killed. This is sufficient for the purpose of this book.

Table 4.3 The contents of the file 'killsJan2011.csv'

Attribute	Exemplary value	Description
No. of kill	42	Each kill in January is attributed a consecutive number
Place	30001409	The ID-number of the solar system in which the kill occurred
Time	03.01.11 10:44	Specifying the time of the kill
Victim	90225239	The ID of the character whose ship was destroyed
Victim's corporation	1000172	The ID of the corporation[4] to which the victim belonged
Victim's ship	670	The ID of the ship that was destroyed
Victim's alliance	99000198	The ID of the alliance[5] to which the victim belonged
Destroyer	756884476	The ID of the character who fired the determining last shot that finally destroyed the ship of the victim
Destroyer's corporation	847592759	The ID of the corporation to which the one who laid the final blow belonged
Destroyer's alliance	100958673	The ID of the alliance to which the one who laid the final blow belonged
Destroyer's ship	346	The ship in which the character flew while he laid the final blow, for example a battleship
Attacker's* security status	–2.0	The security status of the attacker
Attacker's* alliance	1000958673	The alliance ID of the attacker
Attacker*	472395793	The character ID of the attacker
Attacker's* ship	346	The ID of the ship the attacker flew
Attacker's* corporation	847592759	The corporation ID of the attacker
Attacker's* weapon	24692	The ID of the type of weapon the attacker used, for example a laser or a projectile weapon
Attacker's* damage	123	The damage done by each attacker to the ship of the victim in absolute numbers (the higher, the more damage)
Item**	266	The ID of the item
Item's** amount	400	The quantity of the item in question
Item's** amount dropped	200	The quantity of the item in question that was dropped after the kill, that is that was not destroyed due to the explosion of the destroyed ship
Item's** location	0	Where the item was located in the victim's ship, for example in the cargo hold or fitted to the outer hull of the ship

* For each of the potential additional attackers besides the destroyer that also participated in the kil.l

** For each item that was in the ship of the victim (or fitted on it).

Table 4.4 The contents of the file 'characters.csv'

Attribute	Exemplary value	Description
Character	90225239	The individual character ID
Player	7354628	The ID of the account on which the character is created. Each account holds up to three characters
Character's corporation	1000172	The ID of the corporation the character is a member of
Character's create date	12.11.2005	The date when the character was initially created by the player
Player's date of birth	15.08.1984	The date of birth of the account owner
Last logon	14.01.2011	The time when this character last logged in to the game
Character's name	Shul'khan	The fictitious name of the character
Character's gender	Male	The gender of the character
Player's gender	Female	The gender of the account owner
Player's status	Active	Specifying if the account is active or disabled (since the subscription has lapsed)
Player's type	Paying users	Specifies if the character is on a trial or a regular account
Deleted	notDeleted	Specifies if the character was already deleted at the time of the snapshot
No. of logon	02. [6 to 20]	Specifies how often the character has logged in since its creation. Is listed in categories rather than as precise number
Total logon minutes	03. [201 to 300]	Sum of the total logon minutes of this character. Is listed in categories rather than as precise number
Play session	06. [60 to 90] Minutes	Specifies how long the character is logged in on average every time it comes online. Is listed in categories rather than as precise number
Balance	02. [0 to 5000]	How much money did the character have in his wallet at the time of the snapshot. Is listed in categories rather than as precise number
Skill points	01. [0 to 5000]	Specifies the number of skill points the character had at the time of the snapshot. All skills that a character trains translate into skill points acquired. Is listed in categories rather than as precise number
Country	Russia	Country in which the account was registered
Country IP	Russia	Country from which the IP stems with which the character logs in
Language	EN	Specifies in which language the EVE client is used

characters.csv This file is the second most important file for the book. For every character that ever was created in EVE since the publication of this game, it lists several attributes that allow the researcher to further determine what characterizes the players of EVE. The data in this file stems from a snapshot taken at the end of January 2011.

This file allows the researcher to distinguish between all kinds of demographic variables for the real and the virtual world, for example to only consider wealthy characters or to only consider female players. The distinction between *character* and *player*, that is between the *in-game representation* and the *human being controlling it* is important to note.

wallets2011.csv This file specifies all monetary transactions that took place in EVE in January 2011: between two players, between players and corporations, between players and NPCs. For example it lists the value of all the market transactions a player made or every time he gave money to another player. The file contains the following attributes:

Table 4.5 The contents of the file 'wallets2011.csv'

Attribute	Exemplary value	Description
Date	11.01.11	Date of the transaction
Active party	980774468	The character or corporation ID of the active party in a transaction, for example the character ID of the player that gives money to another player
Passive party	974833858	The character or corporation ID of the passive party in a transaction, for example the character ID of the player that receives the insurance payout after he lost his ship
Amount	1,000,000	Amount of the transaction in ISK
Balance	134,002,889	The new balance of the character's or corporation's wallet
Transaction type	Insurance	The type of the transaction. Other types are for example 'market transaction', 'broker fee', 'docking fee' or 'bounty'

wars.csv This file contains a list of all wars that ever were formally declared in EVE. Only corporations and alliances can declare war. The file lists the following attributes:

Table 4.6 The contents of the file 'wars.csv'

Attribute	**Exemplary value**	**Description**
No. of war	1255	Each war receives a consecutive number from the software
Corporation/alliance declaring	98300590	The corporation or alliance ID of the party that declared the war
Corporation/alliance declared	100033438	The corporation or alliance ID of the party on whom the war is waged
Time of declaration	12.11.2005 05:44	The time when war was declared
Ended	15.08.2006 13:22	The time the war ended (either because the war was retracted or because the bill for the war was not paid)
Retracted	15.08.2006 13:22	The time the war was retracted
Corporation/alliance retracting	98300590	The corporation or alliance ID of the party who retracted the war
No. of bill	465	For each war, the declaring party has to pay money in order to start the war and to maintain the warring status. This number specifies the bill ID of these payments
Mutual	0	Wars can be declared mutual by the party on which the war was waged. This has the effect that less war costs have to be paid to the system.

crimesJan2011.csv Certain actions are considered 'crimes' in EVE although they do not cause immediate response from the virtual police force. This file lists the following attributes for each crime committed in January 2011:

Table 4.7 The contents of the file 'crimesJan2011.csv'

Attribute	**Exemplary value**	**Description**
Date	12.01.11	The date and time when the crime occurred
Type of crime	Stole from Jetcan	Further specifies the type of crime committed
Active party	98757583	The character ID of the active party in the crime, for example the player that stole from the jetcan
Passive party	84743883	The character ID of the passive party in the crime, for example the player from whom the thief stole

itemTypes.csv and *avgPricesJan2011.xlsx* The first file is the central item database of EVE. In here, every item that exists in EVE is listed with its ID number and some attributes. Therefore, this file is central when interpreting, that is decoding, the data from the other files, like for example the kill file. Here one can look up precisely which ships were involved in a kill or exactly which items were destroyed or dropped. The file lists the following attributes:

Table 4.8 The contents of the file 'itemTypes.csv'

Attribute	**Exemplary value**	**Description**
Item	245	The ID of the item in question
Item's group	4759	The ID of the group to which the item belongs, for example 'battleships' or 'mining lasers'
Item's name	Gallente Shuttle	The name of the item in-game

The data of this file is especially valuable in combination with the data from 'avgPricesJan2011.xlsx'. In the latter file, the average market price that was paid for every item in January 2011 considering the entire virtual universe is listed. The combination thus enables to price all the ships and items that were lost due to the kills in EVE.

corporations.csv This file lists all the NPC- and player-corporations there were at the end of January 2011. It encompasses the following attributes:

Table 4.9 The contents of the file 'corporations.csv'

Attribute	Exemplary value	Description
Corporation	1000123	The corporation ID of the corp in question
Corporation's alliance	134434345	The alliance ID of the alliance to which the corporation may belong
Corporation's headquarter	2352	The space station in which the corporation has its headquarters
Corporation's name	CONCORD	The name of the corporation in-game
Corporation's ticker symbol	MUYUN	A ticker code for the name of the corporation used in-game from time to time
Corporation's type	NPC Corporation	Specifies if the corporation is a player- or an NPC-corporation
Corporation's size	10. [10001 and higher]	Specifies the number of members the corporation has. Categories are used instead of the precise number of members

alliances.csv, regions.csv, solarSystems.csv, stations.csv, itemCategories.csv, itemGroups.csv, killRights.csv The remaining seven files all contain additional information in order to decode the values from the files explained above. The file 'alliances.csv' for example lists the alliance IDs and names of all the alliances in EVE, as does the file 'solarSystems.

csv' for all the solar systems there are. It is not necessary to go into further detail for these files, since they are of no practical relevance for the results of this book.

4.3.4 Remarks on social institutions in virtual worlds

It is important to note that the rules of the game *EVE Online* do not perfectly mirror the institutions of a real world society – also often termed 'rules of the game'. However, in the following it will be shortly demonstrated that Mantzavinos's (2001, pp. 83–100) distinction between informal institutions (comprising *conventions, moral rules,* and *social norms*) and formal institutions (*laws*) is generally useful and applicable in the virtual world as well, that is that one can work with his concepts to examine the institutions of EVE. In a brief investigation, the few differences that exist between informal and formal institutions in the real and in the virtual world will be elaborated upon to set the framework for discussing concrete evil rules later on.

A new kind of formal institution

The most important difference between real world and virtual world is the role formal institutions play. 'Formal institutions are enforced by law, whereas informal institutions do not need for their enforcement the State as a controller' (Mantzavinos, 2001, pp. 84–85); this fundamental distinction applies to virtual worlds, too. Only that the 'State' in EVE is somewhat different from real world states. In many aspects, the *developers* of the game, *CCP Games,* take over the role of the State in the virtual environment. However, the developers (or 'devs' for short) are not members of a political organization with a legal monopoly on the use of coercion in a specific area, as the State can be defined. First of all, the criterion of the 'legal monopoly on the use of coercion' does not fit. For example, basically everybody can shoot around with his virtual weapons within EVE just as he pleases. The use of force happening in EVE, therefore, is obviously not against the will of the 'State'. And although the devs could enact a legal monopoly on coercion for themselves, they are not willing to do so.

As for the second criterion, *CCP Games* is not a political organization (most importantly not a democratically elected government) but an Icelandic corporation that has to earn money with their business model in order to survive. The players, that is the members of the virtual society, are not able to exert influence on who reigns them and which laws are enacted, which makes something similar to a dictator out of CCP. On the other hand, compared to real life it is very easy for the players to 'vote with their feet', to quit playing the game and switch to another one. This is the reason why the developers generally listen closely to what the community says and tend to follow their wishes.

But the most important difference with respect to institutions is that this peculiar kind of 'State' is not only able to enact 'classic' laws, like forbidding the sale of in-game currency for real world money, but also to define 'natural laws' – which will be called *game mechanics*. The devs are somehow God-like. The virtual world is their creation and every 'natural law', that is every single game mechanic, can be coded. They can determine what the physical surroundings look like, how many solar systems and planets there are and which atoms everything in EVE is made from. They can determine every physical law, too, for example they would be able to make all things fall to the top rather than to the ground. This power stems from the fact that the developers write the game code of *EVE Online*. *Every institution that the devs really want to enforce can therefore easily be given a 100 percent compliance rate.* There shall be no theft? No problem, the possibility of robbing in-game items from other characters is deactivated or not even coded. There shall be no killing? No problem, you just make other characters unattackable. There shall be no drugs? No problem, you just do not 'invent' them in the first place. Whatever the devs want to be, will be in the virtual world of EVE. *In computer games in general, developers (the 'State') have the possibility of enacting game mechanics that resemble the natural laws of the real world. Although the product of human deliberation, these game mechanics are not enforced by the 'State' but by the game software itself: some actions are technically impossible in virtual worlds.*

However, the omnipotence of the developers dwindles when shifting the perspective from the developer-character interaction to the developer-player interaction. Players are real human beings that live in the same real world as developers – and notably they can decide to establish a link between their online and offline activities. Players can decide to sell in-game money to other players via real world markets, for example *eBay*. And suddenly all the developers can do about this is to enact 'classic' laws that forbid this kind of behavior and to sanction non-compliance to their best ability. They can take legal action by going to real world courts or at least 'ban' the player from the game, that is to shut down temporarily or permanently the account of the alleged criminal preventing him from playing. There are many documents outlining legal rules directly related to EVE, namely the 'End User Licence Agreement' (CCP Games, 2011a), the 'Terms of Service' (CCP Games, 2011b), the official 'Chat Rules' (CCP Games, 2011c), the 'User Policy' specifying which character names are allowed (CCP Games, 2011d), the 'Reimbursement Policy' (CCP Games, 2011e), the 'Ban Policy' (CCP Games, 2011f) and so on. All these documents state what the player is allowed to do and what not. The typical sanction for non-compliance is a ban. In this respect, the definition of the 'State' having the legal monopoly on coercion becomes true: *CCP Games* appoints 'game masters' with the right and competences to settle small in-game disputes, acting as police and judges simultaneously, and only the developers are allowed (and able) to ban players, that is to bring about their permanent virtual death.[6]

The category of formal rules is twofold for computer games. A second group of formal rules emerges next to laws, namely the natural laws (game mechanics) of the virtual environment. This is a significant deviation from Mantzavinos's classification, and it is due to the fact that computer games are technologically created environments.

Existence, emergence and change of formal rules in virtual worlds

Surprisingly, the existence of a second type of formal rules in virtual worlds whose adoption/enforcement is 100 percent sure does not seem to greatly alter other characteristics of formal institutions, namely why they exist, how they emerge, or how they change. Mantzavinos states that formal rules enforced by a State *exist* because they provide a solution to 'a twin problem faced by individuals in a society: the problem of trust and protection from the aggression of individuals of the same society *and* of those of different societies' (2001, p. 133). In a large society – and EVE's 778,521 characters surely count as that – the problem of deviant behavior becomes more virulent and an effective enforcement mechanism is needed. This is why there is a market system in place in EVE that guarantees proper transaction. This is also why there is high security space in EVE, in which the virtual police immediately sanctions (that is, takes action against) every hostile attack. This is furthermore a reason why CCP forbids and fights real-money trading, since it is often associated with hacked accounts and credit card fraud (Guðmundsson, 2009a, p. 24). The developers create the laws and natural laws of the virtual environment in order to enable trust and protection – at least to a certain degree. That they deliberately choose not to provide perfect protection and trust is an aspect that has to be intensely discussed but that does not affect the raison d'être of formal rules.

That formal rules typically *emerge* as the final outcome of a deliberation process is true for the real and the virtual world. The initial impetus for a new law may be a new solution to a social problem that *spontaneously* emerged within the community – but in the end it is the 'State' (CCP Games) that consciously decides on the exact scope of the institution. Whether this deliberation takes place among the elected members of a democratic government or among the employees of a corporation is not important here: the analogies are obvious. It is however noteworthy that EVE is the only MMORPG that possesses a democratically elected political organization that formally represents the views of the players to the developers. The CSM, a committee of nine players, is elected every six months, every EVE character having one vote. It provides a formal mechanism for the players to utter their wishes for changes to the game to CCP. Regular meetings between CCP officials and the CSM are held.[7]

Unlike in the real world where formal rules develop after informal rules with respect to time, in computer games formal institutions are the first to exist. This is because at the beginning the game is a product of design through and through. The game mechanics and the laws applicable to the game exist *before* the first player enters the virtual world. Only over the course of time – and notably dealing with the creativity of the player community that (ab)uses the environment and tools the developers gave to them – do the informal institutions of the community and maybe new formal rules emerge. *In virtual worlds, the evolution of institutions does not proceed from informal to formal rules but from formal rules to informal rules back to formal rules.* Of course, natural laws precede the existence of human societies in the real world, too. And most surely the fundamental physics of our world exert influence on which social institutions emerge. Still, natural laws are not the outcome of humanly controlled design processes as are game mechanics. The deliberate creation of institutions, therefore, plays a far bigger role in virtual worlds than in the real world.

Finally, real world formal institutions tend to *change* either because of external aggression leading to the rise of a new protection agency; or the change may be 'initiated by many individuals acting collectively in order to respond to a new social problem' (Mantzavinos, 2001, p. 95). The first reason might not be perfectly applicable to online environments. Although one could argue that CCP Games, being in constant competition with other MMORPG producers, would certainly adapt the formal rules of the game if too many players were about to switch games because they liked the different rules much better. The second reason, however, applies to both real life and virtual life. Consider for example the introduction of the *alliance system* in EVE.

By definition, every player in EVE is always a member of a *corporation*, that is a member of a formal association of players who regularly play together. Soon after the launch of EVE, players were already looking for a way to formally work together on a higher level than the already built-in corporation level. Many new players had joined the game since the first publication, so the institution of a corporation just got too 'small' for organizing that many people. The player base tried to convince the developers of EVE to establish further institutions facilitating cooperation (CCP TomB* et al., 2004a). They reacted to this demand with a first proposal on introducing *alliances* (formal associations of corporations rather than players) that was widely discussed and on some points heavily criticized (CCP TomB* et al., 2004a). After this experience, another, very different proposal was made that was more widely accepted and that finally got introduced (CCP TomB* et al., 2004b). If one looks at the discussions that took place among the players and developers and at the use the players eventually made of the newly introduced alliance system, it is hard to argue that the institutions in EVE are not adaptive just as they are in real life: they are ever-changing and adjust to the needs of the virtual society. Kjarval, Lead Game Master of EVE, states:

> It is hard to tell who has the biggest influence on the evolution of EVE. Alliances for example were there before there was the formal feature to build alliances. The community then just told us: 'Please make this more simple!' We aren't alone in developing the game. (Kjarval, 2011)

Turbefield and Óskarsson (2011; researcher and community manager) add: 'The big new inventions certainly come from the developers but the community does a lot of small things.' This is possible, since the interaction between player community and developers is extremely good in the case of EVE (Kjarval, 2011; Turbefield & Óskarsson, 2011). In this respect, it is characteristic for both real and virtual formal institutions that they can theoretically change overnight, whereas informal institutions tend to be much more resilient.

Informal institutions

Whereas the technical nature of virtual worlds interferes at some points with the concept of formal institutions, all types of informal institutions seem to be readily applicable to virtual worlds, too. The reasons why informal rules *exist* – social coordination problems (conventions), social dilemmas (moral rules), conflicting interests (social norms) (cf. Mantzavinos, 2001, pp. 101–118) – are identical in the real world and in a computer-mediated social environment. There is just no obvious reason why informal institutions should not *emerge* as the outcome of an invisible hand process in online games, since the underlying problem of many people living together and having to structure their interactions just stays the same. Also the aspects of institutional *change* and *enforcement* do not provide any indication as to why one should not be able to discuss virtual worlds in terms of these established concepts. The technical aspects that were dominant in the case of formal rules take a back seat in the case of informal institutions, since the developers are not able to predict what the players are going to do with the tools they provide them with. The best description of this process comes from CCP Oveur* (2006) describing his experiences as a developer of EVE:

> The biggest change for me is probably when I joined CCP, suddenly being in the position of controlling the destiny of EVE instead of just my own.... Well, controlling is far from being the right word, nobody controls EVE. Chief Housekeeper of the Universe is more like it....
>
> That's the problem, we can never be certain before something hits Tranquility [the name of the EVE server; C.D.M.] and anyone that claims they can foresee all changes and their effects is plain ignorant. How can one assume what 130,000 people will do with something? I don't know the answer, but I'm frequently asked that question.
>
> For us, it's simple.... Let's assume we're adding a brick to the game. One person will take that brick and hit you on the head. The other guy will wait till you pass him by, then hit you on the head, to decrease the chance of retaliation.
>
> Then there is a third guy, having watched the behavior of some brick users, waits patiently at a distance for the first guy to hit the other guy over the head with the brick. Then throws the brick at the last guy's head and takes the loot from them all.
>
> Yet another guy will take it and try to trade it for profit. That means some guy is buying the bricks. Why? The guy buying got tired of hitting people with bricks and asked himself, maybe it would be better to build a house with all these bricks so nobody can hit me? Then yet another guy decides this house thing is a good idea, teams up with some friends and builds a castle.
>
> You can insert anything you like instead of that brick, it applies to everything that changes the game, people will do different things with the tools they are given. (CCP Oveur*, 2006)

It all comes down to the phenomenon of an emerging society, be it virtual – it does not matter. All in all, the analogies between online and offline institutions outlined in this section show that – *although there are differences – the concepts developed by New Institutional Economics can be put to use in virtual environments, too.* Mantzavinos's classification of social institutions and their respective way of enforcement therefore only differs for *EVE Online* in one aspect. There is a second type of formal institution in virtual worlds: game mechanics that are third party enforced by the software (cf. Mantzavinos, 2001, p. 85).

4.4 Conclusion on MMORPGs as a field of research

MMORPGs like *EVE Online* are a particularly suitable environment to study evil actions and evil rules because they are complex and controllable at the same time; but there are also important limitations. Firstly, *the most serious limitation for research in these games is the* time *needed to understand what happens in these games.* One cannot just choose a specific game, ask the developer for the server data, and then start evaluating the data. A reasonable guess is that at least six months of play have to be invested before one is able to roughly understand the many ways in which these very complex games are played and to ask the right questions and draw valid interpretations from what is observed. Virtual worlds are 'worlds' also in the sense that some 'ethnographic' work is necessary to understand them. Doing research in MMORPGs means doing fieldwork first of all. The downside of not having to set up an experiment to get access to quantifiable human behavior is that one has to (1) identify those online interactions that are good counterparts to the offline human behavior one is interested in (in a foreign society of 400,000 people which possesses its own codes and rites) and (2) to re-identify these interactions in spreadsheets with millions of rows of only numbers. It is by no means simpler to do such 'descriptive' research in MMORPGs than to conduct laboratory experiments. The data might already be available in a processible form but a one-month-sample of the actions of 400,000 people is very difficult to handle. *Laboratory experiments and research in MMORPGs represent alternative ways of equal value to examine human behavior.* One should not choose the latter because it is easier (which it is not) but because of its great potential.

Studying human behavior in MMORPGs does not mean talking of the virtual behavior of some rather strange people willing to spend a lot of time in an environment without actually caring about what they do. *MMORPGs are not the physical world – but what is observed in them has scientific relevance.* Human behavior in *games* is related to *economic behavior. Online* behavior is related to *offline* behavior. When asked what, for him, is the biggest difference between the online economy of *EVE Online* and the real economy, CCP Games' lead economist answers:

> In my opinion, there are very few differences. The only difference is that the EVE economy fits closer to economic theory than real life. There are less disturbances – products are homogenous, there is a low barrier to entry in tech 1 production,[8] there is no player that has really any purchase power compared to the rest of the economy that he could really affect the market with for a long time....
>
> There is no fundamental difference: these are people making decisions about what to produce, for whom to produce, and how to produce it, and when to sell it – and they determine this based on market prices and information from the market. (Guðmundsson, 2010a)

Not everybody may take EVE dead seriously but these people exist for sure.

> There are players out there who reproduce their real life in EVE. They may have a small company in real life with hundred employees – and they try to do the exact same thing online. They make a business plan, recruit people, start to make profits, and so on.... There are people who just play EVE, doing occasional missions and stuff – and others who really see it as a second job and who take it absolutely seriously. (Kjarval, 2011; Lead Game Master)

Claiming that what these people do does not matter to economics – a discipline that does not believe in inherent values of things but that people themselves are best placed to decide how much something is worth to them – would be looking at these people with illegitimate disdain.

As far as the methodological approach is concerned, this book takes the computer-generated server logs as the main source of data for examining evil actions, that is for conducting microeconomic research in virtual worlds. The framework of the virtual social institutions will be analyzed referring to more traditional sources of data, notably dev blogs, official protocols of player-developer meetings, developer interviews, and discussions that took place in the official forums. Examining this data about the virtual institutions, one has to keep in mind that, compared to the real world, there are two types of formal institutions in virtual worlds: *laws* that are enforced by the 'State', and *game mechanics* (natural laws, so to speak) that are enforced by the game software itself.

As announced in the introduction, this fourth chapter constituted the first part of the endeavor to establish MMORPGs as a valid field for research in the social sciences. By setting out the advantages, limitations, and methodological issues that apply to MMORPGs, some theoretical considerations were provided for this project. The empirical part which now follows forms the second part of the endeavor. By giving an extended practical example of the possibilities and the power of empirical research in MMORPGs it shall further the goal.

The next section is the prelude to the empirical part of this book. It will provide a good impression about what it takes and feels like to play EVE, about basic rules and principles of EVE, about potential playing styles, and about the economic and political landscape of EVE. This information is necessary for analyzing the server data on the virtual interactions that happen in EVE every day and for putting in place the findings on the evil social institutions of EVE.

5
EVE Online

EVE Online (usually only called 'EVE' by players and developers) was published by *CCP Games* in May 2003. In January 2011, EVE had more than 390,000 active players and an average of around 30,000 concurrent users logged in at any time. On January 23, 2011, a new record of concurrent users was achieved: 63,170 users were simultaneously logged on onto the same server (CCP Explorer*, 2011). These numbers make EVE one of the internationally most successful MMORPGs at the moment.

EVE is a science-fiction themed game about trade and conflict in a remote future. The player's main task is to steer a spaceship through a galaxy far away ('New Eden') and to compete with other players – in both economic and military ways. Once you have purchased an account and created a character (one account can hold up to three characters) you can choose freely what you wish to do. Among the most common things are trading virtual goods, exploring the more than 7500 independent solar systems of 'New Eden', producing goods, mining asteroids for resources, patrolling the most important trade routes in order to rob merchants flying by, or fulfilling missions generated by computer-controlled agents (for example to transport things from A to B or to hunt down a wanted outlaw). The typical character is thus a *trader*, an *explorer*, a *producer*, a *miner*, a *pirate*, or a *mission runner* – or a combination of all. The ultimate goal in EVE is 'power' (EVElopedia, 2011a). Whereas many players aim to acquire more and more wealth as a final goal (for example by undercutting the prices of products of competing players and thus raising their sales volume), other players strive to dominate others through military means (Turbefield & Óskarsson, 2011). Instead of spaceships specialized for mining asteroids or transporting huge amounts of minerals from one station to another, they steer battleships equipped with lasers and other high-teach weapons. 'Power' can be said to be the final goal of EVE – with the vagueness of this goal being a characteristic rather than a shortcoming (cf. Section 4.1 on the general role of goals in MMORPGs).

The explicit intention of making EVE a 'sandbox' (Guðmundsson, 2010a), in which everybody can do whatever he chooses to do, in which players create the stories, and in which individual decisions can actually change the course of the virtual history and may have impact on a large number of people, is also furthered by the technical fact that EVE is a *single-shard universe*. Unlike other MMORPGs, in which the players are distributed to different servers (called 'shards'), every EVE player logs on onto the exact same server. This means that there really is only *one* virtual world in EVE. EVE players share the exact same universe and whenever you play EVE, you could possibly run into any other EVE player around – and not only the 3000 German players, for instance.

5.1 Gameplay

In order to better understand the game – and thus also the findings of this book – the best way is to actually play EVE for some time. The following pages can only provide a rough idea of how it feels to play EVE.

5.1.2 Moving around

The first time you play EVE, you will have to create your character – that is mostly to determine its race, gender, physical appearance, clothing, and so on. As soon as you are finished with the design, you will be granted a rookie spaceship and find yourself within this spaceship inside a certain space station. You will find that it is not the humanly looking avatar you just created that you are controlling most of the time but rather the *space ship* in which your character is located. For example, you can undock from the station and fly through space. In fact, this is what players do most of the time: *flying around in space in order to fulfill certain tasks and to make money*. On your journeys you may encounter different space stations, asteroid belts, planets, moons, and wormholes. EVE comprises more than 7500 solar systems that are separate from one another. You are always in one specific solar system and in order to change between them you have to use star gates.

Not every solar system is directly connected to every other, so you may have to fly through a series of star gates and travel through a couple of solar systems in order to reach a space station in a different solar system in which you get, for example, a good price for the merchandise in the cargo hold of your ship. It takes you approximately one minute to get from a station in system A to another station in a neighboring system B, depending on the type of ship you are flying – for example a small, fast *shuttle* or a big, cumbersome *freighter*. It takes you approximately half a minute to fly from a station in system A to an asteroid belt in the same system A – which you may want to visit in order to mine the asteroids for resources. Taking into account the huge number of solar systems in EVE, this gives an impression of the vastness of the virtual universe.

5.1.3 People to meet

The player encounters characters controlled by other human players and characters controlled by the game software itself (so called NPCs). The most notable NPCs are the *virtual police* (called CONCORD: 'Consolidated Cooperation and Relations Command'), *agents* (who might offer him the job to transport something from A to B or to eliminate a known outlaw – and reward him with money for completed tasks), and *NPC-pirates* (who typically try to kill him).

While the interaction with NPCs is standardized (for example text boxes for agents that give you the choice to accept or decline an offered job), there are many ways of interacting with other humanly-controlled characters. You can search for the name of every character in the game and send them an *in-game mail*, you can contact them directly and privately via *text chat* if they are online, or you can use the *public chat channels* to get in touch with other players. The public chat channels are where the social life of EVE takes place. As soon as you have found some online friends, it is highly likely that you will also communicate with them via *voice chat* – using third-party software or the built-in voice chat function as well as a headset.

5.1.4 Atmosphere

EVE is a slow-paced game that mostly does not require the player to make fast clicks and decisions but rather to thoughtfully plan her actions. Long-term strategy and tactics are dominant in all aspects of this game, be it the production of goods or the fighting for territory. EVE tries to bring about the atmosphere of space: its vastness, loneliness, slowness, coldness, and darkness. Colors tend to be dark and the music of the game rather minimalistic, 'spheric', and slow. EVE is intentionally designed to be a dark universe and a harsh environment. There is a famous quote of CCP Wrangler*, one of the lead developers, that gets cited regularly on the forums: 'EVE is a dark and harsh world, you're supposed to feel a bit worried and slightly angry when you log in, you're not supposed to feel like you're logging in to a happy, happy, fluffy, fluffy lala land filled with fun and adventures, that's what hello kitty online is for' (e.g. Del ReyII*, 2007).

The first two rules new players are typically told are: 1. Trust nobody. 2. Do not fly what you cannot afford to lose – because you will lose it eventually (e.g. Luminus Mallus*, 2010). Always be alert and do not fly too expensive spaceships, since killing, treachery, cut-throat business practices, or deception are very common and explicitly allowed by the developers, sometimes even favored by the game mechanics.

5.1.5 To kill and to be killed

In this atmosphere, and with many players out there and some additional NPC-pirates, it is more than likely that you will be shot at or even killed sooner or later. In EVE, death is – compared to other MMORPGs – relatively costly and comes in different variants. The most common case is that some hostile character attacks your ship and destroys it. In this case, you will find yourself in a small rescue capsule. You are then unable to attack your aggressor and pretty helpless but at least you are able to fly to the nearest station and buy a new ship. Although your character has not really died (your avatar is still sitting alive in that rescue capsule), this kind of ship destruction and escape is referred to as a 'kill' in the terminology of the game. When killed, you incur the costs of replacing your equipment and ship (often the most valuable possession you have) and the loss of all cargo you were carrying with you in the cargo hold of your ship.[1]

However, the situation is even worse if you get 'pod killed'. The 'pod' is the game term for the rescue capsule you are in after the destruction of your ship. If you get pod killed, the hostile character does not only succeed in destroying your original ship but also in destroying your rescue capsule. Getting pod killed resembles more what one commonly associates with the word 'death': a virtual corpse is floating through space. Thankfully – and due to the advancements of technology in the coming 20,000 years – even if you get pod killed you do not start anew from scratch. Instead, you are transferred into a clone of yours in a pre-selected space station. You may continue playing immediately and do not have to create a new character – which makes this variant of death non-final, too. However, the costs for getting pod killed are even higher. You may lose some precious brain implants you bought (in order to improve your combat or production skills) and – the most expensive case – some skills and abilities that your character has acquired since

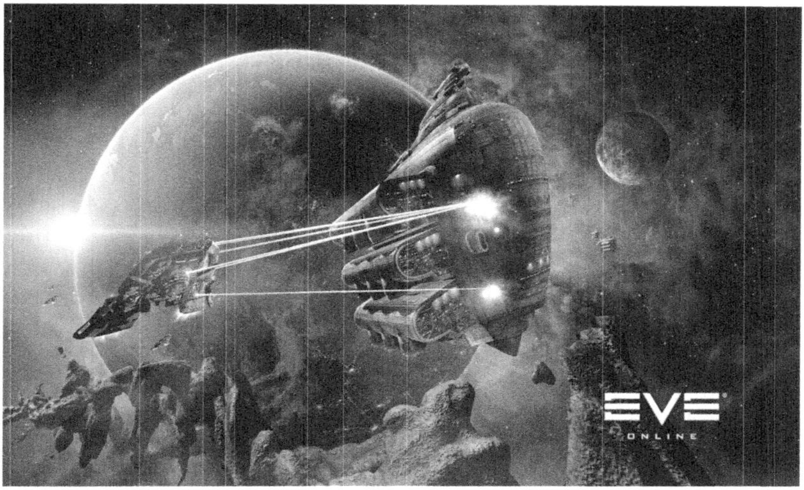

Figure 5.1 Screenshot – a freighter being attacked

you started playing EVE. These costs are optional, though, and depend on decisions you made in-game earlier. Figure 5.1 is a screenshot from EVE which shows a freighter being attacked by a small battle ship.

5.2 Economic environment of EVE

Earning virtual money is one of the main incentives for EVE players – and the accumulation of wealth is one of two dominant long-term strategies in the game. The other one is the amassing of political and military power (which we will have a look at in Section 5.3). However, to build up and keep up an army is a costly endeavor in the virtual as well as in real life; therefore one can safely state that making money is *the* central activity of the game (Hreiðarsson, 2011). A good way to understand the economic environment of EVE is an example of how players can earn 'ISK' (short for 'InterStellarKredit', the in-game currency).

5.2.1 Microeconomic considerations

When you first play EVE, you start out with a rather powerless character in a rather powerless rookie spaceship. In order to advance in the game you will need money – for example to buy a more powerful spaceship. One way of earning money in EVE is to invest the money you were initially granted by the game to buy mining equipment, undock from the station, fly to a nearby asteroid belt, mine some asteroids until your cargo hold is full, fly back to the station, and sell the ores you just mined on the market there. *The different ores mined from asteroids (there are 16 of them in EVE) are the raw materials from which nearly everything in EVE is made (ships, weapons, space stations, and so on) and the mining business is the central backbone of EVE's economy.*

After some time – the player is now the owner of a state-of-the-art mining ship and able to mine many times the amount of ore than when he steered his rookie ship – he will realize that the cargo hold of his mining ship is rather small and that the trips from and to the station take a lot of time that he would rather spend mining. This is the point where specialization and division of labor kick in. What the player could do in order to further raise his profits is to ask another player – who is specialized in the transport business – to continually haul the ores from the asteroid belt to the station for him. *In EVE, the different ships and the equipment fitted on them are designed in such a way that they foster specialization and division of labor.* A mining ship is very efficient in extracting ores from asteroids and can fit more advanced mining equipment than a transport ship. However, it has a comparably small cargo hold and, thus, would have to travel a lot in order to haul all the ore to the station where it can be sold. This is the strength of transport ships. Together the players can mine and sell more ore and make higher profits. So they found a two-man 'corporation'.

This process of specialization soon becomes very complex. You might for example meet a *producer/researcher* who is willing to spend his time refining the ore before selling it on the market – and thus obtaining a higher price. Maybe he is even able to produce primary or secondary goods from the ore, and can then sell goods instead of raw materials. Or an *explorer* might join you. He possesses a ship capable of searching space for the most lucrative places to mine. However, the prospering business of your corporation will most likely not go unnoticed: competitors will start to undercut your prices on the market and you may have to sell your goods in a different, less competitive space station. Perhaps then, a *trader* joins your corporation. He is specialized in finding the best offers for your goods in different space stations and has to pay lower broker fees for setting up buy and sell orders on the virtual market. If you are unlucky, some less peace-loving players may also have heard about your regular shipments from A to B and start attacking your transport ships in order to steal your ores and goods. They are acting as *pirates*. So you will need protection for your convoys and you will want some players capable of flying battleships to join your corporation. The next pirate attack will possibly end with losses on both sides – but, with a little luck, your goods make it to the chosen station.

This brings us to the end of this example. The process of exploring, mining, hauling, producing, trading and fighting is a fairly short but reasonably exhaustive description of how the supply side of the EVE economy works. Figure 5.2 illustrates this process graphically.

Individual players trying to advance their characters and wanting to buy better equipment are an important demand force in EVE's economy. Typically, however, the final goods produced and sold on the market are combat ships and weapons that will get destroyed in combat shortly after. The single most important factor of the demand side of EVE's economy is fighting. 'War is the engine that drives the universe' (Guðmundsson, 2010b).

The skill system: human capital the virtual way

It is not only money that generates more money in EVE (by the means of more efficient equipment) but also the individual *skills* of a character. A skill is an item that you can buy on the market but you still have to

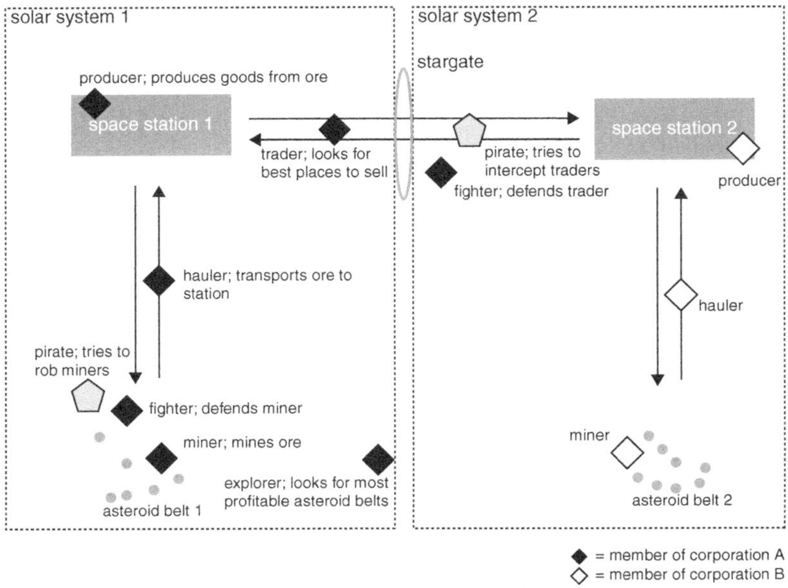

Figure 5.2 The supply side of EVE's economy

'train' the skill after you have bought it. Compare it to the fees for higher education: paying the fees alone will not raise your human capital. You still have to invest time and learn what you are taught. In EVE, for example, if your character trains the skill 'mining' to level one, this will raise your mining yield by 10 percent – irrespective of the equipment you are using to mine asteroids. Training the skill to level one takes around half an hour. Training time flows in the background. You can still do other things in the game while you train a skill. Once you have trained a skill, you will profit from it during your character's entire life.

There are skills for almost anything in EVE and just as with physical capital, skills are highly specialized. Even after years of skill training you will not have learned every skill there is in EVE. *Only after you have spent 8 to 12 months training production skills with your avatar, are you deemed a skilled manufacturer who can compete with the lowest prices on the market.* Since all characters train skills in real-time, and thus at the same pace, seniority is highly rewarded in EVE.

5.2.2 Macroeconomic data of EVE

Thanks to the work of Guðmundsson, lead economist of EVE, and his fellow researchers, a wide range of macroeconomic data concerning EVE is available compared to other MMORPGs. The 'Quarterly Economic Newsletters', which have been published since 2007, are a good source for everybody interested in the EVE economy (Guðmundsson, 2007, 2008a, 2008b, 2009a, 2009b, 2009c, 2010c, 2010d, 2010e, 2010f, 2011).

Demographics

From September 2007 to January 2011, the population of EVE grew from about 195,000 accounts (representing 433,000 characters[2]) to about 390,000 accounts (representing around 780,000 characters) (Guðmundsson, 2007, p. 4, 2010f, p. 8). This equals to an average yearly population growth rate of just over 17 percent. These numbers are impressive for an MMORPG which is – with its eight years of existence – an oldie in the game industry.

At the end of January 2011, 95.7 percent of the players (accounts that are neither disabled, nor banned) are male players and 4.3 percent female. This is a very high proportion of male players even for the MMORPG-genre. The players come from nearly every country in the world, with the top five being the United States (36 percent), the UK (11 percent), Germany (9 percent), Russia (8 percent), and Canada (5 percent). The typical EVE player does not come from a specific country but rather shares some common character traits:

> It is more a question of character than of country. We have a well-educated computer scientist in the U.S. who likes it and a well-educated computer scientist in Russia who likes it. A business guy in Germany, and a business guy in Sweden. (Guðmundsson, 2010a)

The age distribution of the players can be seen in Figure 5.3:

Apart from the outliers at ages 33 and 34 (for which there is no obvious explanation besides players willingly entering a wrong age when registering their account), Figure 5.3 shows a rather smooth age distribution. The average age of the EVE player is around 31 years, which is older than the average age for other MMORPGs. He spends around 17 hours per week on average playing EVE (Guðmundsson, 2009c, p. 12).

> The player base is not representative compared to the real world: we have too many male players and an average age of 30. One could maybe claim that we are a representative sample of male western characters. And we are definitely more representative than taking undergrad students. (Guðmundsson, 2010a)

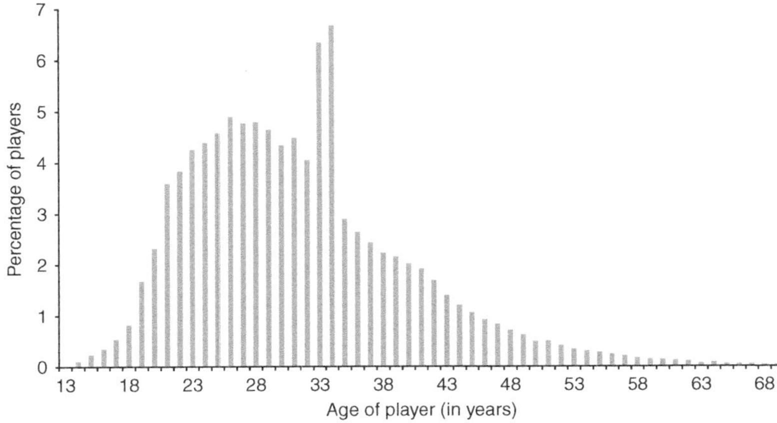

Figure 5.3 Age distribution of the population of EVE at the end of January 2011 from 13 years to 69 years (representing 99.8 percent of the population)

Figure 5.4 shows the age distribution of the characters[3] in EVE, the mean age being slightly under two years (1.93 years).

One also has to take into account that EVE's economy follows a different time scale than real life. Two years in EVE signify a really long time:

> No formal studies have been conducted on the measurement of time across 'fiscal' periods in EVE, but judging from forum-based discussions, markers such as dividend payout frequency and other variables suggest that one year in real life is equivalent to one month in EVE. (Guðmundsson, 2007, p. 6)
>
> We have a weekly economic cycle and an economic cycle that fits around the expansions – about every 6 months. So all this fits well into the monthly view of the EVE economy. (Guðmundsson, 2010a)

Foreign exchange

Although EVE does not have a national, domestic territory because there is just no real 'place' where 'New Eden' lies, one can still calculate a type of foreign exchange rate between EVE's economy and the real world. EVE is a clearly delimited economic area and possesses its own currency that is accepted everywhere in the virtual universe: ISK.[4] *The exchange rate between ISK and EUR in January* 2011 *was about*

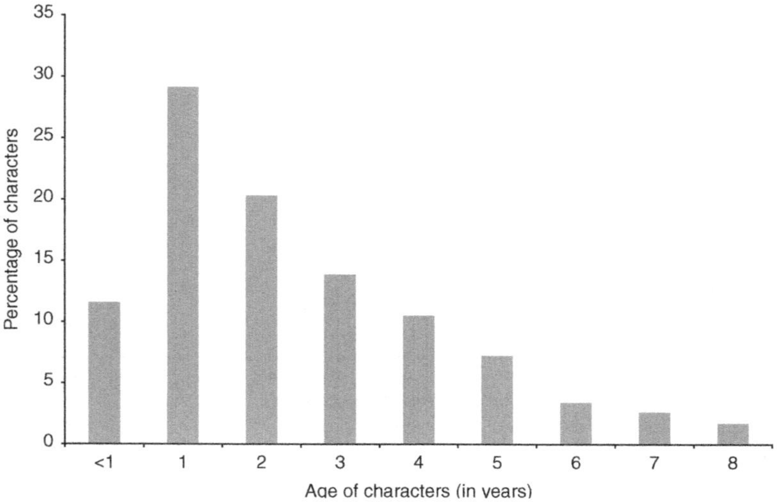

Figure 5.4 Age distribution of the characters in EVE at the end of January 2011

1 ISK = 0.000000051 EUR, or respectively 1 EUR = 19,444,364 ISK. This number can be calculated in the following way.

In EVE, there is the legal possibility of buying in-game currency with real-life money: the PLEX-system. PLEX is short for '30 Day Pilot License Extension'. If a player buys a PLEX for the price of EUR 17.495 (in January 2011) from CCP Games, then he basically buys the right to play EVE for one month. Using PLEX in order to pay for your gaming time is just one more possibility besides having a monthly subscription to EVE (which in January 2011 was EUR 14.95). However, a PLEX at the same time is an in-game item that can be traded via the in-game market. This allows, for example, for paying for gaming time with virtual money that a player makes in the game rather than real money: if you make enough ISK in EVE, you are able to play EVE 'for free'. Experienced players do not have to invest any real money to pay for gaming time.

Figure 5.5 illustrates the prices for PLEX and the volume traded in the most important market hub of EVE – the station IV-4 in the 'Jita'-system(Guðmundsson, 2010c, p. 24) – during the month of January.

Calculating the monthly average for these daily averages (340,179,152 ISK) and dividing it by the cost of one PLEX (17.495 EUR), yields the exchange rate mentioned above. It is, basically, the average number of ISK that you could buy in January 2011 with one Euro.

This type of 'foreign exchange rate' has to be used with caution, since it has several limitations to it. First of all, CCP Games controls the price for PLEX. They can therefore at any time raise or lower the exchange rate ISK/EUR. Second, the rate actually is a one-way exchange rate.

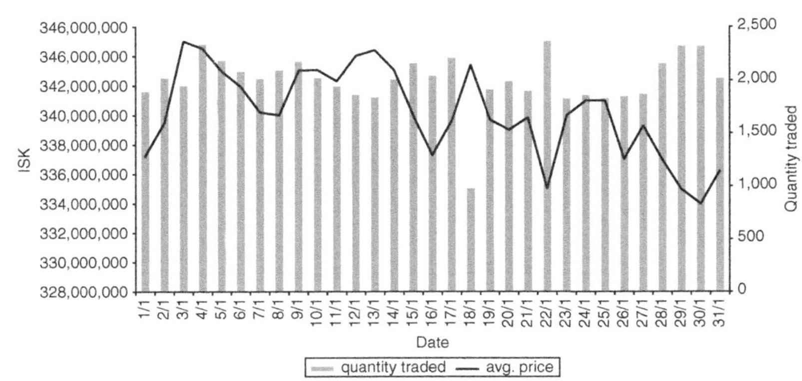

Figure 5.5 The average daily quantity traded (right axis) and prices paid for PLEX (left axis) in Jita IV-4 in January 2011

There is only this one way of legally buying ISK for EUR but not a single legal way of buying EUR with ISK. The latter phenomenon is commonly referred to as Real Money Trading (RMT) in the gaming industry. It is a serious problem[5] known in any MMORPG and since as early as 1989 (Guðmundsson, 2009a, p. 24).

> RMT has grown in lockstep with the MMO industry, and is now estimated to generate somewhere between a 500 million to 1 billion USD in transactions annually. (Guðmundsson, 2009a, p. 24)

Despite these limitations, one should not forget that compared to other MMORPGs there is at least a way of exchanging real money for in-game currency legally – be it only one. Many other MMORPGs can only rely on the prices of illegal transactions to determine the exchange rate.

Figure 5.6 shows that the PLEX-system nowadays is well established in the EVE-economy and accepted by the players. The constant growth with respect to the volume of PLEX traded and the fairly stable price over the years point to the validity of this measure of the 'foreign exchange rate' between ISK and EUR.

Wages and distribution of wealth

The exchange rate should always be seen in connection with the price level of EVE. A low-level spaceship may cost between 200,000 and

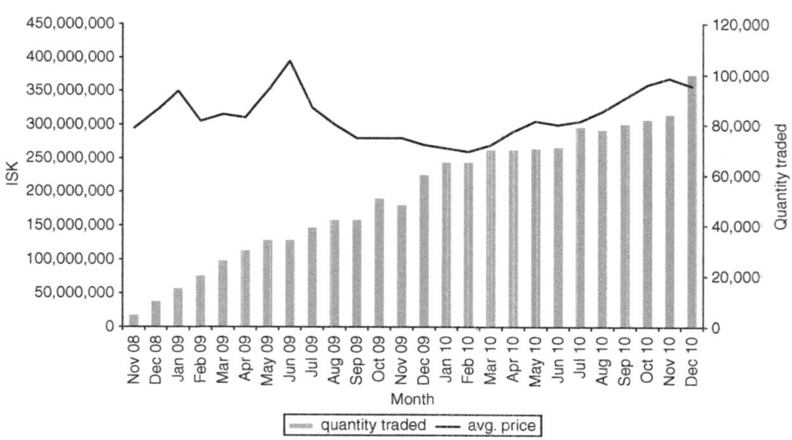

Figure 5.6 Quantity traded and price of PLEX from introduction in November 2008 through June 2010 (Guðmundsson, 2010c, p. 33, 2010e, p. 34)

750,000 ISK, an advanced battleship costs already around 100 million ISK. It is, unfortunately, very difficult to determine average wages for different professions in EVE. This is due to the large differences in the virtual human capital of the characters that greatly influence the efficiency of the virtual work and to the fact that EVE characters typically have more than one profession, which they sometimes execute simultaneously. However, after half a year of playing it should be fairly easy to make 10 million ISK per hour mining in a safe area of space, earning from 25 million to 100 million ISK and more per hour doing missions for agents, or even making from 50 million to 200 million ISK and more per hour by trading on the market (Atima* et al., 2011; CSM & CCP Games, 2011, p. 5). Thus, *earning the equivalent of 2 EUR per hour is no problem for experienced players.*

It is very difficult to measure the wealth of a single character in EVE, too. Especially since the richest characters typically possess rare items that are almost never traded on the market and therefore possess no commonly-known value. However, concerning the distribution of wealth in EVE, one can use the amount of cash held in the character's wallet as a good indicator.

Figure 5.7 shows that the large majority of EVE-characters do not have more than 100 million ISK in cash in their wallet. The general trend is that, as the amount of ISK in the wallet increases, the share of

Figure 5.7 ISK in wallet per character in percentage of population (Guðmundsson, 2009b, p. 16)

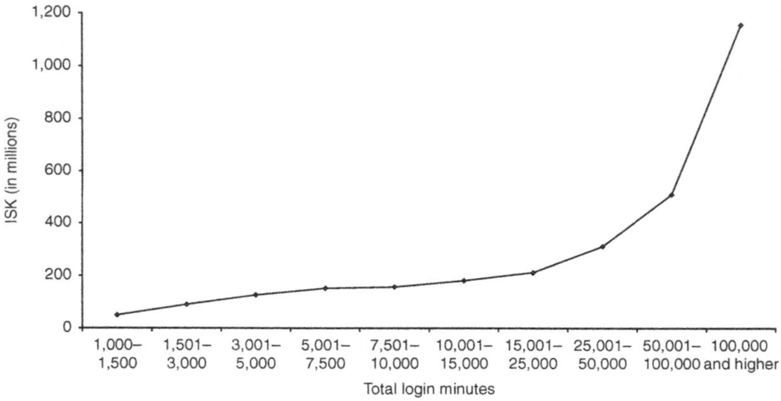

Figure 5.8 Average ISK in wallet per character by total login minutes (Guðmundsson, 2009c, p. 12)

characters in the total population drops – with the exception of the 11 percent of veteran characters who have more than 1 billion ISK in cash. Figure 5.8 highlights more clearly the correlation between total playing time and wealth.

These figures illustrate well that EVE is in fact a 'make-or-break' game. Assuming an average daily playing time of 2.4 hours (which was the case when the data for Figure 5.8 was collected), one finds that *only after 104 days of play* (the equivalent of 15,000 total login minutes) *money making in EVE seems to become comparably easy*. While many new characters are struggling to make enough money, the few really senior characters there are possess considerable personal wealth.

Money supply and the GDP

In December 2010, the money supply M1 for EVE's economy amounted to 445 trillion ISK (around 23 million EUR) – up from 90 trillion ISK more than three years earlier (Guðmundsson, 2007, p. 7, 2011, p. 18).[6] In this connection, the economic system of EVE is best described as a 'sink and faucet' system where currency flows into the system through various sources and leaks out through different sinks. Both the faucets and the sinks are created and controlled by CCP Games (Guðmundsson, 2007, p. 7). Over the years, the money supply has been constantly growing in EVE – as has the population. Periods of mild deflation were always followed by periods of mild inflation and overall EVE turns out to be a very stable economy (Guðmundsson, 2007, 2008a, 2008b, 2009a,

2009b, 2009c, 2010c, 2010d, 2010e, 2010f, 2011). Inflation in EVE is measured based on a mineral price index, a primary and secondary producer price index, and a consumer price index.

Unfortunately, it turns out to be very difficult to determine the GDP of 'New Eden', or rather the GUP, the 'Gross User Product' – defined as the total product 'of the user-controlled characters in the economy'(Guðmundsson, 2008a, p. 12). An initial attempt to define and measure EVE's GUP in 2007 was not continued. For referential reasons, that is for *in-game comparisons* and to evaluate in the following how important certain phenomena are to EVE's economy as a whole, the money supply M1 will be used as a measure. The reasons for this are that it has been constantly calculated since 2007 and possesses a well-documented real-life equivalent as well. Since the definition of the money supply M1 of the European Central Bank corresponds to Guðmundsson's definition (European Central Bank, 2011a), this book will usually refer to the M1 of the European Union for *real-world comparisons*. In January 2011, the M1 of the European Union amounted to 4711 billion EUR (European Central Bank, 2011b).

The market

EVE's economy is almost completely driven by those that participate in playing EVE – and so is its market (Guðmundsson, 2008b, p. 4). The current *daily trade value record* (from December 2010) of trades executed via the market system in EVE amounts to 1.8 trillion ISK raised in more than 1.2 million individual trades (Guðmundsson, 2011, p. 6).

> The industrial and market component of EVE is every bit as harsh and competitive as the PvP[7] aspect of the game. Players compete fiercely with each other as they battle to lower production costs or outbid each other on the open market. They also compete in the mining sector by adding to and advancing their skills in order to boost returns and reduce waste, often investing significant effort to increase their efficiency by just 1% at a time. But that 1% edge is often what makes or breaks a mining mogul. (Guðmundsson, 2008b, p. 4)

The central place for economic competition in EVE is the 'market'. The 'market window' – that you can bring up at any time – is basically a list of all items traded on EVE's market with the corresponding overview of all buy- and sell-orders for each item in the region.[8] It shows how many star gate jumps away from the current position the offers are, which quantity is offered, at which price, in which station exactly, and when the offer expires. The players also have access to historical price information like for example the daily traded volume of an item for the past six months, the five- or 20-day moving average price, and the median day price (presented either in tables or as graphs). *Buying and selling contracts are always kept in EVE, since the game mechanics automatically withdraw the money or item from your assets and hand it over to your counterpart.* The highly reliable, well-functioning, and ubiquitously available market function stands in stark contrast to the rather unclear political environment of EVE – which will be treated in the next section.

Particularities of EVE's economy

The most important particularities of EVE's virtual economy shall not go unnoticed. First, the asteroids which serve as the main resource for the whole economy with the ore they provide, can never be exhausted. They do vanish if players mine them for long enough, but all asteroid belts in the universe get 'reseeded' at the daily half-an-hour 'downtime'.[9] That is, once a day new resources flood the universe and this process will potentially continue forever. There are no limits to growth in EVE in this aspect. NB: As has already been stated, this endless supply of resources does not lead to a price decline.

Second, there is no technological progress in the ordinary way. Players themselves cannot invent new technological solutions but only learn to use the tools given to them by the developers. From time to time, the developers will introduce new technologies to EVE, for example a new powerful weapon system or an even more efficient type of mining. But these 'inventions' or 'technological progresses' are centrally planned. This most supposedly hinders the general economic development of EVE, since no technologically driven entrepreneurship is possible and the pro-competitive role of innovations is severely affected.

5.3 Political environment of EVE

Because of the very clear-cut, ubiquitous and efficient market system of EVE on the one hand, and the uncertainty and instability that characterizes the political system of EVE on the other, an appropriate first approach to understanding EVE is considering it as *capitalist anarchy*.

Generally speaking, *anarchy* can be defined as a social condition in which there is a lack of State-enforced property rights (Buchanan, 1975/2000). In anarchy, consequently, everybody has a right to everything and neither laws nor governmental enforcing agencies exist. From an economic standpoint, then, the characteristic decision to be made by every person living in anarchy is: should I produce goods myself or steal them from others to make a living (Buchanan, 1975/2000; Hirshleifer, 1995)? Anarchy must not be equated with 'chaos' – a condition in which there are no social rules at all, not even informal ones governing the day-to-day interactions of people. Clearly, institutions do arise without States enforcing them, simply through social interaction in an uncertain environment (Mantzavinos et al., 2004; North, 2005). Such institutions *always exist already* before any kind of trade or governmental control can be established – and do not violate the definition of anarchy. In contrast to anarchy, the *State* can be defined as a political organization with a legal monopoly on the use of coercion in a specific area.

Already the first impression, namely that the two single most important actions in EVE are either producing or fighting – just as Buchanan (1975/2000) or Hirshleifer (1995) postulate it in their economic approaches to anarchy – points in the direction of EVE being an anarchy. The developers of EVE very rarely intervene in a way comparable to a protective State – and only if stark inappropriate action takes place. You lost money to somebody who promised you a certain item after you handed him over the money in the first place? – That is your problem! CCP Games tries to stress autonomy and consequence, harshness and unforgivingness in its game and always underlines that careless decisions are the responsibility of the players, not the developers (Hreiðarsson, 2011). The developers of EVE, thus, cannot be characterized as being the minimal protective State that at least enforces property rights.

5.3.1 EVE – an anarchy?

EVE is not a perfect anarchy in all aspects. Speaking of property rights for example: there is a system in place that lets the game know what belongs to whom. For example, you can buy a ship on the market and then board it and fly around in it. Only you are entitled to do so with this ship. On the other hand, nobody keeps your opponent from attacking the spaceship you are currently flying in, or from destroying it and taking away what was in the cargo hold. This behavior is not prosecuted – so the perceived 'property rights' were very fragile ones in the first place. Yet, a virtual, computer-controlled police force and army exist in EVE and the 'State' – not CCP Games (!) but the computer-programmed entities – enforces its property laws in some areas of the galaxy.

Generally speaking, the virtual universe is divided into three areas: *high security space* ('hisec' – security status of the solar system between 1.0 and 0.5) in which the police actively enforces property laws, *low security space* ('lowsec' – security status of the solar system between 0.4 and 0.1) in which there is only passive enforcement, and *null security space* ('nullsec' – security status of the solar systems equals 0.0) in which there is no police at all and no property rights apply. For instance, if you attack your opponent to rob him as described above *in hisec*, police ships will quickly arrive and retaliate by destroying your ship as well. Additionally, your personal 'security standing' will be lowered as a consequence of every crime you commit. The *security standing* is a number between +10 and -10 attributed to your avatar. If your security standing gets too low, you are no longer allowed to enter hisec without getting attacked by the police.[10]

If you commit the same crime *in lowsec* however, the police will not destroy your ship and the security standing decrease is the only sanction. Additionally, there is no lower limit for your security standing that would deny you access to lowsec without repercussions. *In nullsec*, finally, you can do whatever you like. The police will not take notice of what you do there. Anarchy reigns nullsec space: there are neither property rights nor a monopolistic State-agency that enforces them. The only organizations there are in nullsec are 'alliances' – large associations of players that try to enforce *their* idea of property rights and *their* informal institutions in the territory they control. They however only provide *private* enforcement of institutions. NB: The governmental enforcement of property rights by the police is not very effective in hisec and lowsec either. Other people can 'declare war' on you at any time – with the consequence that the police no longer interfere with combat between the warring parties. The legal monopoly on the use of coercion in hisec is as weak as the concept of property rights in EVE. The 'State' accepts war on its territory. *The protective State in EVE is as minimal as it gets.*

> EVE is not governed.... We are not the Gods, we are the janitors of the universe.... EVE might be an example of the minimal State. The market works and some basic rules, but that's it. (Turbefield & Óskarsson, 2011)

You can always choose as a player, whether you want to fly around in relative security (hisec), in an area of lower security but in which still some laws do apply (lowsec), or in a purely anarchic environment (nullsec). The players of EVE thus have the possibility of voting with their feet and choosing their preferred form of government from this set of three alternatives with relatively low effort. And the voting results are quite telling: from March 2009 to June 2010, of those characters that were active in EVE (in the sense that they logged in at any time) around 53 percent of the characters were living in hisec space, 8 percent in lowsec, and 39 percent preferred the total anarchy of nullsec (Guðmundsson, 2010e, pp. 9–10).[11] The preference for a quiet virtual life unaffected by violence thanks to governmental law enforcement is clear – but the fact that over one third of all active players choose to live in the virtual anarchy of nullsec is stunning. In EVE, many people voluntarily continue to live, in an area of a constant 'war ... of every man against every man' (Hobbes 1651/1998, p. 84).[12] *Anarchy prevails in some areas of the virtual universe and a non-negligible minority prefers the natural state over the State.* This is an important finding in itself. Even more so, insofar as one cannot simply state that there is more money to be made in nullsec, that is that the higher risk is offset by higher rewards. The resources to be found in nullsec are more valuable and the population density is lower, meaning there are less competitors (Guðmundsson, 2010c, pp. 10–11). However, the infrastructure is very bad and the big trade hubs all are in hisec. Additionally, you have to always fight for what you earn in nullsec. With respect to profit, fighting and the effects of territorial dominance in nullsec are comparable to business and trade in hisec.

5.3.2 Political organizations besides the State: corporations and alliances

In EVE, *corporation* (or 'corp', for short) is the term for formal associations of players. As division of labor and specialization are highly rewarded, joining forces is a quite logical thing to do. Every corp has a *CEO* (usually the founder), who, by default, is a dictator with respect to every decision to be made: he alone decides, for example, whether the corporation goes to war (but plenty of democratic or even communist corporations exist in EVE).

Corps are the smallest political units in EVE – and for large parts of EVE (namely the hisec and lowsec territories) the most important. Corporations compete with others on the market, cooperate with other, friendly corporations, and go to war with their enemies. There are 'global' corporations with members in every time zone in order to be able to play EVE around the clock, corporations that found virtual banks to which every EVE player has access, and mercenary corporations that take money for hunting down and killing a specific player or for going to war with other corporations. New players automatically join one of the 28 NPC corporations, lead by a computer-controlled avatar. These NPC corporations provide a loose connection and low levels of trust among the members, since players are distributed by chance into these corporations and, thus, typically do not know each other. Around 50 percent of the players stay in (or return to) an NPC corporation (Guðmundsson, 2010e, p. 9). Half of the players are members of one of the 74,000 player-run corporations that range in size from one-member corporations to about 1500 members (ibid.). Players formally apply to become the member of a successful corporation – just as they would for a real-life job (a look in the corporation/alliance-recruitment forums is very enlightening in this context (CCP Games, 2011g)).

Alliances are formal associations of corporations allowing for teaming up on an even higher level, bringing together very specialized corps. They consist of one 'executor corporation' (usually the alliance-founding corporation) and a certain number of 'member corporations'. The *executor corporation* fulfills the same roles for the alliance as the CEO does for a corporation. Alliances are the single most important political, economic, and military actors in nullsec space. Living in nullsec with your character, being part of a big alliance that formally claims territory and defends it against other alliances, is the endgame of EVE, the long-term goal of many players. However, becoming competitive in nullsec alliance warfare takes the average player about two years of gaming (Guðmundsson, 2010f, p. 10).

5.4 An introduction to economic evil in EVE

The archetypical example of an economically evil action in EVE is a *kill*. A 'kill' is essentially the game's term for ship destruction. To destroy the ship of a fellow EVE player you, first, have to find him (which is not easy in the vastness of virtual space), second, you have to 'target' him (that is lock your weapon systems to his ship), and third, you have to activate your weapon systems and start firing. If you succeed in destroying an opponent's ship before he escapes or manages to kill you instead, the system will count this as a kill for you. Since the whole process is rather complicated to execute and since ships are obviously costly, each kill that happens in EVE is an economically evil action: it is *intentional*, it *materially harms* the victim, and the *material payoffs for the perpetrator vary between positive and negative.*

This is why the next sections will all center on kills. The goal is to shed some light on when and where the kills happen, who the victims and perpetrators are, and whether one is dealing with *egoistic actions, wanton actions,* or even *malicious actions* when looking at kills in EVE from the perspective of economic evil. Section 5.4.1 will provide a general introduction to killing in EVE and Section 5.4.2 will discuss some of the fundamental social institutions that guide killing, thus presenting first evidence on *evil rules*. Chapters 6 to 8 will then each narrow down the scope to one specific type of kill: piracy, suicide ganks, and war in EVE – looking not only at the extent of the evil actions occurring but also at the evil rules that guide the different types of behavior.

5.4.1 Economically evil actions in EVE

In January 2011, 327,911 player kills[13] *happened in EVE.* These kills are fairly evenly distributed throughout the month as Figure 5.9 shows:

The number fluctuates around the 11,000 kills per day mark; the remarkably low number of kills on January 18 is explained by the fact that a new patch to the game software was launched that day and servers were offline for some time. Weekends (January 1 and 2, 8 and 9, 15 and 16, 22 and 23, 29 and 30) are high times for killing, since more players are online. *Killing happens at a fairly constant rate in EVE.* Although more than half of the characters 'live' in hisec, more than half of the player kills take place in anarchic nullsec (Figure 5.10). Clearly the players

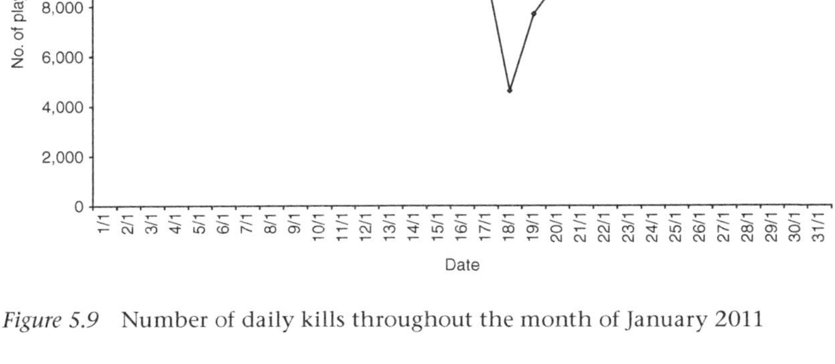

Figure 5.9 Number of daily kills throughout the month of January 2011

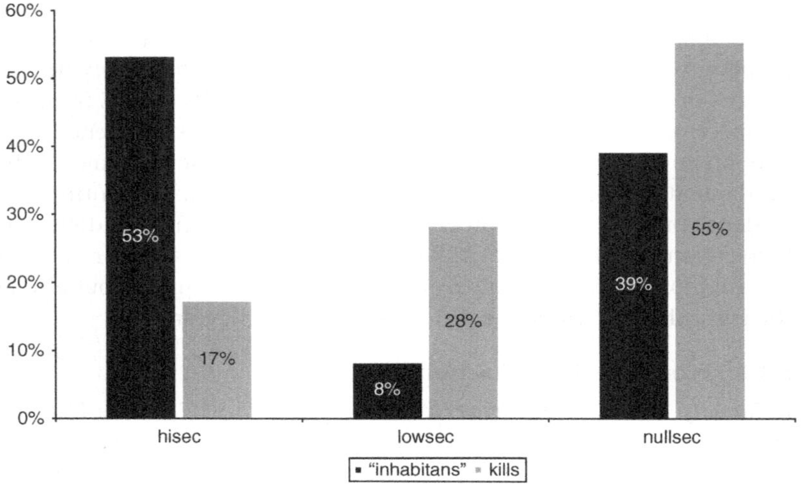

Figure 5.10 Where players 'live' and where they kill

make use of the less strict sanctions for killing in lowsec and especially in nullsec.

The category of player kills can be further divided into five important motives for killing:

1. *War*:[14] Any corporation or alliance in EVE can at any time declare war on another corporation or alliance. Members of the warring parties are allowed to kill any member of the opposing party anywhere in EVE (including in hisec) without having to fear repercussions by the police. Wars will be treated in more detail in Chapter 8.
2. *Factional warfare* (FW):[15] Since 2008, single players and corporations alike are able to join 'factional warfare'. FW is closely tied to the background story and the role-play aspect of EVE: the four main empires (or factions), Caldari, Gallente, Amarr, Minmatar, are engaging in territorial conflicts and the players and corporations are able to join the militias of these four factions. Once you join factional warfare, you are formally allowed to kill any member of the opposing factions – be it an NPC or a player character.
3. *CONCORD*:[16] CONCORD is the virtual, computer-controlled police force. Every time a player transgresses a law in hisec, CONCORD will arrive and destroy that player's ship. CONCORD-kills will be of great importance in Chapter 7 on 'suicide ganks'.

4. *Intra-corporation kills* (ICK):[17] In general, the game mechanics of EVE do not sanction against you if you kill one of your corp mates. One important occasion may be intra-corporation tournaments or training for real battles.
5. *Erratic kills* (EK):[18] Every time a player is killed by another one without obvious reason (see points one to four), this will be counted as an *erratic kill*. This may look like a subsidiary category but should rather be accepted as a genuine type of kill. Often, there is no official or formal reason why a ship is destroyed. Erratic kills, with their anarchic connotation, are the heart of what happens in EVE. Unofficial reasons for killing are manifold, from personal animosities over self-administered justice to economic reasons (for example earning a living as a pirate).

Figure 5.11 shows which share of the total player kills in January 2011 the different motives have.

The largest share is erratic kills (78.3 percent), followed by kills that took place in the context of factional warfare (13.3 percent). Less

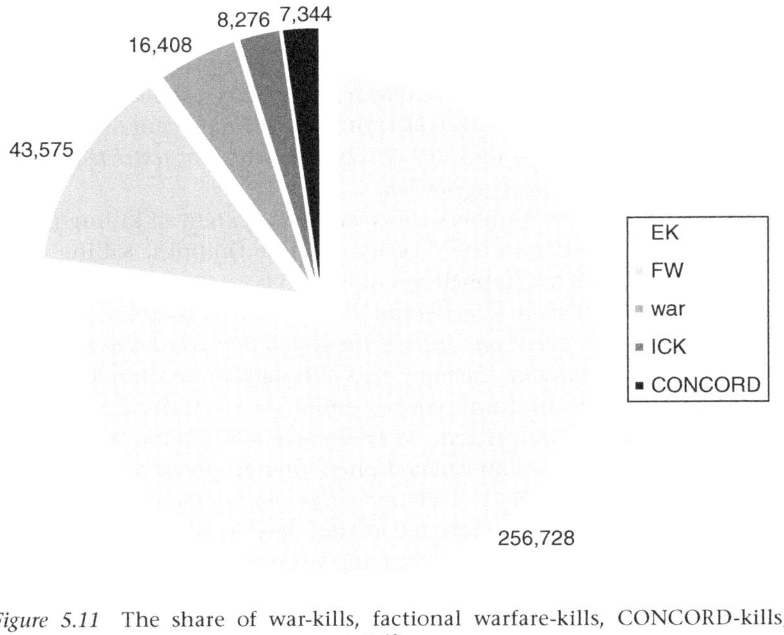

Figure 5.11 The share of war-kills, factional warfare-kills, CONCORD-kills, intra-corporation-kills, and erratic kills[19]

predominant are kills because of formal wars (5 percent), intra-corporation kills (2.5 percent) and CONCORD-kills (2.2 percent).

As for the *victims* of the kills, the proper benchmark in order to determine how many percent of EVE's population fell prey to at least one kill is not the overall number of characters there are in EVE (778,521 at the end of January 2011) but rather the number of characters that logged in at least once during January 2011. If players do not even log on in January, they can hardly be killed. This number – referred to as the *active population* of EVE in January – amounts to 545,438 characters. Taking into account that there were 327,911 player kills, one could say that almost two thirds of the active population got killed during January. However, only 99,870 *different* characters were killed in January 2011. That is to say, that whereas 81.7 percent of the population did not become a victim in January, the 18.3 percent of the characters that actually were killed died more than three times on average. A very similar picture evolves from the data on the *perpetrators*. Only 68,804 *different* characters are responsible for the 327,911 player kills in January. Although only 12.6 percent of the characters became perpetrators in this period, every character that did so destroyed on average almost five ships.

Only 46.6 percent of the victims also acted as attackers in the same period, that is more than half of the victims are 'innocent' in the sense that they did not kill a fellow player in January. *Although those who commit evil are very likely to also suffer from evil* (67.6 percent of the perpetrators became victims, too), *the effects of evil are not restricted to those who willingly participate in aggression.*

The seemingly low numbers concerning the extent of killing in EVE should not distract from the severity of these findings. Killing is not just some common social phenomenon: *12.6 percent of the active population chose to intentionally inflict harm, that is to act evilly on a regular basis.* More surprisingly even: *one fifth of the population gets killed regularly – and still EVE is a thriving economy.* And although more than 80 percent of the kills happen in unsafe lowsec and anarchic nullsec, still *almost half of the population favors living in these areas, where killing is ubiquitous.* Furthermore, evil is not an isolated phenomenon predominant only in certain sub-communities in EVE: *more than half of the victims are innocent.* In fact, the numbers just cited are not 'low' at all. They are the first empirical proof that talking about the economic role of evil actions matters for this economy.

5.4.2 Evil social institutions in EVE

Having argued in the theoretical part that there are no fundamental limitations of applying the concept of formal and informal institutions in EVE, what can be said in general about evil rules in EVE? For example one can say: *killing is fine*. Consider Guðmundsson (2010a):

> I was flying in my freighter to a lowsec system, 0.2. And for some reason I was on autopilot, I forgot, and was doing something else. When I looked again, my ship was destroyed but my pod was still there and I was sitting in there with all my implants. I never saw my ship being destroyed, I did not react, so it would have been easy for the attacker to destroy my pod as well. He didn't. Now, that was a decent guy. (Guðmundsson, 2010a)

In other words: killing/being killed is fine, and you can be happy if you are 'only' killed, that is you did not suffer all the possible damage. Killers can be 'decent guys'. Piracy, that is killing other people for a living, is an officially recommended job (EVElopedia, 2011a). One former member of the CSM, when asked if he thinks that piracy in EVE is something evil, simply replied: 'No, it's just piracy' (Eriksen, 2011). *To commit evil is officially advised by the rules of the game*. EVE is pervaded by evil rules and yet the players still seem to enjoy it. The population is actually growing at a fast pace. These two facts alone constitute a major finding whose importance can only be underestimated: *EVE is an environment with lots of evil rules and still people voluntarily play it, enjoy it, and do not want to change the social institutions*.

EVE is a dark and harsh universe – this is what characterizes it. When asked why EVE was designed that way, the former Lead Game Designer of EVE replied as follows in an interview:

> We wanted to go for a lot of realism. How will it look like in the future in space? You will not be completely safe. There won't be cops standing around everywhere you go.... This game is build around conflict.... We advertise it saying: 'It will make you angry. You will die and you will lose a lot of money if you do'....
>
> The players appreciate what they have and they know that we are never going to get away from it. The only players that we have to push are those longing for a completely different game – however,

> those don't last very long and quit after two or three months. We would never change the atmosphere, how the general experience is.... There is a majority of players who really wants to keep it harsh. (Hinrichsen, 2011)

The developers are eager not to provide too many formal institutions that facilitate the building of trust, for example (Hreiðarsson, 2011). And this approach adapts fairly well to what the players themselves really perceive to be 'evil behavior' according to another Lead Game Master.

> What happens inside the rules of the game is not considered evil by the players. But if things go beyond the game mechanics and things are taken outside of the game – for example macrominers, market botters, exploiters, real money trading, or account hacking – then that is clearly considered evil. It is about people who break the physical laws of the game. (Kjarval, 2011)

Once again, the astonishing aspect is not that the developers opted to make evil rules prevail (or at least hinder the development of conflict-solving institutions) but that *players actually seem to like this*. Otherwise, why would they go on playing?

6
Piracy

6.1 Lowsec piracy

Life as a *pirate* is one of the most typical ways of making a living in EVE. Acting as a pirate means to systematically attack ships in order to destroy them and to pillage what is left over after the kill. Without producing themselves, pirates live off whatever their victims produce and transport, and thus are an empirical example of what Buchanan (1975/2000) and Hirshleifer (1995) had in mind when describing the most basic choice there is in anarchy: to produce or to depredate. Consisting of making money by robbing somebody else, *piracy is an example of an egoistic action*. Like in the real world, there are regions in the virtual world where piracy is particularly predominant: especially trade routes and regions in which the governmental enforcement of law is imperfect. In EVE, 'Lowsec is pirate land' (Kjarval, 2011). In *lowsec* the virtual police do not interfere when ships of innocent characters are attacked. The only formal punishment is a loss of security status for the pirate. This may have consequences for his travel opportunities as he may not be allowed to enter systems of a higher security rating without being attacked. Once the security status drops below -5.0, he is considered an 'outlaw' – and may be killed on sight by anybody and anywhere without any repercussions for the attacker. What makes lowsec also a good region for pirates is the fact that it is not as sparsely populated as nullsec (Guðmundsson, 2011, p. 9) – meaning *more potential victims* – and that often less experienced players stray into lowsec (compared to nullsec where the most powerful players live) – meaning *weaker victims*.

This book considers all erratic kills that happened in lowsec in January 2011 as acts of piracy.[1] Figure 6.1 shows how total kills in January can be broken down into different categories of kills.

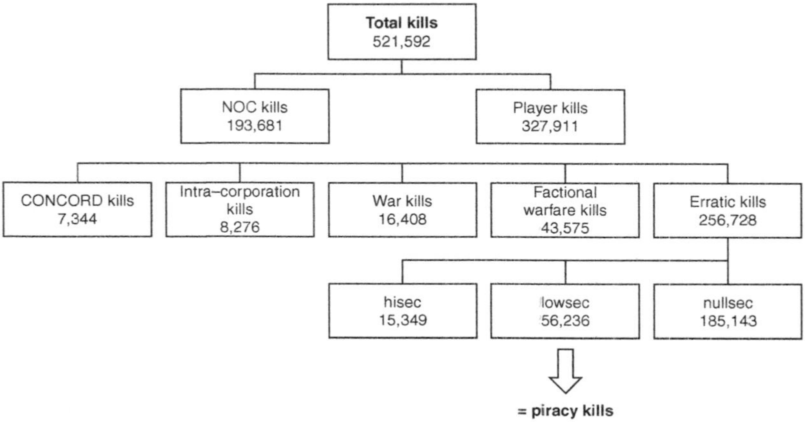

Figure 6.1 A classification of kills – and how often they happened in January 2011

6.1.1 Economic consequences of piracy

The pirate's income stems from different sources: from taking whatever was in the cargo hold of the victim and did not get destroyed in the explosion (the *loot*) and from salvaging the ship wreck (the *salvage)*. Both, loot and salvage, that is goods and raw materials, can then be sold on the market afterwards. The costs of piracy include the price of a ship (sometimes pirates also get shot down by their more tenacious 'victims'), and the costs of ammunition. If a pirate's ship is destroyed, her loss may be partially compensated by an insurance payout (if she opted for insuring her ship in the first place). This book will ignore the benefits of sold salvage and the costs for ammunition, since they are difficult to measure, partly offset each other, and both are negligible compared to the value of loot and the ship losses.[2]

The pirates' benefits

In January 2011, 56,236 pirate kills took place. That is, lowsec pirates account for almost every fifth player kill in EVE. In these killings, 29,233 different victims were attacked by 18,195 different perpetrators, representing 5.4 percent and 3.3 percent of EVE's active population, respectively. Piracy is an important factor in the economics of EVE.

Using the data from the file *killsJan2011.csv* in combination with the file *avgPricesJan2011.xlsx*, the value of the loot for every ship destroyed can be calculated by pricing the dropped items according to their average prices on the market in January 2011.[3] Adding up the value of the loot for all individual kills yields loot worth *663 billion ISK dropped because of lowsec piracy in January.* This is what the 18,195 pirates earned doing their job in January: about 33,000 EUR.[4]

Dividing the total value of loot by the number of kills, the average gain *per ship killed* amounts to 11.79 million ISK (0.60 EUR; *SD* = 1billion ISK). However, the average gain *per pirate and ship killed* is a lot lower, since often more than one pirate is involved in one kill. The per capita gain amounts to 4.23 million ISK per kill (0.20 EUR; *SD* = 267 million ISK). As a further measure to classify these numbers besides the EUR equivalent, remember that in other professions (mining, mission running, trading) an hourly wage of about 20 to 40 million ISK (1 to 2 EUR) can be achieved with comparably low effort. That these average loot values just cited tell only part of the story of how profitable piracy is, is illustrated in Figure 6.2 that plots the value of loot made for all 56,236 kills and shows their frequency.

Figure 6.2 shows clearly that the most frequent case is in fact that no loot at all is gained by the attackers. More than a quarter of the kills fall into this category. In addition, 8 percent of the kills yield loot worth less than 50,000 ISK, signifying practically no financial gain. The second quartile ends just under 1 million ISK made at 954,267 ISK, and the third at 6.3 million ISK. It is telling that the median loot value is at 954,318 ISK (0.05 EUR) compared to the mean at 11.79 million ISK. Piracy seems to pay off *on average*, but most of the time it is just harming innocents for nothing or almost no loot. Piracy is an egoistic action – but one that does not involve really big payoffs for the perpetrators.

Given this data, one might assume that piracy only pays off for the best and most skilled of the pirates and that it is just experience that makes piracy a truly worthwhile activity. If this was the case, then one should expect to see only a small number of different characters being able to steal more than the median value, that is that only the best ever commit more worthwhile attacks. However, almost every pirate was able to score such an above-median-kill at least once: 16,589 of 18,195 registered pirates looted above median value in January. *The small benefits created by piracy are not caused by lacking experience or skills of the players, it is the very essence of piracy that most of the time you harm other players for almost nothing.*

The (theoretical) average hourly wage that can be earned by doing nothing else than pirating is low. January 2011 is a period of 744 hours. The average EVE character from the active population has an *online time*

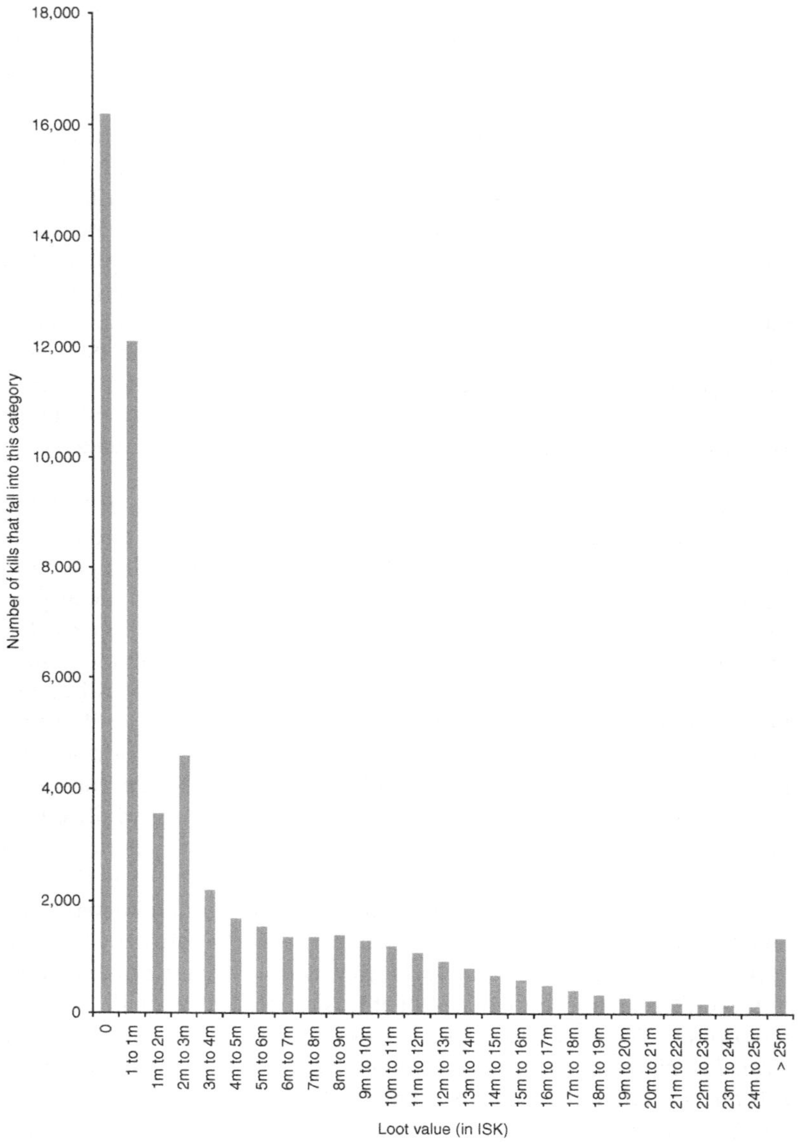

Figure 6.2 Amount of loot made and frequency of those amounts

of about 4 minutes per 1 hour of *real time* (6.73 percent online time per real time).[5] This yields an effective period of 50 online hours in which the 56,236 piracy kills took place. That is, there were 1125 piracy kills *per online hour* or 0.06 piracy kills *per online hour and pirate* (18,195 pirates) in January: 0.06 times the average loot value per attacker (11.79 million ISK) yields a theoretical average hourly wage of only 707,400 ISK (0.04 EUR). Compared to the hourly wages that can be made through mining, mission running, or trading (from 10 to 250 million ISK per hour for a decently experienced character; about 0.5 to 10 EUR), it clearly shows how unprofitable pure piracy is. *The economic impact of piracy is not due to the fact that the individual kill is so profitable but rather due to the fact that there are so many people out there doing it.*

The pirates

The most important demographic distinction criterion in EVE with respect to economic evil is how wealthy a character is in-game. More wealthy players may get over the meager profits of piracy more easily than the poorer players struggling to advance in the game. Figure 6.3 shows the distribution of wealth[6] of the overall active population, those perpetrators that participated in player killing in general, and of those that acted as pirates.

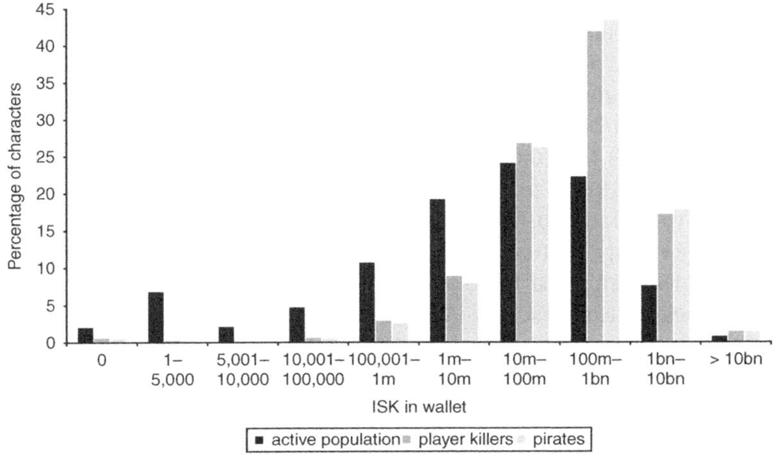

Figure 6.3 Distribution of wealth for the active population, player killers, and pirates

The straightforward interpretation of this chart is that those characters involved in player kills and piracy, while not possessing large differences among each other, differ heavily compared to the active population as a whole. The more 'meaningless' the kill becomes – from living a quiet life in EVE to committing player kills for a reason (for example war), to focusing on erratic kills mostly – the richer the characters tend to be. This is evidence supporting the idea that you have to be capable of affording evil before you actually commit it.

The overall economic effect of piracy

The economic effect of piracy does not limit itself to the pirates' gains. Piracy only redistributes income but is not productive itself. Furthermore, it does so in a very ineffective, even destructive way. Piracy in EVE is empirical evidence for one of the recurring themes and assumptions made in the field of the economic theory of conflict (Hirshleifer, 2001b, p. 1): '*The way of production and exchange* enlarges the social total of wealth. *The way of predation and conflict* merely redistributes that total' (Hirshleifer, 2001b, p. 2). Every time a ship is destroyed, only a fraction of the items that were in the cargo hold of the victim are actually dropped and can be picked up by the pirate (in January on average: 52.3 percent). Following the game mechanics, the other half of the items is destroyed during the explosion of the ship – and nobody can tell beforehand which items are going to persist.[7]

In absolute numbers: whereas the perpetrators made 663 billion ISK worth of bounty (33,000 EUR), the victims lost 1.26 trillion ISK worth of cargo to pirates in January (65,000 EUR). The mean loss per victim amounted to around 10.6 million ISK (0.55 EUR) per kill, the median loss to 709,529 ISK (0.04 EUR). These numbers suggest an analogous distribution of losses for the victims as compared to the distribution of gains of the pirates shown in Figure 6.2.

Two more aspects have to be integrated into the general picture: the value of the ships lost for the victims and the value of the occasional ship losses for the attackers. As for the pirates, although the top pirates reach success ratios of up to 150:1 (150 ships killed compared to only one own ship lost), a fairly average ratio seems to be 15:1 (BattleClinic, 2011). The value of every fifteenth pirate ship amounts to 1.1 trillion ISK (57,000 EUR). The victims lost ships worth 1.4 trillion ISK (72,000 EUR). It may be surprising that one fifteenth of the total value of the pirates' ships destroyed is still only slightly below the total value of the victims' ships destroyed. This can be explained, first, by the fact that the pirates' ships have to be more powerful than those of their victims (otherwise they would not be able to destroy them); and more powerful means more expensive in EVE. Second, many of the ships flown by the victims are really cheap or possess no market value (rookie ships and capsules). After all, what ship would a rational actor choose if he knew that he were about to fly into pirate territory?

Adding up all the different sources of loss for EVE's economy through piracy, the significant number of 3.1 trillion ISK in January (160,000 EUR) is reached; around 7 percent of EVE's M1. Compared to real world economies, 7 percent of the money supply M1 of the EU means 330 billion EUR destroyed in one year.[8]

Summary

Piracy, an economically evil action, has a significant economic impact on EVE's economy. More than every twentieth inhabitant of EVE fell prey to lowsec piracy in January. However, the process of 'redistribution through piracy' is very inefficient: the pirates do not earn decent hourly wages, and the loss of capital stock in EVE's economy is almost five times as big as the individual gains for the pirates. Egoistic actions play a huge role in the online economy although they feature all the shortcomings that are typically brought up in economic theory against the persistence of conflict over a long period of time. *Egoistic actions matter in EVE.*

6.1.2 Comparing pirates and civilians – individual effects of piracy

Since piracy is such a destructive activity on the social scale, it is interesting to see how these effects break down to the individual pirate's income and wealth. However, before analyzing the wealth development of pirates in January, some fundamental principles of making money in EVE have to be explained in more detail.

What influences money making in EVE

The shortest way of summarizing how your ability to make additional ISK is influenced by what you have already acquired in EVE is to follow Atima* et al. (2011): 'Mining and mission running scale with SP [skill points; C.D.M.]. ... Trade scales with wealth.' In other words, making money by mining and doing missions for NPC agents becomes more and more easy as the character becomes more experienced, more precisely as his skill level rises. On the other hand, for trading things on the market not many skills are needed but a big fortune to start with. In EVE this means that a character that has six additional months of playing experience can make one million times the money of a new character (cf. also Figure 5.8 above). *One cannot simply compare the wealth development of pirates to those of civilians* (that is the part of the active population not involved in any player kills in January, either as attacker or as victim) *by considering global averages.*

Therefore, the way to proceed will be to look at a clearly defined subgroup of all pirates and a representative sample of the civilians with comparable characteristics. The characters considered in this section have to be comparably experienced, skilled, and wealthy. As an indicator for the playing experience of the *player*, the total login minutes of a character will be used, that is the total number of minutes this character was logged onto EVE. The character's total skill points (that is how powerful/skilled the character is in-game) will be used as a measure for the experience of the *character*. And as a measure of initial wealth, the individual wallet balance will be used. All three attributes are listed in the file *characters.csv*, however, not as precise numbers but in categories. Table 6.1 lists how *CCP Games* assigned the different categories.

It is the rule rather than the exception that a character falls in different categories with respect to different attributes. For example, a

Table 6.1 Categories for total login minutes, skill points, and wallet balances in *characters.csv*

Category	Total login minutes	Skill points (millions)	Wallet balance (in ISK)
1	0 to 100	0 to 5m	0
2	101 to 200	5m to 10 m	1 to 5000
3	201 to 300	10m to 20m	5001 to 10,000
4	301 to 400	20m to 30m	10,001 to 100,000
5	401 to 500	30m to 40m	100,001 to 1m
6	501 to 750	40m to 50m	1m to 10m
7	751 to 1000	50m to 75m	10m to 100m
8	1001 to 1500	75m to 100m	100m to 1bn
9	1501 to 3000	> 100m	1bn to 10bn
10	3001 to 5000	–	> 10bn
11	5001 to 7500	–	–
12	7501 to 10,000	–	–
13	10,001 to 15,000	–	–
14	15,001 to 25,000	–	–
15	25,001 to 50,000	–	–
16	50,001 to 100,000	–	–
17	> 100,001	–	–

character can have 12,000 total login minutes (category 13), 21 million skill points (category 4) and 11 million ISK in his wallet (category 7).

Figure 6.4 gives an overview of how important criteria concerning money-making abilities are distributed among pirates and civilians overall. Total login minutes are shown in black, the skill points in dark grey, and the wallet balance in light grey. The solid bars always represent the pirates, the framed bars represent the civilians. Figure 6.4 shows that the players who act as pirates are on average way more experienced than those players acting as civilians in-game. Whereas the distribution of the total login minutes for the civilians has three local peaks at category one, nine, and seventeen, there is practically no pirate that falls in category eight or below. *Pirates are on average very experienced players.*

In addition, *pirates tend to have more skill points on average and tend to be a little bit richer than civilians.* As for the former aspect, the civilian population has a noticeably large share of characters with no or almost no skill points (category one).[9]

The comparison opted for will be between *all* pirates that simultaneously fall into the categories 14 (total login minutes), 2 (skill points), and 7 (wallet balance) (n=82) and a *randomly drawn sample* of the same size of civilians that fit into the same categories. The category of 15,001 to 25,000 login minutes was chosen, since Figure 5.8 (above) shows clearly

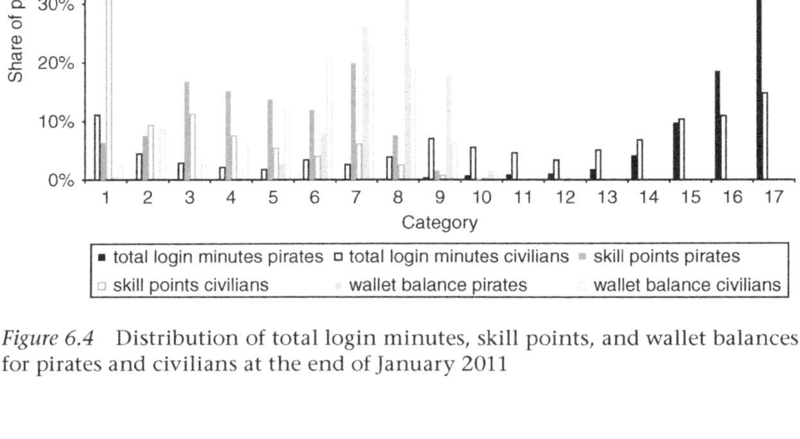

Figure 6.4 Distribution of total login minutes, skill points, and wallet balances for pirates and civilians at the end of January 2011

that at that time and with this much experience money-making typically starts to get easier in EVE and deviations in wealth development may be identified more clearly. Within the subset of those pirates and civilians falling into category 14, the most frequent combination was category 2 for skill points and 7 in respect to wallet balance. This group of characters will be referred to as the *14–2–7 group*.

Comparing the wealth development of pirates and civilians

Figure 6.5 shows how the average daily wealth for pirates and civilians developed in January 2011. The numbers depicted are the means of the average daily wallet balances of pirates and civilians for the 14–2–7 group. These numbers were calculated by using the average wallet balance for each day and each player, and then calculating the daily mean of these means. The thin, fluctuating grey (black) line represents the mean daily average wallet balance of the group of pirates (civilians) on that particular day, whereas the thick grey (black) line shows the general, linear trend in this period.

Since piracy is economically evil with negative material consequences for the whole economy as well as financial disadvantages for the individual player (perpetrators and victims alike), it is not surprising to see pirates doing worse than their peace-loving fellow players. Whereas the general trend for the civilians is upward sloping at a pace of around

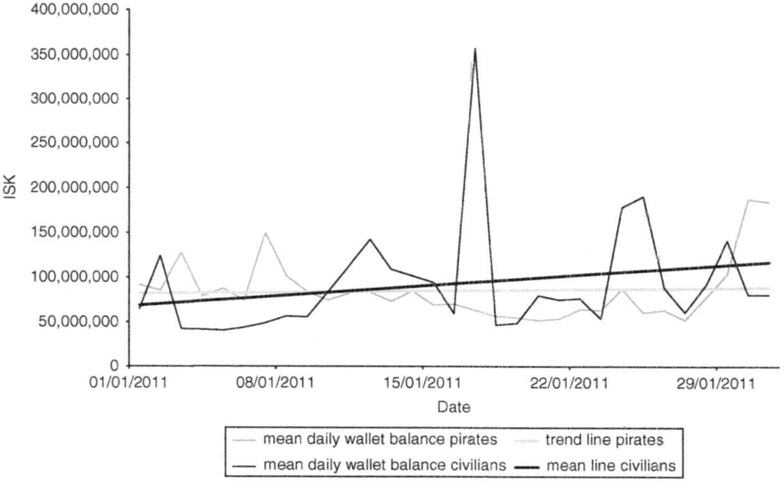

Figure 6.5 Development of mean average daily wallet balances for pirates and civilians of the 14–2–7 group

1.6 million ISK per day, the average wealth of the pirates of the 14–2–7 group almost stayed the same in the observed period (average growth of 0.2 million ISK per day).

The implications of this finding are important: the wealth of the 82 pirates of the 14–2–7 group does not only stagnate – it does so in an environment in which acquiring further wealth typically is mere child's play. *The pirates stand out from the trends of the long-term path of wealth development in EVE* shown in Figure 5.8 (above), and from the general trend of the active population of EVE in January 2011 shown in Figure 6.6 (average daily growth of 16.6 million ISK per day).

Simple linear regression reveals that, for the active population of EVE in January 2011, progression in time significantly predicts the growth in average daily wallet balances according to the equation: average daily wallet balance = 16,648,782 * day of month + 483,858,047. The regression line's slope β is significant with $t(29) = 3.68$ and $p < 0.01$. Time also explains a significant proportion of variance in average daily wallet balances ($R^2 = 0.32$, $F(1,29) = 13.57$, $RMSE = 225.05$ million).

But unfortunately, neither for pirates nor for civilians is progression in time able to significantly predict the growth in the average daily wallet balance. The *pirates'* regression line features an intercept of 81.85 million and a slope β of 0.19 million ($t(29) = 0.28$, $p = 0.78$). Time is not able to explain a significant proportion of variance in average daily

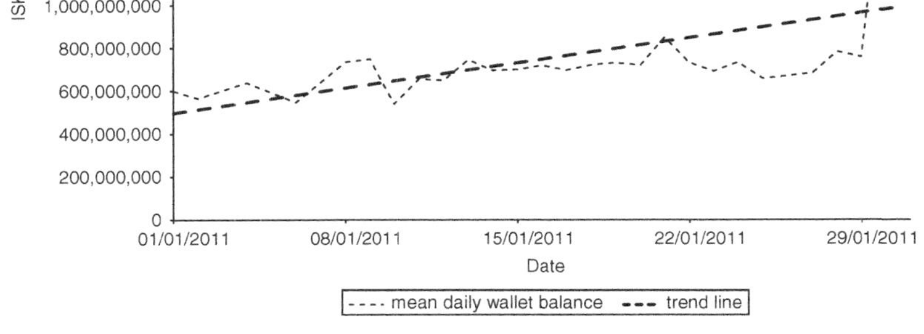

Figure 6.6 The development of the mean average daily wallet balance for the active population in January 2011 (random sample of n=300)

wallet balances ($R^2 = 0.003$, $F(1, 29) = 0.08$, $RMSE = 34.84$ million). The *civilians'* regression line has an intercept of 67.46 million and a slope of 1.57 million ($t(29) = 1.26$, $p = 0.22$). Time does not explain a significant proportion of variance in the average daily wallet balance of civilians either ($R^2 = 0.05$, $F(1, 29) = 1.59$, $RMSE = 62.13$ million). These findings impede further statistical tests, notably the test whether growth in average daily wallet balance differs significantly between pirates and civilians.

Commitment to evil

Some further investigations concerning *how* the pirates play the game emphasize the impression that they are *voluntarily abstaining from making more money* if they also have an opportunity to harm others. This would suggest that there is more to be considered than just a potentially lower savings ratio compared to civilians. Furthermore, the findings presented in this section contradict the idea that pirates might 'just not know better'. Instead they suggest that pirates in EVE are highly committed to evil and willing to incur the losses inevitably tied to this playing style. Two signs point in this direction:

1. *Although pirates generally seem to know how to make money by fighting, they prefer the less profitable fighting against other human players.* Nobody is really a full-time pirate but many people earn their money killing NPCs in the name of NPC agents in missions. Pirates seem to be 'born' fighters and tend to fight more than other players, be it against NPCs or humans. Although nothing stops pirates from becoming full-time mission runners and earning a lot of money without committing economic evil (they are already adept at fighting!), they choose to use mission running only as a way of financing their pirating.
2. *Pirates tend to be more active players and still earn less.* As in real life, time is money in EVE. With a higher average login time per day, pirates would be able to make more money than civilians. Only that they seem to spend this extra time for unprofitable piracy rather than for profitable activities.

First sign

Using the data in the file *wallets2011.csv*, one can find out where the money for civilians and pirates comes from (income) and what it is spent on (expenses). Figure 6.7 shows – for the three most important[10] sources of income and expenses – a comparison between civilians and pirates.

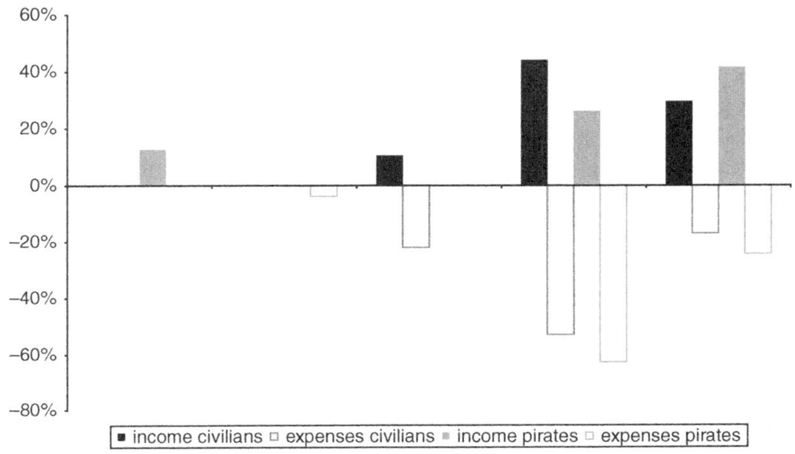

Figure 6.7 Share of income and expenses for most important transaction categories for civilians and pirates

The three most important sources of income for civilians are 'market transactions', 'player donations', and 'market escrow'. The first and the last are directly linked to buying and selling goods on EVE's market, whereas 'player donations' refers to direct transfers of money between two characters. Player donations and market transactions also are the two most important sources of income for pirates. However, their third foothold is 'bounty prizes', that is money paid out by the virtual police for hunting down and killing NPC-pirates: 12.5 percent of the pirates' income stems from this source, whereas civilians only earn 6.4 percent of their income this way (fourth most important category for them). This points towards the suggestion that pirates in general make their virtual living by fighting rather than by producing or trading goods. Even more so as the category 'market escrow' only accounts for 0.4 percent of their income (rank 12) compared to the 10.6 percent for civilians. Additionally, pirates are even more dependent on money transferred from other characters (probably a well-earning second character under their control that mainly trades or payments from a corporation that maintains them) than civilians. And even if they sell all their captured loot on the market, their sum of market transactions is smaller than that of the civilians.

The side of the expenses is almost a mirror image of the income side. However, it is striking that with respect to expenses the third most important transaction category for the pirates becomes 'contract prices' – that is money paid for acquiring goods from other players by using the *contract system* instead of the market – and that the pirates' share of market transactions is even higher than that of civilians. This may suggest that pirates have to spend a lot of money on buying the most advanced fighting equipment, which is costly and rare (therefore they use the *contract system*). They constantly have to buy new ships and equipment, unlike peaceful civilians.

All in all, Figure 6.7 shows that pirates generally tend to earn their money by destroying other ships. Sometimes, these ships are controlled by NPCs (and thus feature a bounty paid out), sometimes they are controlled by other human players. Pirates know how to fight and want to fight. But given their meager wealth development, pirates often seem to choose to hunt for human targets (not very profitable) instead of making money by chasing down NPCs (profitable).

Second sign

In order to determine which group of players is more active, the daily online times of both groups have to be compared. The simplest way of doing this is by calculating the quotient of *total login minutes* and *total minutes since character creation* for every character. The result is a ratio that determines for each character how much of *each minute of real time* a character was actually *online*.[11] This measure of playing activity is not perfect since characters can actually be logged into EVE without doing much. For example you can be logged into EVE and still be watching TV. On the other hand, it is as close to measuring playing intensity as one can get based on the available data. In a second step it can be determined how these ratios are distributed in the pirate population and civilian population. Figure 6.8 displays the outcome of this comparison.

On the x-axis in Figure 6.8, the quotient of total login minutes divided by the minutes since character creation is displayed; on the y-axis the share of the population that possesses the respective quotient. The peak of about 8 percent of the pirates around the quotient of 10 for example means that 8 percent of the pirate population was logged in 10 percent of the time since character creation. This means also 10 percent of the time per day equating to slightly less than two and a half hours.

Notice that Figure 6.8 does not consider the total civilian population but only the 80 percent that were most active – thus eliminating the first (and laziest) quintile of civilians with the lowest online time. This was done in order to prevent alt-chars from blurring the picture.[12] Figure 6.8

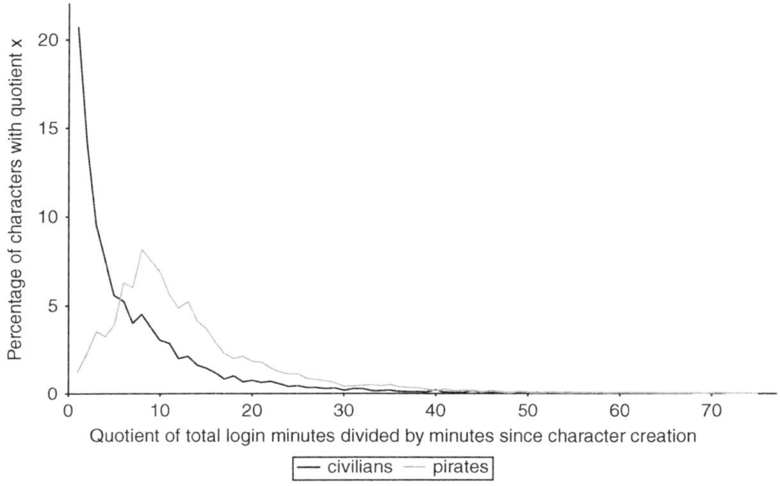

Figure 6.8 Comparison of daily login time of pirates and civilians (without lowest quintile)

shows that, even if the comparison is based only on the most active 80 percent of the civilians, *on average pirates do play more*. Their mean play time amounts to 12.7 percent of real time (*SD* = 9.6) compared to 6.8 percent of average play time (*SD* = 8.8) for the four most active quintiles of civilians.

Summary

The two signs – pirates generally know how to make money by fighting, pirates play more than civilians – should actually enable the pirates to make comparable amounts of money as do civilians. The fact that they do not, shows how committed these players are to being pirates, to committing economic evil. Although the pirates have all it takes to make money in EVE – sometimes even to a greater extent than the civilians – they do not live up to their economic potential. Instead, *they seem to display a 'taste for harming'.* Eriksen, former member of the CSM and now CCP employee puts it another way:

> [Civilians] do missions for profit and fun. PvPers[13] do missions for profit and PvP for fun. Their fun is that they have an impact on somebody else. It's about 'me versus you' for them. (Eriksen, 2011)

6.2 Ransoming as a pirate

6.2.1 Ransoming as wanton action

In the preceding section, piracy in EVE was presented as *egoistic action*. However, the more perturbing (and fascinating) phenomena for economists are *wanton* or *malicious actions*. This section on ransoming in EVE leads the way to the more severe forms of evil actions.

Preliminaries on ransoming in EVE

In EVE, pirates are able to demand a ransom in two cases: either just before they lay the final blow to the victim's ship or just after they laid the final blow to the ship before destroying the escape capsule (the 'pod') as well. Both scenarios are difficult to bring about for the pirate. *The first scenario* requires a militarily one-sided battle in which the victim's ship is close to destruction whereas the aggressor's ship is still in good shape. Then, the victim is no longer a threat to the pirate and he can offer (via text chat) a cease-fire. In this case, the victim would be willing to pay an amount up to the total value of his ship and all the cargo in it, the pirate would accept any amount bigger than the estimated value of the dropped (that is not destroyed) cargo. This should leave ample room for negotiation and for reaching a mutual beneficial deal; even if some information asymmetries and uncertainty may blur the picture. After the ransom was accepted and paid, the pirate has the incentive nevertheless to destroy the victim's ship, cashing in on the cargo dropped as well. Only *expected discounted future gains of honoring ransoms* (the pirate can raise his income by successfully ransoming victims but in the long run no victim will continue to pay ransoms if they get killed afterwards anyway) might prevent him from doing so.

The second scenario requires the pirate to be able to prevent his victim from escaping in the rescue capsule. This requires a lot of dexterity from the pirate's side (and some lack of it on the victim's side). If the pirate succeeds in trapping the victim, he can demand a ransom for not destroying the 'pod'. In this case, the victim would be willing to pay any amount smaller than the value of his character's brain implants (quite expensive items that raise the skills of a character and that are always destroyed as the pod is destroyed). The perpetrator on the other side would accept any positive amount as a ransom. He cannot gain materially from destroying the capsule in any way.[14] He may try to guess the worth of the trapped victim's brain implants and demand the highest ransom that can rationally be expected to be paid by the victim – but any single additional ISK made should in principle be welcomed (cf. on ransoming in EVE: EVElopedia, 2011b, 2011c; Verone*, 2007). Since there are no material gains in the short run, the expected discounted future gains of honoring ransoms should theoretically be enough to tip the scales in the favor of the victim in the second scenario, leading to the pirate honoring the ransom and not destroying the pod. In the second scenario, the pirate's expected discounted future gains do not have to be higher than the estimated value of the cargo dropped on destruction in order for the pirate to honor the ransom but only bigger than zero.

The act of ransoming itself is not economically evil as it can lead to a mutual beneficial outcome (starting from a very bad status quo for the victim, though). *Only if the promise not to kill the ransomed party after the money transfer is not kept one can talk of economical evil.* In the first scenario, this would be just another example of an *egoistic action*. In the second scenario, assuming the expected discounted future gains of honoring this specific ransom to be only infinitesimally bigger than zero,[15] one witnesses a *wanton action*. What follows is an empirical investigation of the second scenario of ransoming (with the ransom being paid).

Ransoming as a sequential bargaining game

Examining the second scenario of ransoming in EVE is a good example to support the claim made above that laboratory experiments and research in MMORPGs are alternative ways of equal value to examine human behavior. The proceedings of ransoming are similar to a sequential, repeated bargaining game of the structure shown in Figure 6.9:

The pirate having offered a ransom to the amount of r (>0), the victim has to decide whether to pay. Examining only the cases with paid ransoms, only the upper-right section of Figure 6.9 is of interest, that is only the cases in which the pirate made a good guess of the value v (>0) of the victim's brain implants and offered $r < v$. Assuming the pirate wants to continue ransoming victims in the future (and since the pirate does not directly profit from destroying the pod), the pirate's choice whether to destroy the pod is solely determined by the expected discounted future gains of honoring this ransom (ε; assumed to be infinitesimally bigger than zero). Figure 6.10 shows the possible payoff combinations for victim and pirate (with $v = 5$, $r = 3$, $\varepsilon = 0.001$).

Given the discussion of evil actions and evil rules in EVE, it should be clear by now that the case of defection from the victim's side followed by cooperation from the pirate's side is most unlikely to happen. Once

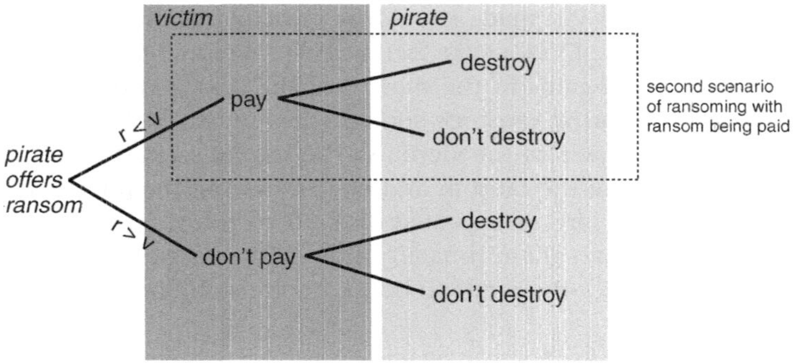

Figure 6.9 Structure of the second scenario of ransoming in EVE

victim	pirate: don't destroy (cooperate)	pirate: destroy (defect)
pay (cooperate)	–3 ; 3.001	–8 ; 3
don't pay (defect)	0 ; 0	–5 ; 0

Figure 6.10 Typical payoffs of the second scenario of ransoming with ransom paid (the first number in each cell referring to the victim's payoff; the number past the colon referring to the pirate's payoff)

a pirate has managed to bring about a situation suitable for ransoming, she most likely will not just let the victim go without paying anything. However, for the general line of argument it is more important that honoring ransoms weakly dominates any other strategy for the pirate. Taking into account that some accidental pod-kills may happen, *the null hypothesis to be empirically tested in the following shall be a population proportion of $\pi \leq 5$ percent of dishonest pirates in the second scenario of ransoming (with the ransom being paid)*, that is that practically no wanton actions take place.

Method

Instead of conducting a laboratory experiment with the given parameters, the MMORPG-approach can be used to test this hypothesis. It involves identifying all instances of ransoming in the second scenario with ransoms being paid in the data of what 390,000 people did in the course of January 2011. This was achieved by identifying all characters that fell prey to a pirate kill with not more than five attackers[16] and yet directly transferred a sum of money to at least one of their attackers on the exact same day. It means searching a combination of the files *killsJan2011.csv* and *wallets2011.csv* for a certain pattern. In a second step, it has to be determined whether the paid ransom was not honored, that is in technical terms whether not only the *ship* of the character paying the ransom but also his *pod* was destroyed in a successive kill.

Besides the requirement to define appropriate indicators to scan the data, this approach presupposes a thorough understanding of the virtual universe of EVE: that there is something like ransoming, that there are different scenarios of ransoming, how the involved players proceed, how the players think about it. It is not the point that no experiment *was conducted* (meaning that 'only' descriptive work was done) but that no experiment *had to be conducted* (the data being already there). The MMORPG-approach should not be chosen because it seems easier to manage but because of its great potential for huge sample sizes and long-term observations of repeated interactions in a complex and lifelike environment.

Results

Overall, there were *255 instances of ransoms paid* in lowsec piracy in January. As one should expect, given the incentives outlined above and the difficulties of actually bringing about a ransoming situation as a pirate, the quota of only 0.5 percent of victims of piracy kills paying a ransom is fairly low. Sixteen instances of ransoming featured two killed ships for the victim, the second one being a capsule. That is, 6.3 percent of the encounters with ransoming pirates ended with an additional pod kill. Furthermore, there were 19 instances of ransoming (7.5 percent of total ransoming instances) in which pods were killed without prior destruction of a real ship. *Adding these two numbers, 13.7 percent of all ransoming incidents involve a pod kill – that is pirates breaking their promise and causing harm without personal benefit, thus practicing wanton actions.* Using a *z*-test, the null hypothesis H_0: $\pi \leq 0.05$ that no wanton actions take place is rejected ($z = 3.99$, $p < 0.01$ one-tailed). One should also keep in mind that a substantial fraction of the 220 victims that got away with only a *ship* (not the *pod*) killed might also have fallen prey to unkept promises – in the first scenario of ransoming, however, representing egoistic actions.

Overall, there were 82,951 pod kills in EVE in January. Just as is the case with ransoming, no perpetrator ever earns anything from killing a pod. The only potentially beneficial effect for the perpetrators is a relative one, namely to make the victim incur even higher costs and make him even worse off in comparison to himself – which might be reasonable in wars. Be that as it may, *there are 82,951 instances of wanton actions in EVE in January 2011.*

6.2.2 Evil rules regarding ransoming

Woodward (2009) argues that it is a valid approach to look for unexpected characteristics in the results of simple bargaining games (for example a surprising modal offer, or a significantly high number of dishonest pirates in the case of ransoming) in order to draw conclusions on social norms influencing the player behavior (for example by defining a reference outcome). With about 14 percent of dishonored ransoms, one might ask whether there is an *evil moral rule* in place that advises pirates to *generally* disrespect ransoms and to go for the additional kill, *even if the player finds himself in the second scenario of ransoming,* that is about to impair his own income. In a dev blog from 2006, CCP Oveur* highlights his point of view on ransoming:

> If there is anything which I've seen through all this time come up, again and again it's the brutal life of an EVE pilot. There have been a couple of large threads popping up on the issue....
>
> This is a brutal universe where your decisions and actions can severely affect yourself – as well as others. Did you perhaps put all your eggs in the same basket?
>
> This is the brutal beauty of EVE, this is the reason manufacturers have buyers for their ships, this is the reason mission and complex runners can sell their loot, this is the reason minerals are actually worth something, this is the reason the ISK that you earn can get you something....
>
> Think about the pirate that ransomed you and did let you go....
>
> Those are the real heroes of EVE. (CCP Oveur*, 2006)

The interesting point is that CCP Oveur* highlights that brutality is a central feature of EVE and that not honoring ransoms is a typical example of this brutality. However, those pirates that honor ransoms are 'heroes'. This sounds much like the description of the *good* moral rule 'Do honor ransoms!' But things are not that simple, as shown by looking at the players' reactions to CCP Oveur's* blog. Table 6.2[17] gives a quick overlook of some of the reactions.

Table 6.2 Reactions on ransoming

Character	Opinion
Jim McGregor*	'I'm one of the heroes in this game (ransoming pirate)...[but] Eve needs to be brutal.'
Llucan Dleaur*	'As Papa Oveur reminds us, this game is designed to be brutal and raw. Yes, the designwork is balanced toward PVP, but that is exactly how it should be. There is no hand-holding. We survive using our brains, or die from the lack thereof. God, I love this game.'
Spy4Hire*	'They [the real heroes; C.D.M.] don't exist.'
Polydectes*	'I dont like that he said the hero's of eve are the people that dont shoot you, the people that dont shoot you are just nice, or done think they can kill you. I have to disagree obviously. I think the heros are the people that make the game fun, the ones that punish you for make a bad desicion, ie, undocking, or flying a hauler alone....But without people to show you when you goof up, then eve wouldnt have those wonderful consiquences. Every game needs bad guys.'
Spaja Saist*	'There's a difference between a brutal game and a griefers paradise. It's obvious that the devs don't give a **** that the game has turned that way....Personally I find Oveur's attitude about it pathetic. I can see which side of the fence he's on. Obviously he enjoys that pathetic form of game play....The devs love people acting like griefing children in this game.'
Kalixa Hihro*	'Life in eve is cruel, that's the main attraction.'

Source: CCP kieron* et al. (2006).

The community is far from being agreed on what is 'good' and 'evil' concerning ransoming. Many people hold the view that brutality, mistrust, and constant awareness are the essence of EVE and that, therefore, dishonoring ransoms is at least appropriate, if not even advised. For them, it is a moral duty not to honor ransoms *in any case* and so to keep the 'spirit of the game' alive, to keep people smart and wary, to punish bad decisions; for them, dishonoring ransoms is a just (sic!) punishment and to dishonor ransoms even in the second scenario an evil moral rule.

The question which rule applies best to EVE – the good moral rule to honor ransoms or the evil moral rule to dishonor ransoms – is still open and alive. Players who got ransomed, paid, and were nevertheless killed continue to complain on the forums (for example, Greygal*, 2009; Kennedy Lincoln*, 2008; Lona Lwyd*, 2008). Other players will not stop pointing out how stupid the former ones are for, first, getting into a situation in which they can get ransomed, second, for actually paying the ransom, and third, for complaining about it on the forums. One very recent and typical example is the forum post by Azhpol* complaining about getting ransomed and killed and asking why. Table 6.3 lists some of the answers to his question.

These examples of players arguing about what is good and evil in EVE also reproduce an interesting characteristic mentioned in the psychological primer. When discussing how to evaluate a certain action, victims tend to intensely describe the background of a certain 'evil' act; all the events that lead to it as well as all of the consequences it had.

Table 6.3 Reactions on lamenations on dishonored ransom

Character	Opinion
Father Fondle*	'Why would you fly into Amamake[18] with a shipful of skillbooks and BPOs [i.e. with such valuable cargo; C.D.M.]? Son, I am disappoint.'
Lady Spank*	'I don't think you "get" Eve.'
Xenuria*	'A good question is why the hell there was a gatecamp in your route to your destination? If you had any kind of wisdom you would have scouted first and if you have an intel network you dont need scouts. I am just so trolled by your situation.. It's like you were flying by the seat of your pants and paid the price for it and now your shocked? Never fly anywhere you dont have intel.. The only time I have ever lost ships was because I was not watching my intel channels. Learn from your mistakes.'
Dalryn*	'Why are you butthurt that you got ransomed for the potential value of your implants and time spent for replacing them? U mad?'
daddys helper*	'Tears[19] are more valuable than isk.'
Kalixa Hihro*	'You claim to be a nullsec pilot.. then how the hell did you lose a pod in lowsec? No bubbles[20].... apparently you're just completely full of fail.'
Dracoliche*	'Nobody owes you any courtesy.'
Zaveed*	'So long as they let you go if you pay, then they're shining bloody paragons. If someone got into piracy with the idea that they're gonna get infinitely rich from it, they're not in the right profession. Well, unless you count a wealth of tears.'

Source: Azhpol* et al. (2011).

The perpetrators, on the other hand, typically only describe the event itself, do not see any serious consequences of their actions, and tend to tell happy endings (Baumeister & Vohs, 2005, p. 87). In all of the four exemplary forum posts mentioned (Azhpol* et al., 2011; Greygal*, 2009; Kennedy Lincoln*, 2008; Lona Lwyd*, 2008) the victims closely describe what happened to them and why they think it was unfair. The comments of the pirates on the forums are always rather short and tend to stress the good in what happened to the victims: they learned to be careful, to mistrust, and not to pay ransoms. This shows two things: the data from EVE seems to be valid in the sense of really representing instances of *evil* actions and that there is not one singular moral rule in place governing behavior.

The 14 percent of pirates not honoring ransoms are not just the defectors typical for any moral rule, whose characteristic is not to be respected by anybody (Mantzavinos, 2001, p. 106). There are lots of pirate corporations which explicitly condemn dishonoring ransoms (cf. for example Alucard Strat*, 2011; are34*, 2011; SkwisgaarSkwigelf*, 2011; yopparai*, 2011), whereas other pirate corps explicitly say: 'Every activity must have one goal in mind; how much ISK can we make off the back of others today!' (Azael Lightshade*, 2011). This statement is in fact intended to make the corporation attractive for new players to join, since it was posted in the forum dedicated to recruitment. There have been two general opinions on ransoming in EVE since the very first days. *The evil moral rule to dishonor ransoms even in the second scenario may not be predominant in EVE but it emerged and prevails.*

This evil moral rule could very well have emerged spontaneously in an invisible hand process, following the mechanics of the emergence of evil moral rules outlined in Section 3.3.3. It was not put in place by CCP Games, but by pirate corporations who learned that it is 'beneficial' not to honor ransoms. First, it could be beneficial for corporations that had established this evil moral rule in the sense that they were able to provide their members with very simple rules guiding their behavior in-game. Not honoring ransoms seems to be appropriate behavior for a pirate in an MMORPG. From a cognitive standpoint, not to honor ransoms probably is the behavior most expected by authentically evil pirates and the evil rule advising to do so structures social interaction effectively. Second – from a motivational standpoint – some pirate corporations could have realized that it is beneficial not to honor ransoms *in the first scenario of ransoming* and then they *mis-extended* the evil moral rule to hold also for the *second scenario of ransoming*, in which not keeping promises is a wanton action at best. In fact, the first ransoming scenario features an incentive structure similar to a prisoner's dilemma. In the theoretical part, however, it was argued that such situations are very ambiguous learning environments in which misapplications (not to honor ransoms even if in the second scenario) could happen too easily and even truly evil rules providing benefits in the short and the long run could emerge.

The rule not to honor ransoms even in the second scenario of ransoming is therefore a good example of an evil moral rule: it is first-party enforced and tells players to defect, even if this may diminish their material income and that of their counterpart. It is followed only by part of the population. Nevertheless, it is possible that it emerged spontaneously in an invisible hand process. *In EVE, evil moral rules may emerge and persist.*

6.3 Discussion on piracy

Piracy is an example of an egoistic action that cost the virtual economy about 7 percent of its M1 in January. Although in the large majority of the cases no or almost no loot is gained by the pirate, still 3.3 percent of EVE's active population participates in lowsec piracy. Ransoming, on the other hand, is an example of wanton actions in EVE – at least every seventh promise concerning ransoming is not kept. Overall, 82,951 pods were destroyed in January – that is, more than every fourth player kill is a wanton action. These are the brutal facts showing that *economically evil actions exist and matter.* The more important finding is, however, that *the economic evil described is of a different kind than the harming behavior currently known to economists.* In stark contrast to the three economic theories mentioned in the theoretical part, the evil just described is *unconditional.*

Buchanan (1975/2000) and Hirshleifer (1995, 2001c) argue that we may harm other people if this increases our material payoff directly and in the short run (for example by fighting). But lowsec piracy in EVE does not look for direct profit in the short run; this was shown by the unprofitability of piracy compared to other less risky and less demanding professions. By choosing to act as pirates instead of running missions, they voluntarily accept a slower wealth development although playing more than other groups of players. And even if a small profit is made, we are certainly not observing pirates trying to maximize their material income by exploiting their comparative advantage in fighting (Buchanan's reasoning) or pirates who 'lean in the direction of conflict or lean in the direction of cooperative production and exchange, whichever is more profitable on the margin' (Hirshleifer, 2001b). In addition, this virtual world is far from overcoming the natural state. Fighting will not end in the near future.

Pirates cannot be said to have other-regarding preferences in the proper sense. Fehr and Schmidt (1999) and Hirshleifer (2001d) state that if humans possess other-regarding preferences, emotions like envy and anger may cause them to give up own income only to lower the income of their counterpart in a strategic situation, too. But pirates do not kill *conditionally* based on the outcome or behavior in some previous interaction but *unconditionally*. A piracy kill is not even an *inter*action. The pirates are not envious or angry, they just shoot. 'There is nothing personal in piracy usually. They [the victims; C.D.M.] have done nothing to make you [the pirate; C.D.M.] angry at them' (Eriksen, 2011; former CSM member and current CCP employee). Pirates might care about the victim's payoff but not in a way that could be captured with theories of fairness, altruism, and reciprocity. They only care that the victim's outcome is bad.

Finally the question of reputation: Hirshleifer (2001d), Schelling (1960), and others highlight that reputation building may lead people to give up income only to harm others. The suggested goal of being able to increase their own material payoff in the long run, backs up their arguments. Some pirates in fact do cultivate a reputation of being evil. Consider for example what former Lead Game Designer Húni Hinrichsen (2011) says:

> Griefing noobs[21] gives you a feeling of power. You are making sure that the new players coming into the game will remember your name and fear you for what you did. It comes down to reputational things.

But the reputation pirates build up does not fulfill the function of raising material income in the long run, as economists suspect. First, the reputation of the most evil pirates in EVE is publicly shown to everybody via their security status – nobody trusts them or would want to interact with them in trade affairs. That is, it seriously hurts their potential to earn money by other means than fighting. However, these other means (trade, producing, or 'business' in general) are typically more profitable than fighting. Second, they incur severe limitations to their freedom of travel, particularly preventing them from going where the money is made in EVE (the big trade hubs in hisec). And third, if Schelling (1978), Duntley and Buss (2005) and others cited above, reason that having a bad reputation is a good way of avoiding being attacked or exploited by others and evolutionarily speaking reasonable, this is not what the pirates want to achieve. They *do not want to avoid being attacked and robbed* by others; they rather *actively look for trouble*. This is the very reason why they started out being evil pirates in the first place. 'There are many lowsec pirates who enjoy to be mean, who like getting angry mails from the people whose most precious ship they destroyed.... The conflict itself is entertaining to them' (Turbefield & Óskarsson, 2011; researcher and community manager in *EVE Online*). One side effect of acting as a pirate is that the individual security status of the character slowly drops. A security status of –5.0 and lower, however, will make the pirate an 'outlaw'. Outlaws can be attacked by anybody in the universe at anytime and anywhere, even in hisec, without the attacker having to fear governmental sanctions. Thus, pirates achieve the exact opposite of having a bad reputation that scares attackers. Killing is a dangerous and costly strategy.

Pirates do not intend to maximize their own material income, either in the short or in the long run – contrary to the basic tenets of the 'fighting in anarchy' approach or the reputation approach. Furthermore the perpetrators do not care about their victim's prior behavior or payoff (as long as it is negative) – contrary to the basic tenets of the fairness approach.

The case of not honoring ransoms is even clearer in this perspective. There are no material benefits from not keeping promises not to kill the victim's pod, neither in the short nor in the long run. All the pirates achieve is to harm their long-term potential to cash in on ransoms. They do not cultivate a bad reputation only to cash in on it later. Finally, the response not to honor a ransom is *conditional* only in the sense of requiring a victim willing to pay that ransom in the first place; but this is not the domain of fairness and reciprocity. The pirates are not envious because their counterpart has more or angry because he treated them unfairly. Instead, as was shown, they make fun of their victim afterwards saying that he is plain dumb.

At present, there are theories explaining why people spend money in order to *harm* others – because they either profit from it in the short run or in the long run. There are also theories explaining why people spend money to *help* others – because of unconditional altruism and conditional reciprocity. But there is no theory able to explain why people spend money to *unconditionally harm others, although they do not profit from this*. This is what is called the human *'taste for harming': it is an unconditional commitment to evil*. The evil committed in EVE has no instrumental value. It is unprecedented, and hostile.

7
Suicide Ganks

7.1 Suicide ganks as malicious actions

Eighty percent of all player kills take place in lowsec and nullsec. However, this chapter about *suicide ganks* and the following chapter on *wars* will show that evil does not only happen in clearly delimited regions with lower State-guaranteed security. Even if very efficient mechanisms to punish evil exist, the 'taste for harming' is strong enough to pave its own way and to erupt in the midst of a 'secure' area.

7.1.1 What suicide ganks are

When you steer your space ship through hisec and attack an innocent[1] fellow player whom you stumbled upon, police will arrive very quickly and kill you. This is a game mechanic of EVE and everybody knows it. The police (*CONCORD*) will arrive so fast that you probably do not even have the time to destroy the ship of your victim. They arrive *every time* you attack an innocent and will *always eventually kill you,* no matter how powerful your character is.

However, these game mechanics do not prevent player killing in principle. In a *'suicide gank'* (SG), a group of perpetrators joins forces, that is firepower, to quickly kill their chosen victim in a hisec system only to get killed themselves by the police directly afterwards. NB: Every perpetrator that acted aggressively will be killed. Often the attacking group will bring along one character that stays passive during the encounter only to be able to collect whatever is left over after the battle – notably the *victim's* cargo. Since this specific character stays passive during combat, he is not destroyed by CONCORD. Suicide ganks are a very risky endeavor with respect to profits for the attackers: it is not always clear what cargo the victim has got in his hold and they can never be sure which part of the cargo will be destroyed in the explosion. Additionally, especially in small groups it is difficult to judge whether the attackers will be able to destroy the ship quickly enough before CONCORD punishes them. On the other hand, the coordination effort is significant: a whole group of characters has to wait for victims, either flying around or 'camping' at a star gate. They have to agree whether a specific, potential victim flying by is actually worth attacking and coordinate the strike to kill quickly. After the combat, they somehow have to share the potential gains among the group members.

Considering the harm done to the victim, all SGs are economically evil actions, but they may not be detrimental in terms of material payoffs for the perpetrators. The loot dropped by the victim could offset the worth of the ships lost by the attackers and allow for a decent profit. Many gankers claim that they commit SGs for the sake of profit, not for the sake of evil. This section will address the question to what extent suicide ganks do happen in EVE and it will show that, despite the gankers' claims, this kamikaze-tactic typically is an example of a malicious action, involving material losses for both victims and gankers. The first null hypothesis to be empirically tested is that the *median gain per attempted SG* is positive (H1). The stronger, second null hypothesis to be tested is that the *median gain per successful SG* is positive (H2).

7.1.2 Multi-person suicide ganks

Defining suicide ganks technically

Every time that *CONCORD killed two or more different characters* within a *short time period* (less than one minute) and in the *same system*, this situation was classified as a suicide gank-attempt. If, in addition, *at least one of the characters that got killed by CONCORD acted as an attacker in a player kill* in the *same system* that took place *less than two minutes before or one minute after the CONCORD-kill*, then this situation is considered a *successful* suicide gank. If there is no player kill by the characters killed by CONCORD in the preceding two minutes or following minute, the situation qualifies as a *failed* suicide gank.

There are several reasons for this definition. Firstly, there is no reason why two or more different characters should be killed by CONCORD in short succession in hisec in the same solar system other than an attempted suicide gank. One character may be killed by CONCORD because he accidentally attacked another player but two players misclicking in a short period of time in the same system is very unlikely. Second, CONCORD takes some time to show up and kill the attackers, but two minutes after the player kill are plenty of time for this. The reason why also player kills carried out *after* the time of the CONCORD kills are considered is that CONCORD response is not triggered by the actual killing of the victim but by the first aggression towards it. Sometimes the last volley from the attackers before getting destroyed by CONCORD is the final blow that kills the victim. The player kill that caused CONCORD to intervene is then listed *after* the CONCORD kill. Nevertheless, this is a suicide ganking incident. The fact that victims get killed by the last volley of their attackers – that are dead themselves by the time the rocket hits the victim and destroys it – shows just how intense and risky a business suicide ganks are. Figure 7.1 shows the timeline of a typical suicide gank and the period examined for identifying related kills.

This also means that there are always several kills that belong to just one SG.[2] The basic unit for suicide ganks is not one kill, but rather one attempted suicide gank.

The money in SGs

A total of 616 attempted suicide ganks happened in EVE in January 2011: 221 of these attempted suicide ganks failed and consequently 395 were successful (failure ratio: 36 percent). A total of 2322 perpetrators participated in the attempted SGs and at least[3] 647 victims were attacked. Most SGs only involve two attackers (about 40 percent), and as the number of attackers rises, the number of attempts declines steadily. In the average SG, there are four attackers engaging one victim.

In January, the 395 successful SGs yielded a total value of 12.9 billion ISK (660 EUR) of captured loot. This corresponds to a loot value of about 21 million ISK *per attempt* (1 EUR); almost double the average captured value in a pirate *kill* (12 million ISK). Even if divided by the number of

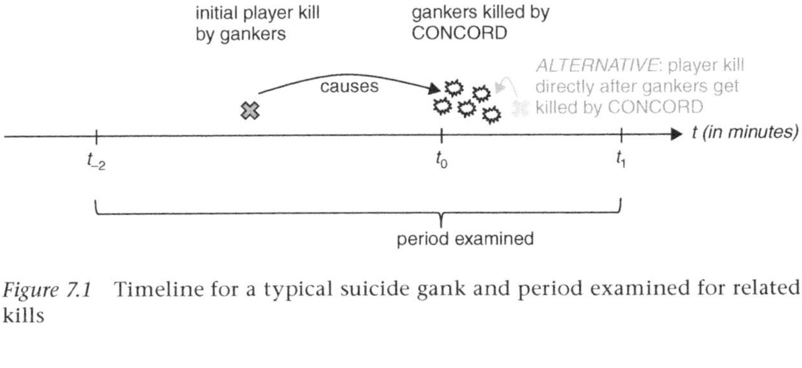

Figure 7.1 Timeline for a typical suicide gank and period examined for related kills

attackers, the benefits of SGs are comparably high: about 5.5 million ISK (0.30 EUR) *per attempt and ganker* (piracy: 4 million ISK *per kill and pirate*). SGs are more people-intensive yet promise higher gains.

However, the suicidal nature of this tactic changes the overall payoff drastically. The losses add up as follows: the value of the gankers' ships destroyed by the police, plus the value of the items fitted on the gankers' ships (for example weapons) destroyed in the explosion, minus the effect of the insurance payouts for the destroyed ships.[4] Overall, SGs in January led to a loss of 24.6 billion ISK (1300 EUR). *Adding up the benefits stemming from killing and robbing the victim and the losses stemming from being killed oneself by the police directly afterwards, the total profit of suicide ganking in EVE in January amounts to -11.7 billion ISK (-600 EUR).* This is a first indicator that SGs are malicious actions.

The median loss per attempted SG amounts to 2,446,729 ISK. A chi-square test for goodness-of-fit reveals that the normality assumption for the underlying distribution of SG-gains has to be rejected based on the sample ($\mu = -19$ million ISK, $SD = 200$ million ISK, $\chi^2 = 232.28$, $p < 0.01$). Since the distribution is at least approximately symmetrical (cf. Figure 7.2), a Wilcoxon signed-rank test for one sample is used to test H1; the number of attempts for which $d_i \neq 0$ being $n = 613$, a normal approximation to the W distribution can be applied. Hypothesis 1 that the median gain per attempted SG is positive is rejected on this basis ($W = 49{,}666$, $z = -10.13$, $p < 0.01$ one-tailed). *Suicide ganking in EVE is an example of a malicious action.*

Even the stronger null hypothesis H2 that the median gain of the 395 successful SGs is positive has to be rejected. In an analog approach, one can first show that the underlying distribution of gains for successful SGs is very likely not normally distributed. Given a mean gain of 1.5 million ISK per success ($SD = 226$ million ISK), a chi-square test for goodness-of-fit rejects the hypothesis of a normally distributed population ($\chi^2 = 580.71$, $p < 0.01$). The median loss per successful SG amounts to 758,420 ISK. A Wilcoxon signed-rank test for one sample with normal approximation then leads to the rejection of H2 ($W = 30{,}406$, $n = 395$, $z = -3.83$, $p < 0.01$ one-tailed). *Even successful SGs in EVE are examples of malicious actions.*

The finding that SGs generally speaking are malicious actions (rejected H1) might not be too surprising given the average failure ratio of 36 percent. But that even successful SGs, whose perpetrators profit from the value of the loot dropped by the victim, are malicious actions (rejected H2) is a very important finding. On average, every ganker in January spends more than 5 million ISK per attempt. One might argue that these 5 million ISK are only worth about 0.26 EUR in real world currency. But still the finding remains: people are willing to spend money to harm other players. The decision to be made is whether to spend 26 cents in order to harm somebody, or rather to earn 4 cents and still harm somebody (the hourly wage of piracy), or to earn about 2 EUR per hour without harming anybody (doing missions or mining).[5] Obviously, some players nevertheless opt for the first alternative.

Considering the losses of the victims: in total more than 105 billion ISK (5400 EUR) were lost in January (worth of ship and cargo minus insurance payouts), or 247 million ISK (13 EUR) per victim. These high values indicate that the attackers do not pick random or even unprofitable targets for their actions. Due to suicide ganking, the EVE economy lost 155 billion ISK (8000 EUR) in January[6] – only to redistribute 12.9 billion ISK, so to speak. Comparing these numbers with those from lowsec piracy – that was identified above as a *very inefficient* mechanism for redistribution (3.1 trillion ISK lost for redistributing 663 million ISK) – shows that SGs are an *even worse* mechanism. While lowsec piracy causes costs of more than four times the sum redistributed, SGs causes costs of more than 12 times the sum redistributed.

Suicide ganks are conscious actions of people committed to doing evil Given the way SGs function, nobody can seriously doubt that the perpetrators are consciously inflicting harm, that is committing economic evil. However, even if H1 and H2 assuming profitable SGs have been rejected, some gankers claim that they do it for the money (for example, Destiny Corrupted*, 2011) and one might ask the question whether the gankers realize that they themselves also lose money in such encounters, that is they not only commit egoistic but rather malicious actions. Figure 7.2 illustrates that there are no noteworthy exceptions to the rule that suicide ganks do not pay off. It shows the distribution of the perpetrators' gains and losses in the 616 successful and failed SGs.

The vast majority of failed attempts are slightly unprofitable. Only 29 percent of attempted SGs are profitable. But nowhere near as profitable as mining or trade. One should expect players to learn very quickly about this fact, since there are no highly profitable outliers, inducing them to think that SGs might not pay off on average but at least do for them personally, that blind them. In fact, the curves of failed and successful SGs presented look surprisingly similar taking into account that only successful SGs can profit from the value of the loot dropped by the victim. Although a Kolmogorov-Smirnov test leads to the rejection of the hypothesis that gains in successful and failed SGs follow the same distribution ($D = 0.584$, $p < 0.01$ two-tailed) this

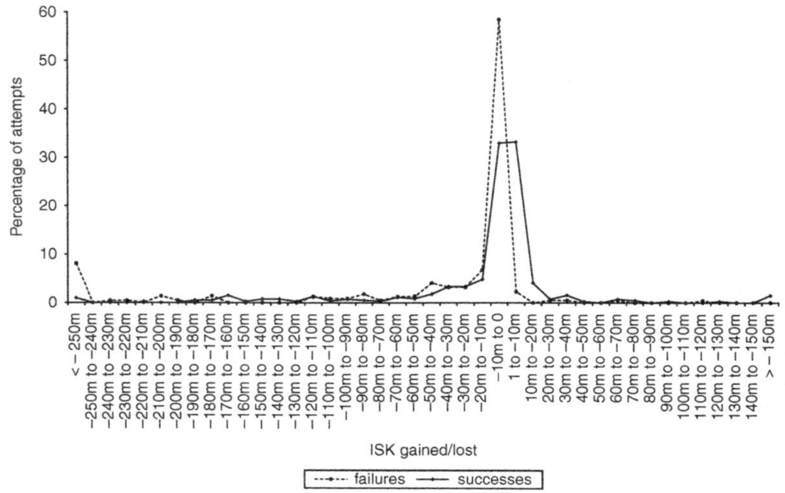

Figure 7.2 Distribution of gains and losses for the gankers of the 616 SG attempts

does not change the general line of argument. The median gain for failed (successful) SGs amounts to -5.3 million ISK (-0.8 million ISK), and the standard deviation is 133 million ISK (226 million ISK). In other words, it almost does not matter if a suicide gank is successful or not – SGs equal losses.

The most probable explanation for this is that successful suicide ganks require more advanced ships and equipment or simply more participants (indeed the failure ratio drops as the number of participants rises) – which in turn also cost more if eventually and inevitably lost. The gains from the loot captured in the successful cases are therefore directly offset by the higher losses the attackers incur themselves. Figure 7.3 and Table 7.1 show how the average per capita profits are distributed with respect to the number of attackers (for two to ten attackers) and support this reasoning.

The best way to do an SG seems to be to bring three people (mean loss: 7.1 million ISK; if you belong to the lucky and successful you even make a mean gain of 2.3 million ISK), since three participants guarantee a comparably low failure ratio and yet only bring along a little capital. But even if players learned this best strategy in the course of time, they would incur losses in the long run. The only strategy

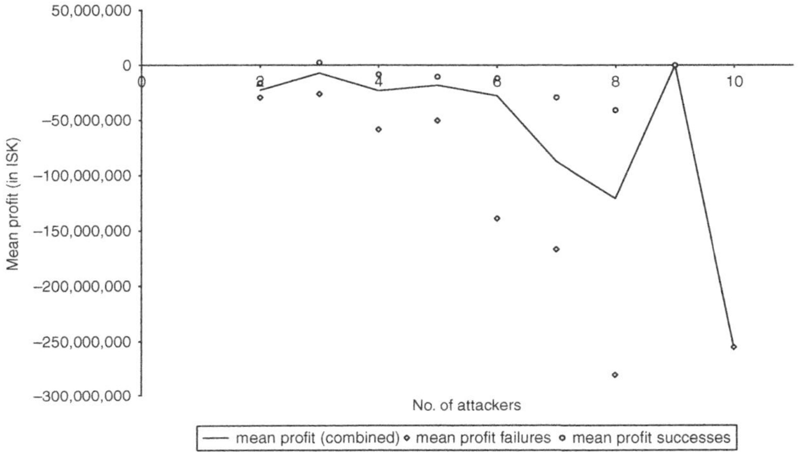

Figure 7.3 Mean per capita profit of suicide ganks with respect to number of participants (two to ten attackers)

Table 7.1 Number of SG attempts and mean profits with respect to number of participants (two to ten attackers)

Participants	**No. of attempts**	**Mean profit (combined; in million ISK)**
2	253	-22.5
3	124	-7.1
4	85	-23.0
5	58	-18.1
6	32	-27.6
7	19	-87.2
8	12	-121.0
9	1	0.6
10	1	-256.1

that seemed to do even better was to bring nine people. However, given the general trend of the mean profit curve, this seems to be an outlier: there simply was no *failed* SG with nine people in January (no four-sided dot in the figure) and only a single successful suicide gank with nine attackers – that yielded a mean per capita gain of just above 600,000 ISK.

Summarizing this data on making money by doing suicide ganks is straightforward. There is no good way of making money by committing SGs. On average the players will always lose money, even if they optimize their way of approaching this tactic: in the long run, losses are guaranteed. Even successful SGs are malicious actions with both victims and gankers incurring losses. Players can be expected to learn about this quickly, and thus seem to be motivated by a 'taste for harming'.

The people committing suicide ganks

Figure 7.4 follows the same rules as Figure 6.4 above, and shows the most important demographic attributes of attackers and victims of SGs. Gankers are on average a little bit more experienced with respect to skill points and total login minutes, and also possess a slightly higher wealth than the victims. It is not the case that poor people are teaming up to rob the rich, as one might believe (in 'Robin Hood' style). Generally speaking, gankers and victims are more experienced and richer than the population average for EVE.

This makes sense since victims have to be relatively rich to serve as worthwhile target and gankers have to be reasonably experienced in order to plan and execute an SG. It is not the case either that only a

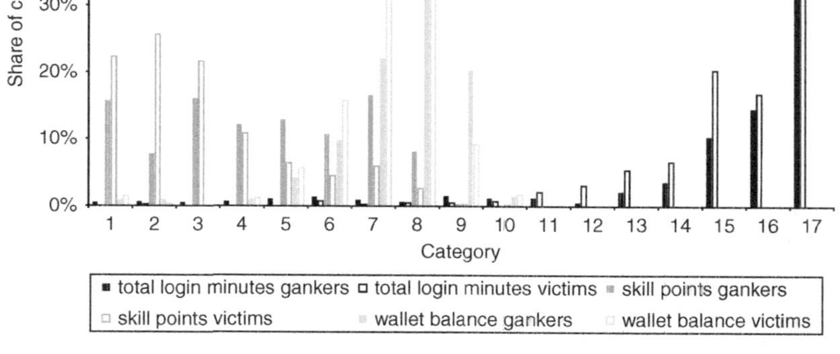

Figure 7.4 Distribution of total login minutes, skills points, and wallet balances for gankers and victims at the end of January 2011

small group of perpetrators is responsible for most of the SGs. Of the 2322 perpetrators involved in SGs in January there were 1218 *different* characters; on average every ganker participated in only about two SGs. This number is small compared to the average of more than three piracy kills per pirate in January. And even the top one percent of those committing such a suicide most frequently represents only 8.4 percent of gankers killed. In SGs, it is not the poor (with little to lose) that kill the rich or some small group of 'sadists' wreaking havoc.

With respect to the *players*, a z-test reveals that the average age of the gankers (29.1 years) is significantly lower than that of the active population (30.9 years) (population $SD = 8.53$, $z = -7.36$, $p < 0.01$ two-tailed). Additionally, the share of female gankers (2.4 percent) is significantly lower than the active population average (4.1 percent) ($z = -2.99$, $p < 0.01$ two-tailed). Just as in real life, young males seem to fall more easily for aggression. That trends well known from the real world can also be identified in the data from EVE supports the validity of the data.

7.1.3 One-person suicide ganks

The following data on one-person suicide ganks is intended to complete the picture of suicide ganking in general. It is very difficult for single characters to execute a suicide gank – nevertheless it happens. These one-person suicide ganks are not considered in the main discussion of multi-person SGs in the previous section, simply because it is impossible to identify *failed* one person suicide ganks compared to failed multi-person SGs, in which many CONCORD kills take place without prior player kill. But one cannot discern a random CONCORD kill because the character accidentally committed a crime from a failed one-person SG. Only successful one-person suicide ganks can be observed *directly*. However, it is possible to infer an estimated number of failed one-person suicide ganks from the success ratio of multi-person suicide ganks, that is to approach failed one-person SGs *indirectly*. Assuming a 50 percent failure ratio (that of *two-person* SGs being 49 percent) should be appropriate to avoid overestimating the losses involved in one-person SGs.

In January, there were 376 *successful* one-person suicide ganks in EVE. The 376 successful attackers shot down 428 victims. Adding up all the benefits for the successful attackers in these successful SGs, the number of 3.4 billion ISK (175 EUR) is reached. However, as is the case for multi-person SGs, these benefits are outweighed by the losses due to the suicidal nature of the attacks, which amounted to 4.8 billion ISK

(250 EUR). Successful *one-person SGs, just as multi-person SGs, therefore are a losing deal, costing the perpetrators 1.4 billion ISK in total in January (70 EUR).* Also the distribution of gains and losses for the perpetrators in these 376 successful cases very much resembles Figure 7.2 (above), with a maximum in the category between -2 million ISK and 0 ISK (Figure 7.5).

Comparing the distribution of *per capita* gains of successful multi-person SGs with that of the successful one-person SGs examined here supports the idea that the latter show the same characteristics. The average loss per successful one-person SG amounted to almost 3.8 million ISK (median loss = 550,894; SD = 78 million ISK), meaning that one-person SGs seem to be slightly less costly than two- or four-person SGs, yet less profitable than three-person SGs (cf. Figure 7.3 (above)). The average per capita loss per successful multi-person SG amounts to 2.7 million ISK (median loss = 288,312; SD = 24 million ISK). One cannot reject the hypothesis that the median gain in the two groups is equal (Mann-Whitney $U = 76407.5$, $n_1 = 376$, $n_2 = 395$, $p = 0.49$ two-tailed). *One-person SGs seem to constitute no exception from the generalized findings for multi-person suicide ganks.*

For all the numbers presented one has to keep in mind that these are only the *successful* SGs, which tend to be more profitable (at least this is the case

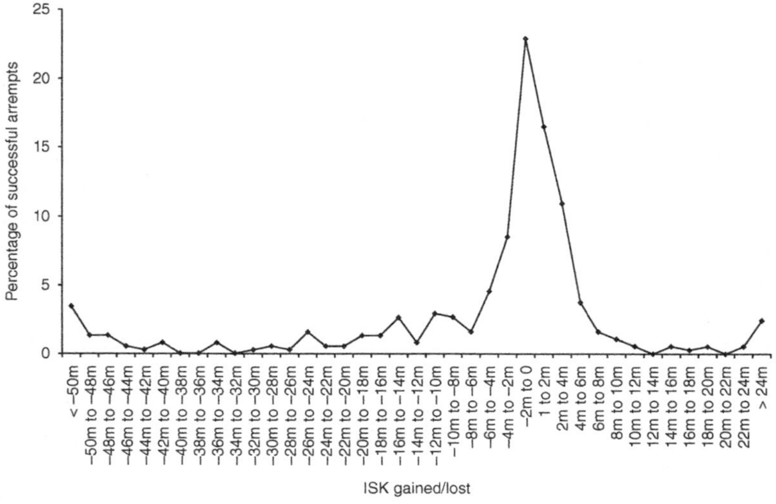

Figure 7.5 Distribution of gains and losses of the 376 successful one-person SG attempts

for multi-person SGs). Cautiously assuming a failure ratio of 50 percent implies an additional 376 unlucky perpetrators. Furthermore, cautiously assuming that these attackers lose just as much as their successful counterparts per time killed by CONCORD, then the overall losses for the EVE economy (that is combining the losses of victims and gankers) due to one-person SGs probably add up to about 67 billion ISK (3400 EUR).

7.2 Evil rules regarding suicide ganking

Whether suicide ganking is a legitimate action in EVE is not in question: 'Suicide ganking is an accepted game mechanic', this is the clear standpoint of CCP (CSM & CCP Games, 2010, p. 15). As long as one is willing to incur the costs inevitably tied to this (destruction by CONCORD), it is fine to attack other ships in hisec. *Even a sanction that is 100 percent effective is not able to deter the gankers from what they want to do: kill and rob other players in hisec.* The formal institution, that is the game mechanic behind suicide ganking (that it is even possible to attack other players in hisec), explicitly allows these acts. It is an evil formal institution of the game mechanics type: it is software-enforced, the outcome of a deliberate action of CCP Games, and it incites social conflict. *Players are formally allowed to commit evil.* This section traces the history of this evil formal institution, notably asking how it is possible for a rule *publicly known* for fostering evil to survive in this virtual society.[7]

7.2.1 The historical development of the rules governing SGs

Since the first launch of EVE, CCP has tried to attain two sometimes conflicting goals (Hinrichsen, 2011). First, EVE is designed to be a harsh and unforgiving universe in which you always have to be very cautious whom you trust and where you steer your ship. On the other hand, there shall be some relatively safe areas, notably intended to allow new players to get used to this new environment a little bit before actually being shot at. The first goal embraces suicide ganking, since SGs bring danger even to the safest places in the universe, whereas the second goal requires less player killing.

When EVE started out on May 6, 2003, there were even less rules preventing players from attacking others in hisec. This quickly led to pirates invading hisec and killing new players. CCP was forced to take action very early in the history of EVE.

> We definitely underestimated the need for security in the first place. A lot of effort went into making hisec safer, as we intended it to be.

> The main efforts were to secure new players who are not profitable targets for griefers. The intention was to allow profitable piracy but making new player griefing more difficult. (Hinrichsen, 2011; Lead Game Designer at that time)

Only four weeks after publication, a dev blog by CCP LeKjart* (2003) was written stating: 'Players seem to be using some laxity of CONCORD to actually pod kill players in high security systems. We will ... make them more efficient.' The 'laxity' of CONCORD that CCP LeKjart* mentions, was in fact total ineffectiveness: they fought with weak weapons and arrived too late to actually destroy the ships of the attackers. In those days, suicide ganking was often not even suicidal, since the virtual police force was not powerful enough (CCP LeKjart* et al., 2003).

Measures taken against suicide ganking 1: CONCORD gets tougher

The first measure that was taken to relieve pressure from the victims was to give CONCORD ships better weapons (CCP LeKjart* et al., 2003). Additionally, static cannons at the star gates and stations (where many attacks happened) were introduced (CCP Hellmar* et al., 2003a). The most discussed event, however, was a direct intervention by the developers in the game. The developers literally got in their virtual space ships with superior weapons and themselves (!) destroyed lots of pirate ships that gathered at a particularly infamous location. This is remarkable, since by doing so the developers acknowledged that the built-in institutions against SGs just were not enough to deal with the problem at that time. The CEO of CCP himself wrote the explanatory dev blog justifying the intervention of the game masters (GMs):

> Empire controlled space [hisec and lowsec; C.D.M.], means that the space is controlled by the empires. If the police are not cutting it against players ..., reinforcements will be called, be it special NPCs or GM-controlled NPCs (special-ops).
>
> Do as you please in non-empire space but please don't complain when the empires take action against you in their space, when you are obviously violating their rules.
>
> The actions taken today were within the rules of the game, the ships being used are ships in the game. The empires have ample resources to manufacture them and the pilots controlling them have up to 3+ years experience flying EVE vessels. (CCP Hellmar* et al., 2003b)

As a last resort for restoring order, the developers had to actively intervene in the virtual universe – a singular act in the history of EVE. This shows just how serious the problem was, one of the foremost rules for CCP being not to actively control 'New Eden'. It was later acknowledged that this intervention was a mistake; the in-game problem should have been solved with in-game organizations and institutions. The rule to stay passive as a developer was reinstalled as top priority. Lead Game Master Kjarval explains:

> In the beginning, the GMs were a lot more active. They intervened more often and tried to punish what they considered bad behavior. There is this quote from Hilmar [the CEO of CCP Games; C.D.M.]: 'In the beginning, we were like the God of the Old Testament. Hands on. Now we are more like the God of the New Testament. Letting things go their way.' Nowadays, the GMs really try to stay in the background. (Kjarval, 2011)

Measures taken against suicide ganking 2: increased security penalties

The increased power of CONCORD solved the problem for some time but the community kept complaining about the evil formal institution. In 2008, the player-elected CSM decided to ask CCP to further impede suicide ganking (CSM, 2008). The protocol of the meeting of CSM and CCP officials details:

> CCP realized that even though they *do not plan to remove suicide ganking completely,* today's suicide gank mechanics are too biased in the ganker's favor, and they have set up a task force to look into suicide ganking...
>
> For the short term, they plan to increase the security hit for crime in high-sec space and make sure that all ship kills will be counted as kills, with the matching sec hit, for everyone that participated....
>
> Mid term, the plans are to look into suicide ganking and the insurance payout, *once they have made sure that new players are not impacted by this too much* and have extra security in place so that accidents should not be punished. (CSM & CCP, 2008, p. 9; emphasis by author)

This source shows the discrepancy between CCP's goals to allow SGs yet to protect new players. The mentioned changes to the security status reduction were introduced shortly afterwards (CCP Fear*, 2008). The main effect of this was that, first, the costs of suicide ganking were raised by a bigger decrease of the offender's individual security status, and second, repeated offenders were prevented from ganking over and over again in a short period of time. The latter is due to the fact that if the security status of a character is too low, it is difficult for him to even enter hisec systems. If he tries to do so, the computer-controlled navies of the Empires who patrol at the star gates immediately attack him. Between every SG committed the gankers therefore had to bring back up their security status.

It is important to note that this decision to raise the security status reductions was by no means made unanimously: 'Alex (CSM Bane Glorious) said that most suicide gankers already thought of... regain[ing] security status as painful' (CSM & CCP, 2008, p. 9). Furthermore, it is important to note that this decision did not have all the desired effects. Many suicide gankers simply found a way to circumvent this new institution by exploiting another institution of the game. The game mechanic that neither Empire navies nor CONCORD attack characters flying around only in their rescue capsule *even if they have a very low security status and try to enter hisec space* was abused by the gankers:

> A certain tactic is currently being employed by criminals, which allows them to operate in high-security space despite their negative security status. The tactic is as follows:
>
> - Fly into empire in pod
> - Let neutral alt pile up ships in safespot (either with Orca or by ejecting)
> - Board ships and fly to belt/station/gate
> - Activate smartbombs or otherwise gank some targets
> - Let neutral alt loot the wrecks
> - Repeat. (CSM Ankhesentapemkah*, 2008)

People obviously are adapting to new institutions in EVE that make committing evil more complex but they do not stop to profit from the overall evil formal rule that attacking innocent players even in hisec is made possible by the game mechanics. It is surprising to see to what lengths players will go to commit evil for evil's sake.

Measures taken against suicide ganking 3: insurance payouts revalued

Eventually, the mid-term counter measures promised by CCP came into effect: the insurance system of EVE was overhauled (CCP Chronotis*,

2010). By lowering the insurance payouts, CCP encoded one of the traditional main complaints of the opponents of SG, namely that insurance payouts subsidize suicide ganking. This concession was in fact a compromise. CCP did not abolish insurance payouts altogether for ships being destroyed by CONCORD – which was the initial goal of the opponents. 'It was made clear that suicide ganking is an accepted game mechanic' (CSM & CCP Games, 2010, p. 15).

'Flame wars' in the forums: about carebears and PvPers

Not only the developers want to establish a safe but harsh environment. The player base is divided, too. Since the first days of EVE, there are constant discussions between 'carebears' on the one side and 'PvPers' (PvP is short for 'player vs player') on the other side.

> When PvPers and carebears meet, that is usually the problem. It is a pretty different gameplay for both. That's the biggest clash we usually see. (Hreiðarsson, 2011; Lead Game Master)

These discussions are also known as 'flame wars', since each group is trying to 'flame' the posts of the other group in the official forums. Flame wars are a good example of the antagonistic competition between good and evil taken to the verbal level, theoretically described by Duntley and Buss (2005, p. 115; cf. Section 2.2). Whereas the carebears want to avoid combat against other players, just run their business, and try to influence the developers to make aggressive actions more difficult, the PvPers want to engage in combat as often as possible and seek to diminish the possibilities of avoiding attacks. This is also a quarrel between the two potential lifestyles in anarchy: between *producers* and *fighters*. There are many technical terms used in these discussions that may hinder an easy understanding. To overcome this problem and to give at least a slight overview of the arguments exchanged, Table 7.2 reproduces some of the comments. It is structured in analogy to the three measures taken against suicide ganking just cited: for every measure there are some pros and some cons listed that were brought up by the players. The fact *that these discussions are readily available is one of the priceless advantages of doing research on the development of social institutions in MMORPGs.*

It is in these forums and in discussions like these that the players decide which institutions they want to see implemented or changed. It is a public parliament in the literal sense.

Table 7.2 Comments on institutional changes affecting suicide ganking over the years

Character	Comment	Source
Measure 1: What the PvPers say about a more powerful police and the dev intervention		
Stavros*	'do not do this, areas are secure enough as it is. Carebearing the game like this will drive off many legit pirates, in space concord would have a long reaction time of hours or days at least, so this is at least realistic.'	(CCP LeKjart* et al., 2003)
MORPHEUS*	'pirates would never "take over secure areas and kill newb corps right away" – it's not profitable'	(CCP LeKjart* et al., 2003)
Axelay*	'I would like to state that I am not happy with the fact that GMs log on with maxed skills and hop in their uber ships and come kill us. It would be one thing if a player(s) came in one of those ships and disrupted us (they would have worked for it etc) but to have fabricated ships piloted by day-old characters with maxxed stats popping up from no-where and killing us is cheap in my opinion. CCP could have organized the players and held an "event" for the players to come take us out, or even come in reasonably similar ships (even if they were more powerful) and we would have had fun fighting them. This, however, is pointless.'	(CCP Hellmar* et al., 2003b)
Measure 1: What the carebears say about a more powerful police		
Hippey*	'Stavros is just a pirate and wants his life easier. Drive off legit pirates?? come on.. who cares about 10 legit pirates when they ruin the gameplay for 1000 players.'	(CCP LeKjart* et al., 2003)
Yakzan*	'These are secure systems after all, CONCORD should be given the same tools as the pirates and not be outnumbered or outgunned as to modules and such.'	(CCP LeKjart* et al., 2003)
Tigsen*	'In 1.0 security systems I would like to see the police come in and stomp any would-be pirates in a heartbeat. I think that if you don't have this happen then you will eventually end up with PK[8] corps taking over the newby starting systems and killing the new players right away. That does nothing but harm the game…'	(CCP LeKjart* et al., 2003)

Lijah Reaper*	'I think a permanent police presense in 1.0 areas near asteroid belts would be an excellent solution, making police protection visible and comforting to the new (or scared) player.'	(CCP LeKjart* et al., 2003)
drunkenmaster*	'what makes a pirate "legit"? 1.0 systems shouldn't even be accessible to pirate corp members'	(CCP LeKjart* et al., 2003)
Weaselsmasher*	'The age-old argument of "a PK's money is as green as a carebear's" is simply not true. When PKs sweep through newbie areas, ruining the game for people who have just bought the game, they leave a wake of unsubscribed accounts. While this may boost the fragile egos of the newbie-killers, it directly costs the developers money.'	(CCP LeKjart* et al., 2003)
Ralimenua*	'This is an excellent idea. I'd go further: killing newbs should cause CONCORD to break out the heavy-duty quantum entanglement viral mind weapons that bust jackasses back to skill kindergarten. Wankers that podkill newbs belong in diapers, and CONCORD should put them there in a drooling syphillitic clone.'	(CCP LeKjart* et al., 2003)
Zyrla Bladestorm*	'[quote] "I would not support CCP creating a bunch of uber pirates from nothing and going around slaying you either."[/quote] they didnt create uber pirates .. they merely deployed the top end of law enforcement .. it's not like concord battleships are a big secret .. there in several of the POTW's[9] even. You chose to Pk in empire space and the empires responded .. simple as that.'	(CCP Hellmar* et al., 2003b)
Vlamina Trescu*	'As far as I know this is what an empire does: it controls its claims with high-tech, state-of-the-art hardened military units when its laws are broken. The Empires are finally doing what they are supposed to do. If they didn't protect their laws and control their territory then what would be the point of even having the Empires in the game?'	(CCP Hellmar* et al., 2003b)
Ends*	'Great job CCP! PKers are WEAK, listen to em whine, it's like music to my ears!'	(CCP Hellmar* et al., 2003b)

Continued

Table 7.2 Continued

Character	Comment	Source
Measure 2: What the PvPers say about increased security reductions		
Lysander Kaldenn*	'As long as suicide ganking remains possible…I don't really care about doing it, but i always thought high sec violence made the game more credible.'	(CCP Taera* et al., 2008, p. 1)
Bellum Eternus*	'It's sad to see CCP cave again. Oh well, it wasn't unexpected. On the flip side, this'll keep the lesser players away from killing in high sec and let the pros get on with culling the braindead carebears and taking their ISK. The funny thing is, this won't even slow down the high sec killings that much. It may raise the bar a bit on what is considered worth killing, but it won't stop it. Thank God.'	(CCP Taera* et al., 2008, p. 1)
Scout R*	'This game get nearer and nearer to being carebears online every day'	(CCP Taera* et al., 2008, p. 1)
Dungar Loghoth*	'Keep bending over for the whiners CCP, it's really what's made this game unique among the sea of other MMOs.'	(CCP Taera* et al., 2008, p. 1)
Kyguard	'Sad, so sad.'	(CCP Taera* et al., 2008, p. 1)
Plave Okice*	'Have you forgotten what this game was supposed to be about? Where are the old devs who made this game a dark and harsh universe?'	(CCP Taera* et al., 2008, p. 2)
Nautsyn Thome*	'CCP you took my only weapon against Makrominers away! Please do not let them destroy our game. If you take suicide ganking away, PLEASE remove THEM first!'	(CCP Taera* et al., 2008, p. 2)
THE GREAT LOBO*	'Anymore whiners you want to give into ccp ? What the hell is happening to this game? You are very lucky there is so little competition in the sci fi mmo market.'	(CCP Taera* et al., 2008, p. 3)
Measure 2: What the carebears say about increased security reductions		
Wen Jaibao*	'I can't wait to see the whines from the people who abuse the insurance system.'	(CCP Taera* et al., 2008, p. 1)

Ralitge boyter*	'Finally CCP does know how to make a game fun it just takes them a while to actually implement these kinds of things. Current ganking is really taking some of the fun out of playing EVE, even in high sec space moving around in anything smaller then a Battle Cruiser[10] is basically waiting to die.'	(CCP Taera* et al., 2008, p. 2)
Merin Ryskin*	'These changes are long overdue. For all the people crying about it: *suicide ganking still works*. The only difference is now you'll have to work a little harder, and you'll have to actually pick your targets instead of just ganking every ship you see.'	(CCP Taera* et al., 2008, p. 3)
Measure 3: What the PvPers say about less insurance payouts		
Shepard Book*	'More steps in the wrong direction helping people stay safer in empire.... Where did the vision go to make people want to go to low sec and 0.0? This does not help the sandbox grow. It just makes the weak want to stay in high sec.'	(CCP Fallout* et al., 2010, p. 6)
Measure 3: What the carebears say about less insurance payouts		
Furb Killer*	'More steps in the right direction, gives additional incentive for the suicide gankers to move away from their carebearish concord hugging where they are afraid of any risk. This way they will sooner decide they might try the scary low sec and 0.0. Face it, it doesnt make sense you profit from suicide ganking even if you shoot an empty hauler. Yes it should be possible, but it also should hurt your wallet if you randomly gank around.'	(CCP Fallout* et al., 2010, p. 6)
Nye Jaran*	'Really disappointed to see that the devs continue actively supporting terrorism within Eve by leaving intact insurance payouts on ships attacked by Concord (read: suicide ganking).'	(CCP Fallout* et al., 2010, p. 1)
TheLostPenguin*	'Mentioning suicide ganks this wont "fix" the issue, but at least now it's a bit of an outlay for the ganker(s) rather than the current situation'	(CCP Fallout* et al., 2010, p. 6)

Summary

There is indeed a need for solving the twin problems of protection and trust (Mantzavinos, 2001, p. 133), even in virtual societies. Over time, the rules regulating the effects of suicide ganking got more and more severe. These were all changes demanded by the community. On the other hand, one has to clearly acknowledge that the fundamental evil rule is still in place – and that CCP shows no signs of changing it. After all, as the comments in Table 7.2 point out, even many carebears are not per se against SGs but just against too biased a version of it. The fact that the evil rule is still in place is astonishing, since it really would be no technical problem to change the game mechanics to make attacking innocents in hisec generally impossible. The argument that EVE might just be 'too young' for such a radical institutional change to happen should be weighed against the fact that – for a computer game – being eight years old means being as old as Methuselah. *Evil rules represent a kind of natural evil in that they instigate evil actions but are external to the actors. Such evil rules exist in EVE. And they matter for economic performance. And they persist.*

There is a need for protection and trust-enhancing institutions but there also seem to be people who like war, who like fighting – and who therefore do everything they can to establish evil rules and to keep them in place. This might well be one reason for the great problem of overcoming conflicts in the real world, too. It is not only a question of profits or power for the 'warlords' – it may also be a question of personal taste. A question of a 'taste for harming' being institutionalized.

7.2.2 Effects of economic evil on the income of new players

In the historical discussion surrounding the rules of suicide ganking the argument that SGs make new players quit the game is often to be found. However, Figure 7.4 (above) contradicts the idea of new players immediately falling prey to this tactic: victims of SGs typically are more experienced and richer than EVE's population average. But the question of the effects of an evil action on the victim (beside the immediate material loss) nevertheless is of great interest. In order to examine the effects of being killed in EVE, a particularly suited subgroup are new players who started playing EVE in January 2011, since for them being killed has bigger consequences than for more experienced players. Additionally, it is possible to track every kill they ever suffered from based on the data at hand. All new players face the exact same starting conditions in-game, that is comparisons between different groups can be made more easily without the disturbing effects of already acquired skill points and wealth.

This short section will examine the effect of being killed on the income development of all new EVE characters that were created on January 1. The null hypothesis to be tested is that for players that did not become the victim of a kill in their first month of play (*civilians*) the median profit they generated is bigger than that of *victims* (who suffered from at least one player kill). This hypothesis seems reasonable given the fact that victims have to replace their ship – a costly action that might also prevent them from being as efficient in acquiring income for some time.

Findings and discussion

Overall, 1515 new characters were created on January 1, 2011. Eliminating secondary and tertiary characters since these are not controlled by new players,[11] and ignoring all those characters that were online for less than 5 hours in January since these players probably did not like the game very much and quit quickly, one reaches the number of n_1 = 565 civilians and n_2 = 217 victims. On average, every victim was killed three times in January. Adding up all the different sources of income (from mission running to mining and trading) and subtracting all the expenses (notably for ships and equipment bought on the market), the profit can be determined for victims and civilians. At the end of January, the former have earned an average profit of 60 million ISK (SD = 205 million ISK) and the latter of 36 million ISK (SD = 1033 million ISK). The hypothesis that civilians have acquired a higher profit is rejected (Mann-Whitney U = 52,436, $p < 0.01$ one-tailed).

A part of the difference in profit can be explained by differences in playing time: whereas civilians only have an average online time quotient[12] of 8.7 percent (125 minutes of play per day), victims play on average more than four hours per day (online quotient: 17.2 percent). The importance of the loss of three ships for the overall profit made in January dwindles in the face of almost twice as high online times. Given the data at hand, it is impossible to tell whether those who play more are more likely to get killed more often or whether those who get killed are motivated to play more eagerly in order to avenge themselves more quickly.

However, some additional evidence suggests that the negative effect of becoming a victim on profit generated is indeed small. Table 7.3

Table 7.3 The victims' Spearman correlation coefficients for five variables (n = 155 victims with profit < 100m ISK)[13]

	Profit	Online quotient	Times killed	Date first killed	Joined player corp?	Mean	SD
Profit	1					18.42m	20.72m
Online quotient	0.408**	1				0.16	0.11
Times killed	0.055	0.118	1			2.89	2.07
Date first killed	0.159**	0.063	−0.139*	1		11.45	7.91
Joined player corp?	0.101	0.201**	−0.048	0.039	1	0.60	0.49

*, ** indicates significance at the 90 percent and 95 percent level, respectively (Student t-test, two-tailed).

displays the victims' Spearman correlation coefficients for five variables, as well as means and standard deviations for: profit in January, the online quotient, how often the victim got killed, the date he was first killed (1 = January 1; 2 = January 2, and so on), and whether or not he had joined a player corporation by the end of January (0 = no; 1 = yes).

It is not surprising that the online quotient is positively correlated with profit and the player's decision to join a player corporation: you can only earn money in EVE while online and you probably spend more time online if you have some friends with whom you enjoy playing. That victims being killed later in the course of January exhibit higher levels of profit is not astonishing either; even more so since getting killed later seems to imply getting killed less often.

However, the most important finding is that being killed more often is not significantly negatively correlated with profit generated by victims in January. In fact, the data even suggests a positive correlation. While the null hypothesis rejected above suggests that victims do not do worse in comparison to those not killed, this correlation suggests that even getting killed more often does not impair total profit generated. *The negative effects of evil actions on the profit of the victims do not seem to be large in EVE Online.*

Unfortunately, the correlation coefficients found are too weak to construct a meaningful regression model able to predict the profit of new players that become victims early on based on the variables examined here. Aspects like the character's chosen profession (miner, trader, producer, or pirate), the player's type (achiever, socializer, explorer, or killer), or the player's experience in playing other MMORPGs probably greatly affect the total profit generated but cannot be accounted for given the data at hand.

7.3 Discussion on suicide ganks

Suicide ganks are not among the most common incidents in the vast universe of EVE. There were about 4000 SG-related kills in January in EVE; that is 1.2 percent of all player kills. The economic losses amounted to 222 billion ISK in January (11,000 EUR), or 0.05 percent of EVE's M1, respectively. Translated into the terms of Europe's economy, this corresponds to a yearly damage of 2.4 billion EUR. An estimated[14] number of around 3000 different characters (0.5 percent of EVE's active population) was involved in SGs. For comparison, in the EU this would be around 2.5 million people.[15] Figure 7.6 shows the extent of suicide ganking with respect to the total number of active characters and the total number of player kills compared to other evil actions examined in this book.

Gankers are a minority of people that consciously conduct malicious actions – but the actions of this minority have comparably important consequences, economically speaking, in that their behavior is way more destructive than for example classic lowsec piracy. The conclusion

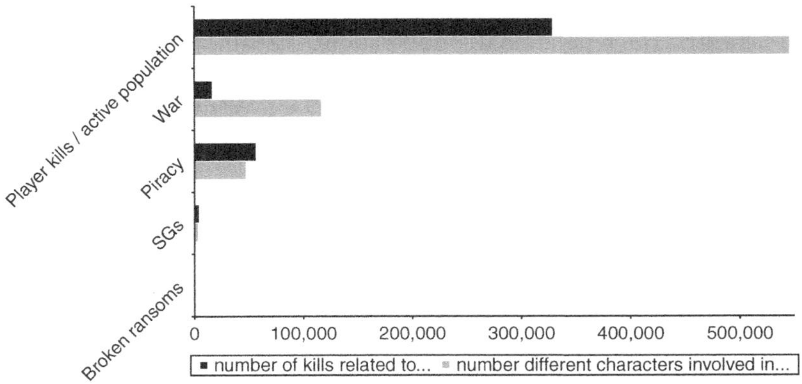

Figure 7.6 Number of kills and different characters involved for certain phenomena

comes to mind that gankers may be the 'sadists' of EVE, that is that one percent of the population is responsible for a lot of the overall evil actions in a society (cf. the discussion of Baumeister & Vohs (2005), Bodholt et al. (2000), and Hare (1991, 1999) in the psychological primer). But for this book it is only important that SGs are a good proof for the existence of malicious actions. That their extent is not as big is less important than their sheer existence.

Like piracy, suicide ganking is not explicable by referring to the economic theories of harming outlined in the theoretical part. Firstly, suicide ganking is *not profitable in the short run*. No matter how sophisticated your approach to suicide ganking, you will always end up losing money on average in the long run. Suicide ganking is not a planned thing but rather an outburst of violence because of boredom (Eriksen, 2011). Interestingly, this reproduces another finding on evil actions known from the theoretical part, namely that impulsivity is a design-feature of evil actions, necessary to circumvent the evolved protection mechanisms of the victim (Duntley & Buss, 2005, p. 118). A suicide gank is precisely that, a violent outburst targeting an unsuspecting victim. Although SGs could be stopped easily from a technical perspective, no effective institution has evolved yet in this direction.

Secondly, to gank someone is not at all *conditional* behavior out of fairness considerations. It considers neither the person ganked nor his wealth. Sure, the target should be worthwhile being ganked – but again, gankers are typically richer than their victims. Gankers cannot be said to have other-regarding preferences in the sense implied by Fehr and Schmidt or Hirshleifer: they do not care for the payoff of the victim as long as it is negative.

Thirdly, as for reputational considerations, the same limitations already mentioned for piracy apply. However, SGs are particularly unsuitable to even build up a bad reputation in the first place. Whereas the individual security status of the ganker inevitably drops (that is he experiences the negative effects of a bad reputation in EVE), he does not automatically experience the 'positive' effects of being feared by others. Suicide ganks are a group effort and groups blur responsibility; this has a double effect in this case. Not only are perpetrators more inclined to commit evil, but the victims also have less knowledge of who actually attacked them. Hence, if the victim does not know whom to fear or to avoid, then the very idea of building up a bad reputation by SGs is vain.

Suicide ganking shows that *malicious actions exist and matter*; it is another example of evil behavior probably best explained referring to a 'taste for harming'. Looking at the procedure outlined in the section

'Measures taken against suicide ganking 2: increased security penalties' and seeing the depth of thought that went into this procedure, the creativity used in circumventing the game mechanics, and the outstanding coordination efforts necessary for accomplishing this type of suicide gank, one has to wonder: why would anybody exercise such effort for doing something that yields no gain when he could just use his skills for actually productive activities? Suicide ganks are the most striking example for the existence of evil actions. They manifest a characteristic of evil highlighted by Eagleton:

> It is as though individual bits and pieces of the project made sense, but not the overall operation.... Evil [typically] is committed in the name of something else, and to this extent has a purpose; but this something else does not itself have a point.... [I]t is purposeful action taken in the name of a condition which is not itself purposeful. (Eagleton, 2010, pp. 97, 104)

Defining evil this way is particularly fruitful for economics. Evil actions are not forms of irrational behavior; it is just that the goals they aim to achieve are not easily explicable in economic categories of material self-interest or even other-regarding preferences.

As far as the discussion on evil rules goes, it was shown that *evil formal institutions exist and matter in EVE*. It is not only the people committing SGs that are responsible for what happens but also the instigating circumstances allowing them to do so. The game mechanic allowing for suicide ganking is a typical example of an evil formal rule: it is software-enforced, deliberately put in place by CCP Games, and incites social conflict. The most astonishing finding in this respect is probably that *this evil rule* persists *in EVE*. Although it is publicly known that allowing attacks on innocent players in hisec instigates social conflict, developers and community decided that they wanted to keep it the way it is. The perfectly carried out sanction by CONCORD that retaliates SGs to 100 percent (that is a perfect rate of detection and punishment) does not prevent ganking from taking place.

There is, however, one big problem with classifying the rules governing for example ransoming and suicide ganks or the general harshness and darkness of the universe as evil rules in the strict sense: *they are not perceived as being specifically* evil *rules by the community*. Actually, the game mechanic allowing for ganks is not a problem if you abide by the most important rule there is in EVE: you should not fly what you cannot afford to lose. Although it might be surprising that somebody tells the victim of a suicide gank not to be angry, since if he is angry this only shows that he flew what he could not afford to lose – this is exactly what Eriksen (2011) proposes. Guðmundsson (2010a) reasons: 'Anything that happens within the boundaries of game mechanics cannot really be considered evil behavior.' Or more precisely on lowsec piracy:

> There are some regions where the pirates can't operate. If you deliberately go to where the pirates live and you have been warned – is it really evil if they destroy your ship and take your loot? The question is hard to answer if you stay inside the game. Now there is no question, if you take things out of the game – if you hack accounts for example – then that is evil behavior. (Guðmundsson, 2010a)

This is the general standpoint of most developers and the community. If asked what they consider evil behavior in EVE and what the players mostly complain about, the answers range from actions that break laws (like macrominers and real money trading), to spamming chat channels, offensive language, or account hacking (Kjarval, 2011), to market scams (Hreiðarsson, 2011), and abusing trust in general (Hinrichsen, 2011). It is not the rules allowing for player killing that players complain about. Asked whether players of EVE *like* the unique atmosphere of EVE with all of its consequences or if they *only accept* it, almost all developers agree that they do actually like it (Eriksen, 2011; Guðmundsson, 2010a; Hinrichsen, 2011; Turbefield & Óskarsson, 2011). Of course, players complain when they get ganked and threaten to quit playing the game but 'people may rage on the forums but they don't quit' (Guðmundsson, 2010a). Furthermore, Guðmundsson explains:

> The universe is not evil, it is harsh. It punishes you for wrong decisions.... The distinction between evil committed by humans and an earthquake that causes harm is wrong. You may not prevent an earthquake from happening but you know it will happen – and you can prepare. Same is true for what happens to you in EVE.

It was already mentioned in the psychological primer that it is the individual normative perspective that makes a value-free action either 'good' or 'evil', and that good and evil are cognitive categories (Duntley & Buss, 2005, pp. 111–113). More importantly with respect to evil rules, when talking about how to 'evaluate evil' (Section 2.3), it was argued that the definition of *evil* social institutions as rules that incite social conflict and induce harm being caused is but a definition. Calling certain rules 'evil' is just following the *principium diiudicationis* allowing to distinguish between what is considered as good and evil in this book. It came to call 'evil' what causes material harm – the EVE community generally evaluates things that do not break the known rules of the game as 'good' (or at least as morally neutral) and things that circumvent game mechanics and transgress the boundaries of the game as 'evil'. The strictly material approach of this book to discern between good and evil – judged to be the economic approach proper – has at least one important advantage. It tends not to underestimate the importance of evil actions and evil rules, when falling short in targeting evil rules may have severe consequences.

8
Wars – Other Forms of Natural Evil in EVE

If there ever was a good example for evil rules fostering conflict instead of productively overcoming it, then it would have to be the rules governing *war* in EVE. War in EVE is not an issue of states but of corporations and alliances. Each player corp or alliance can declare war on every other player corp or alliance at every time.[1] In EVE, 'being at war' means that the members of the warring corporations are formally allowed to shoot down ships of the opponent every time they encounter them and everywhere in EVE. The rules governing war are evil formal institutions: the game mechanic of war is software-enforced, deliberately put in place by CCP Games, and incites social conflict. In essence, the war mechanics allow corporations to fight even in the territory controlled by the virtual State without having to fear any governmental repercussions. *The 'State' formally allows the use of coercion on its territory, resulting in a partial state of nature for the warring parties.*

The following discussion on war in EVE will, besides giving another example of an evil social institutions, highlight other forms of natural evil, known from the psychological primer (Section 2.2) that are present in EVE as well: ideologies, changed vocabulary and semantics, role-play, and deindividuation.

8.1 Some numbers on wars

In January 2011, there were 4100 *active wars* in EVE. This number is reached by ignoring all wars that were declared February 1, 2011 or later, and also those wars that ended on or before December 31, 2010. These 4100 wars lead to 16,408 kills all over the universe (for example compared to more than 56,000 lowsec piracy kills). Although more than half of the total kills in EVE happen in nullsec (cf. Figure 5.10

(above)), 90 percent of war-related kills happen in hisec. Players, thus, make ample use of the tools at hand when they want to attack other players in hisec despite the fact that this space is controlled by the virtual state.[2] In January, 116,250 characters belonged to corporations participating in active wars that led to actual casualties – either on the wardeccing or on the wardecced side. That is to say that 21.3 percent of EVE's active population was subject to wars involving *people killing or being killed* in their circle of friends. Wars, thus, have a high impact on playing experience for many people.

However, players are using war declarations ('wardecs' for short, with the verb 'to wardec someone') not only when they have 'good reasons' for going to war – like for example to scare away a competitor entering the market in which one has a regional monopoly – but in a much more unsystematic way or just 'for fun'.

> Hisec wardecs certainly are a griefing tactic, too. Often you do not get systematically smashed if you're being wardecced like that but you are attacked if you are at the wrong place at the wrong time. There are also 'vanilla pirates' out there – that's what we call them – who just want to have a lot of targets to shoot [and thus wardec as many people as possible; C.D.M.]. (Kjarval, 2011; Lead Game Master)

Grief play, that is intentionally acting in a way so that others enjoy the game less and enjoying this play style, is a phenomenon known from many other MMORPGs as well (Foo & Koivisto, 2004). Basically, the problem the EVE society faces with Empire wardecs is the same as for suicide ganking. Not surprisingly, there are similar discussions around the changes of the war mechanics as around the changes of the rules governing suicide ganking discussed in the previous chapter: PvPers and carebears argue about how much harm-doing should be officially allowed for.

8.2 The Privateers nerf

To avoid redundancy, only one change to the evil game mechanics shall be highlighted here. It is commonly called the 'Privateers nerf'.[3] In EVE, wardeccing corporations and alliances have to pay fees in order to keep the war in effect. In 2007, for alliances, the size of this war fee was affected by the number of member corporations (the more member corporations, the higher the fee) (CCP TomB* et al., 2004b). Additionally, the total was dependent on the number of wars already declared against the *wardecced* corp, that is the more wars the wardecced corporation was already a victim of, the higher the costs for the wardeccing alliance (CCP Atlas*, 2007). But then some changes were enacted, as outlined by CCP Atlas* in his dev blog:

> Previously a war issued by an alliance would cost 50M + 50M/week. If the alliance or corporation being warred *against* was already the victim of another war that fee would increase by 50M for each war declared against the victim.
>
> Money-grubbing CONCORD has decided that the number of wars declared *by* the aggressor will now also count to increase the war prices and the larger of the two is used to determine the war instigation and upkeep fees.
>
> **Example**: Alliance **P** has ten wars in progress. They will have to pay 500M/war/week to keep the war machine running. If they now declare war on the eleventh corporation or alliance that war will cost 550M to start and the upkeep cost will be 550M/war/week for all the wars until any of the wars is canceled. (CCP Atlas*, 2007)

This unsuspicious change in war mechanics came to be known as the Privateers nerf, since the example of 'Alliance **P**' was by no way a random example. The 'Privateer Alliance' at that time was a powerful player alliance comprising thousands of players. The purpose of the alliance was to provide players with the opportunity for PvP-combat against the biggest possible number of potential targets (EVE-history.net, 2007). They simply wardecced everyone around and thus explicitly subscribed to grief play. The leader of the alliance described the idea as follows:

> You may join as you wish and take part at no cost. Fight anywhere, with alts, mains or trials. There are no rules for you to follow. If you can shoot it, it's a valid target. 24/7 365 we war dec alliances. (Surreptitious*, 2006)

And the historical wiki on EVE continues: 'Pilots in the Privateers had no strategic aims beyond forming ad hoc gangs and patrolling the lanes between major trade hubs looking for targets.... No assets, inexpensive ships and no purpose than to fight made the Privateers difficult to harm' (EVE-history.net, 2007). But due to the changes, suddenly, their way of playing the game was associated with exponential costs for every new wardec.

8.3 Other forms of natural evil related to wars

The negative reactions to the enacted changes were very loud at the time and continue to the present day: even almost four years after the changes new forum topics with the subject 'Unnerf the privateer nerf' are published (HeliosGal*, 2011). In the discussion that directly followed the announcement of the nerf, all kinds of natural evil known from the theoretical part can be identified (cf. Section 2.2). Table 8.1 lists some examples for *acceptable justifications and rationales*, as well as *altered vocabulary and semantics*.

It is interesting to see how the justification that EVE is a massively multiplayer game and therefore should not be governed too much by the developers is brought into play. Or, how perpetrators become 'tough guys' and killing many people an 'innovation'. However, the Privateers nerf not only shows how ideologies and vocabulary are used to justify the existence of evil rules, *role-playing aspects* and *deindividuation* can also be found. For example, many of the members of the Privateer Alliance adopt the role of a pirate who is, of course, supposed to be bad. For example ae1* who states: 'Being BADD never felt so good...' (CCP kieron* et al., 2007, p. 10). The word 'yarrr' which is supposed to be the battle cry of pirates is also frequently used. It is often added at the end of comments to show who the other forum users are dealing with. Consider for example sorted*: 'We have always ganked in empire, and we have always been somewhat indiscrimate about the targets we choose...The changes are coming Tuesday- We aint dead, not even close. We will still be here next week, and the week after that, and the week after that,...in anycase.. YARRR' (CCP kieron* et al., 2007, p. 10) or also '1 More week – Yarrr' (CCP kieron* et al., 2007, p. 11). The latter post was even accompanied by an emoticon that clearly shows which role sorted* assumes: . After all, these examples of role-play are not very surprising, keeping in mind that EVE is an MMORPG – a massively multiplayer online *role-play* game.

In addition to role-play, the Privateer Alliance also benefited from deindividuating effects. The members surely *felt more anonymous* in this huge alliance where everybody could join and leave at will as opposed to other, more structured corporations or alliances. Additionally, it was often *a group committing evil*, which frees individuals from feelings of personal responsibility when killing other characters. The victims are *taunted as 'carebears'* and even *environmental anonymity* was raised by the Privateer Alliance. Their operating mode managed to make hisec – which is normally believed to be a region of space where CONCORD

Table 8.1 Examples for different situational influence factors on natural evil in EVE

Character	Comment	Source
Acceptable justifications and rationales		
Roule*	'Seriouly are you really going to take away the *freedom* that this MMO is valued for over any other.'	(CCP kieron* et al., 2007, p. 1)
murder one*	'CCP is yet again *crushing any sort of imagination and creativity* when it comes to piracy.'	(CCP kieron* et al., 2007, p. 2)
ae1*	'The great thing about Eve is that *it mimmicks the world we live in*... So tell me, is there anywhere you can think of that you're 100% safe outside Eve???... You can always join an NPC corp if you think the risk is too high to pilot your ship in space. WAR-DEC'ing an NPC can NOT be done. So I don't want to hear all the whining about how PA[4] pilots are killing all these noobs undocking from stations. They chose to join a corp that COULD be WAR-DEC'd.'	(CCP kieron* et al., 2007, p. 3)
Captain Thunk*	'*Eve is all about Risk vs Reward*. Remove all the risks through sheer volume of complaint and sit there reaping the rewards day after day.'	(CCP kieron* et al., 2007, p. 3)
SlaineMor*	'I spent 6 years playing UO[5] and that pretty much died when they introduced Trammel (carebear) facet.. ruined the game... If CCP continue to do this they will *loose the life of this game*...'	(CCP kieron* et al., 2007, p. 4)
GuntiNDDS*	'*eve really isnt that "sandbox" its marketed at*. in theory the game has alot of potential for creativity and inventions, hower any time players actually do event something original, be it g2g bookmarks or the privateer-thing, the borders get tightened. whats left in the end is a *false sense of freedom*. *"yah, you can play the game however you want, as long as you do it this way"*'	(CCP kieron* et al., 2007, p. 5)
Captain Thunk*	'The whole ethos of Eve-Online has moved dramatically from *a game that appealed to the more mature player to a kiddies paradise* where every whim is met, where CCP will do anything asked for, so long as you don't mention the Elephant in the Living Room, that being the perils of a game developer getting too close to a particular section of the community, to the extent that they could be considered, as Sir Molle put's it, *"Socially Engineered"*.'	(CCP kieron* et al., 2007, p. 9)

Nimrias*	'*Is this a Massively Multiplayer Online Game or a Massively Moderated Online Game?* If only 10% of the effort that went into "OMG PA BREAKS EVE" threads were used in-game, this whole issue of PA would have sorted itself without CCP intervention. Where is the player run anti-PA alliance? Please remember that *no one can force you to do anything in Eve*. That is what keeps this game great. Eve is (I hope) still *a thinking person's game*. PA came up with an original idea (afaik) which everyone obviously has strong opinions both for and against. But the disappointment for me is the "Dev's help us, save us, take us away" mentality that responded, mainly with anonymous alts, here in the forums.'	(CCP kieron* et al., 2007, p. 10)
Altering vocabulary and semantics		
Vastation*	'I hate the changes to war decs.... Privateers brought an *interesting concept* to the game and made life a little harder on the god damn carebears.'	(CCP kieron* et al., 2007, p. 2)
ae1*	'*Tough guys* are a fact of life, and Eve: Get use to it.'	(CCP kieron* et al., 2007, p. 3)
Crazy Tasty*	'This game needs fewer *restrictions*, not more.'	(CCP kieron* et al., 2007, p. 3)
Liang Nuren*	'It's not even a nerf in as much as a crushing obliteration to any *aspirations* anyone has of Empire PVP.'	(CCP kieron* et al., 2007, p. 4)
SlaineMor*	'I think we need to hear from more alleged "victims" of the PA alliance!! I think in the main, altough it may have cost them some isk before they surrendered that it was an *educational experince* for them and most will have found some enjoyment in it!!!!! They definately would have learned more about the machanics of Eve and whats do-able!I'm also sure that returning to their normal mission running and manufacturing etc will seem much *less exciting*!'	(CCP kieron* et al., 2007, p. 4)
Nullity*	'At least the Privateers add some much needed *content*, and *excitement* to Empire.'	(CCP kieron* et al., 2007, p. 4)
maGz*	'As usual CCP seem to think it's a good idea to change something *innovative* (albeit lame to some), and **** it up completely. Is the main goal to completely destroy any type of *fun* in the game and have us all act the same way?'	(CCP kieron* et al., 2007, p. 5)
Captain Thunk*	'Remove all *risks* and reap the *rewards* – welcome to Eve-Online.'	(CCP kieron* et al., 2007, p. 5)
Botschafter Mollari*	'I also have to say that I liked the *thrill*, somehow.'	(CCP kieron* et al., 2007, p. 6)

Source: CCP kieron* et al. (2007; all emphases by C.D.M.).

takes care of evildoers – an area immune from prosecution. All four aspects commonly associated with deindividuation (and raised levels of evildoing) are therefore met in EVE in the instance of the Privateer Alliance.

8.4 Conclusion

It was shown that, first, not only evil rules exist in EVE, but also many other types of situational influencing factors known to foster natural evil. And second, when evil rules are seemingly changed for good, not everybody is happy. The players were particularly unhappy that the developers enacted a change that was so obviously directed against the play style of one single alliance and thus the belief in the freedom to be able to do whatever one wishes in EVE (Blasterella*, 2009; Unvisibility*, 2007). This freedom is often thought to be essential for EVE (Hinrichsen, 2011) including the ability to shoot whomever you like wherever you like whenever you like. It is the freedom not only to do nice things but also to commit evil actions. The players – even if not killing all day long – at least want to be able to kill others in principle. This is a fundamental issue for them and also the reason why the Privateer Alliance got nerfed and the war mechanics still allow for Empire wars up to this day.

9

Altruism in EVE – A Simple Experiment of Online 'Dictator Games'

EVE is considered and desired to be a harsh universe by the player base – and even intentionally designed by the developers to be unforgiving; it is a seemingly anonymous environment guided by evil social institutions. Given this characterization of EVE, one big question has to be addressed: is EVE an instance of a virtual dystopia? Maybe the extent of economic evil is as important in EVE because, unlike in the real world, the positive deviations from the idea of economic man are missing: there are neither *good people* ('moral good') nor *good situations* ('natural good') in EVE and consequently no *good actions*. Based on this opinion that EVE is a 'corrupted' environment not valid for doing research on human morality, one hypothesis could simply be: there is no such thing as altruism in EVE.

A good way of testing this hypothesis is to conduct a *dictator game* online and to compare the results to dictator games conducted offline in laboratory experiments. Dictator games, in which there is a proposer *P* – endowed with a sum of money by the experimenter – who can decide how much of his endowment he wants to allocate to a recipient *R* without *R* having any means to punish *P*'s behavior, are said to measure altruism (Camerer, 2003; Fehr & Schmidt, 2006). Based on the assumption of rational and self-interested utility-maximizers as players, the game-theoretical prediction for dictator games is that the proposer allocates nothing to the recipient. It was demonstrated that this is not the case in reality across a wide range of experiments (e.g. Bohnet & Frey, 1999a; Forsythe et al, 1994; Frohlich & Oppenheimer, 2001; Hoffman et al., 1994). Fehr and Schmidt (2006, p. 8) summarize the findings: 'In experiments, proposers typically dictate allocations that assign the recipient on average between 10 and 25 percent of the surplus, with modal allocations at 50 percent and zero.'

If there is no altruism in online interactions, one should expect a result close to the game-theoretical prediction, that is that all offers concentrate at the single point of nothing being allocated to the recipient. The first null hypothesis to be tested is that in the online dictator game, the median allocation to the recipient amounts to $m = 0$ ISK (H1). *A second, weaker null hypothesis is that the level of altruism found online for the virtual reality is significantly lower compared to offline games.* H2 holds that the median offer in the online dictator game is lower than that for offline games (H_0: $m_{online} \leq m_{offline}$). In both cases one might be more legitimate in calling EVE a badly chosen example for examining the importance of economic evil since good actions are generally underrepresented, if the null hypotheses cannot be rejected.

Apart from the claim that EVE is a corrupted environment, it is also interesting to ask whether EVE is a *corrupting* environment. Given the evil social rules described in the preceding chapters and given the fact that these rules have to be learned by new players who have to adapt to the new environment in the first place, one might reason that, even if levels of altruism are high for new players, they have to drop significantly after some time. This drop would then be accountable to the natural evil predominant in EVE. Another reason for the supposed lower level of ISK paid back by more experienced players could be that the more altruistic and sympathetic players quit playing EVE altogether as they learn about the harshness of the social interactions in EVE. This is the third hypothesis to be tested (H3): *If the level of altruism found online differs for new and experienced players and if it is lower for the latter, this points into the direction that EVE is a badly chosen example for examining economic evil, since it corrupts the high moral standards of players or scares away the 'good' players altogether* (H_0: $m_{new} \geq m_{old}$).

Unfortunately, one cannot simply conduct a dictator game in EVE that would be easily comparable to the ones conducted in real-life laboratories and discussed in the literature. First, because EVE is by no means a controlled lab environment – for better and worse, as outlined above. It would be difficult to teach the players of EVE the rules of dictator games in detail and in a controlled way before starting to play this game. Second, although it would be theoretically feasible to reproduce the triangular structure of a dictator game (experimenter gives money to proposer who may allocate money to recipient) this would seriously transgress the normal boundaries of play in EVE. The character controlled by the experimenter could give money to the subject's character and ask him to transfer it to yet another character (also controlled by the experimenter without the virtual proposer knowing it) – but by no means would this be a 'natural' transaction in EVE. The players would question what is going on and probably adjust their behavior instead of responding with their normal (learned) EVE-appropriate behavior. *That is, by designing the virtual dictator game too close to the offline version, the very behavior intended to be observed would be destroyed.* The question is not what the outcome of EVE players playing a standard laboratory dictator game (be it online or offline) would be but whether EVE players exhibit any sort of altruism *while playing* EVE.

Therefore, the only possibility is to conduct an experiment measuring altruism that resembles a classic dictator game and yet stays within the normal gameplay of EVE. This means sacrificing controllability and comparability but creating a 'lifelike feel' (Camerer, 2003, p. 63) and conserving the phenomenon to be observed.

9.1 Method

The experimenter's character transfers a sum of 50m ISK to another, randomly chosen player. Only characters that were online at the time of the transaction were considered in order to raise the probability of them noticing the transaction and to allow for interaction between sender and proposer. The monetary transaction is followed up by a short message:

> Hi! Sorry, I did not want to give you 50m ISK. It was a mistake. Could you give it back to me please? Thanks! Fly safe.

That is, the recipient of the money gets the impression of accidentally having gained 50m ISK and is asked – kindly, not pitifully, without begging too much – to give it back. The sum of 50 million ISK (≈ 2.50 EUR; about the earnings for two hours of work for a decently experienced player) was chosen to be substantial yet not immoderate. NB: The virtual proposer who was endowed with the money and who is immediately asked to give it back *cannot be forced* to give the money back with in-game measures. Appealing to the game masters to transfer the money back would not be a valid measure either: their standpoint of not compensating for individual mistakes is very strict. The whole scenario resembles a person accidentally dropping a 20 EUR bill in a bustling pedestrian zone – with only the bystanders noticing it.[1]

As it was conducted, the experiment comprised two samples, each consisting of 70 randomly selected online players. However, the first sample only considered players with less than one month of playing experience (the *noob group*) whereas the second one did not consider the age of the characters in any respect and was designed to deliver a representative picture of EVE's society (the *normal group*).

The players of the noob group were selected by flying to the 12 solar systems in EVE in which new characters enter the universe for the first time. From the players online in these systems, five (twice) or six (ten times) characters were selected by randomly creating a three letter sequence (for example 'aig' or 'bdu') and then searching for all newly-created online characters whose name contained this sequence. The first character fitting these criteria was then transferred the money. Then the next character was selected using a new three letter sequence. If no character was found fitting the criteria, a new sequence was generated immediately. *The players of the normal group* were selected in an analogous way, only that no attention was paid to the age of the characters or the solar system they were currently located in.

9.2 Findings

The average age of character for the noob group was 12 days, whereas that of the normal group was slightly under two years. From the 70 players of the noob group, 36 transferred back money: 89 percent of these players gave the money back without asking for *further* explanations from the sender in addition to the one already given in the message – most of them gave the money back without even contacting the sender (64 percent).

Of the 70 players of the normal group, as many as 43 players transferred back money (98 percent without asking for further reasons, 77 percent without any communication with the sender). Figure 9.1 gives an overview of the amounts paid back.

Of those who transferred money back, the vast majority of the players paid back the exact same amount they were transferred in the first place. In the noob group, only one player paid back a fraction of the amount (48 million ISK) and one even paid back more than he received (55 million ISK), apologizing for not having noticed the accidental transfer for so long and thus paying interest (when he had the money for only one day). Within the normal group, three players transferred a fraction of the received amount (twice: 45 million ISK; once: 40 million ISK). The people paying back a fraction have in common that they gave reasons like a

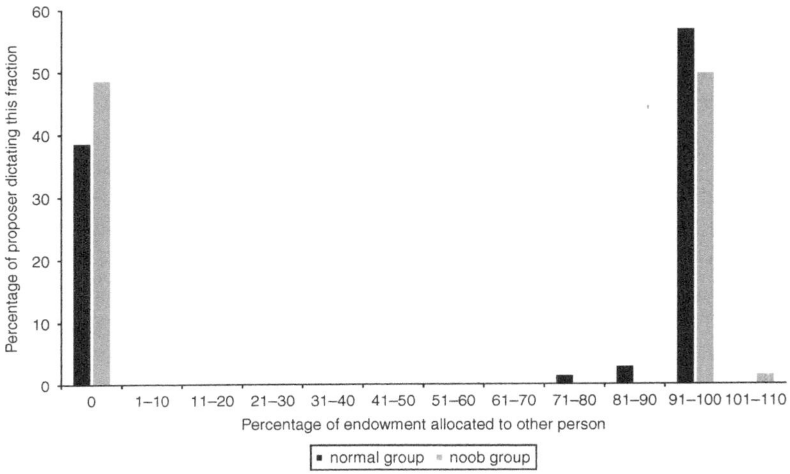

Figure 9.1 Distributions of allocations in the virtual dictator game, noob group, and normal group

'finder's fee' or 'having to pay at least a little bit for one's mistakes' in their replies to the message sent. The mean allocation for the noob group was 51.5 percent of the endowment (SD = 25.2 million ISK); that for the normal group 60.9 percent of the endowment (SD = 24.3 million ISK).

The median dictated amount for the normal group was 50 million ISK; a Wilcoxon signed-rank test for one sample with normal approximation leads to the rejection of H1 that the median allocation for the online dictator game amounts to $m = 0$ ISK ($W = 946$, $n = 43$, $z = 5.71$, $p < 0.01$ one-tailed). *There are positive levels of altruism in EVE.* The median allocation for the noob group being 49 million ISK, one cannot reject H3 (H_0: $m_{new} \geq m_{old}$) based on the sample data (Mann-Whitney $U = 2259$, $n_1 = n_2 = 70$, $p = 0.18$ one-tailed).

Whereas 87 percent of the players that did not give the money back did not get in touch with the sender, the 'honest finders' tended to reply to the message sent (30 percent) and give further reasons as to why they were returning the money. In the light of this book, it is particularly interesting that 12 of the 79 players paying back something stated something similar to 'be more careful man, most won't return it', 'not everyone in EVE would give it back', or 'looks like you found the only honest pod pilot in New Eden'. That is, they are well aware that EVE is generally a rough environment and would not expect many other players to do the same.

Eleven of the 140 proposers (eight out of the noob group, three out of the normal group) stated that they were on *trial accounts*[2] and that they tried to give back the money but found out that the game mechanics will not let them. They promised to give the back the money as soon as they actually bought the game or found another way to transfer the money. These statements, although potentially cheap talk, seem to be rather credible in this specific context. First, the error message that you cannot transfer money from trial accounts (of which two even made a screenshot to convince the sender of their efforts) only appears at the very end of the intended transaction, that is when you have already entered the person to whom you want to send the money and the amount. Second, two weeks after the experiment (that is, when the trial time was definitely over) at least three people stuck to their promise, with one buying EVE sooner than he originally intended to. Third, two of the players on trial accounts in vain tried three different methods for giving back the money (direct transfer of money, private trade of goods, via the contract system) and finally found the fourth and only, very complex way of circumventing the game mechanics (the experimenter setting up a highly overpriced, public market sell order for a cheap item, which is then filled by the proposer). Overall, seven of the 11 players on trial accounts (seemed to) follow up on their promise. To summarize: those who contacted the sender and promised to pay back seemed to really be committed to doing so.

9.3 Discussion

Based on this simple online 'dictator game', the first hypothesis, namely that there is no altruism in EVE could be rejected. Overall one cannot only state that roughly every second player gives back the whole amount transferred but also that most players acted kindly and comprehensively in the interaction that followed the transfer. The third hypothesis that experienced players give back less than new players could not be rejected. The slightly higher willingness to transfer back the money in the normal group could be explained by the fact that 50 million ISK mean a lot more to new characters than it does to experienced characters – the temptation to keep the money thus is higher for the former, although some newly created characters might also be alternative characters of experienced players. However, these small differences are not significant.

Based on this experiment, one cannot decide whether the level of altruism is significantly lower online than offline, that is one cannot reject H2. The modal offers at zero and 100 percent alone (instead of zero and 50 percent as usual) and the fact that the mean allocations for the noob and the normal group are a lot higher than in standard dictator games (above 50 percent compared to 10–25 percent) are not enough. This is due to the fact that the claim of the tested scenario resembling a dictator game is not unproblematic.

The most obvious difference is the lack of the triangular structure that may cause the proposer to feel less entitled to his endowment. It is not the same *to give money* and *to give money back*. However, Hoffman et al. (1994) were able to show that such entitlement effects influence the outcome of laboratory games. If the subjects were asked general questions before the experiment and the role of the dictator is assigned to those who answered most of the questions correctly, then the 'entitled' dictators lower their offers by half. That is, part of the higher online mean allocation could possibly be explained by referring to a very low feeling of entitlement of the online proposers.

Secondly, Bohnet and Frey (1999a) found that interaction between proposer and responder raised the offers in laboratory dictator games and that face-to-face bargaining generally raises offers. If the recipients are allowed to talk with the proposer and to say something about themselves, the mean offer can rise to 50 percent and more than 40 percent of the dictators even allocate more than 50 percent to the recipients. Even if the experiment conducted featured no face-to-face bargaining but contact only via text messages, and even if a high percentage of the proposers do not start communication with the sender, a part of the higher mean allocation found may also be due to effects of identification. One might also interpret the fact that those who paid back something contacted the sender more often than those allocating nothing in this direction.

Thirdly, one might also reason that unlike in standard dictator games – in which a 50/50 split is normally considered the 'fair' allocation (Bohnet & Frey, 1999b, p. 335) – a different fairness norm applies for the online scenario, inciting the proposer to give back the whole amount.

Besides these three aspects known from laboratory games that make plausible higher than average allocations, there are also additional influence factors due to the virtual environment in which the experiment was conducted – most of them suggesting lower than average allocations than in offline dictator games. Table 9.1 lists these factors that may affect the outcome and that could not be eliminated or controlled for.

Table 9.1 Potential influence factors for the amount paid back in the experiment

Effect	Description	Probably lowering or raising the amount transferred back
Fear of spams	People asking you for money or trying to trick you out of profit interest ('spammers') are a common thing in EVE. The transaction and the message might be regarded as a spam, for example inducing people to accidentally pay back 500m ISK or something similar. Also corporation or alliance espionage might be possible this way. Some of the players asked the sender directly whether this was a spam.	Lowering
Language	The message was sent in English. Although English is by far the most spoken language in the game, not everybody may understand what happened and what was expected of him. This is also the reason for the rather bad yet supposedly clear English of the message sent.	Lowering
Players on trial accounts	If the randomly chosen player is playing on a free 14-day trial account, he is *technically* not able to transfer the money back aside from very complex transactions. EVE does not allow for money transfers from trial accounts.	Lowering
Inattention and people being offline	Although the message sent should make the recipients notice the transaction, there is no guarantee of this. In addition, the players might go offline immediately after the transaction to return only several weeks later.	Lowering
Pity with noobs	Although the recipient can easily and quickly check for the age of character of the sender (2 years), players may assume that the accidental transfer was the mistake of a very new player and thus be more willing to pay back the money out of pity.	Raising

All the effects mentioned are limitations to the descriptive power of the experiment conducted. We are not speaking of a perfect counterpart to offline dictator games, as both setups might not measure the same kind of 'altruism'. There are various reasons why the amount paid back might be higher in EVE but also a lot of valid considerations suggesting lower sums could be given back. One should keep in mind the fact that it is not *lower* levels of online altruism that have to be accounted for but rather *what seems to be higher* levels: a mean allocation three times higher compared to standard dictator games was found. Given the initial second hypothesis that online altruism is significantly lower, this is telling in itself.

9.4 Summary

Entitlement effects and fear of spams, to name just two influence factors, may hinder the direct comparability of offline dictator games and the data from the EVE experiment; but not the general ability of the latter to account for altruistic behavior. *EVE is neither a totally corrupted nor a very corrupting environment.* Although there is a lot of economic evil going on in EVE, one cannot simply disqualify the findings by stating that EVE players are all brutes or that EVE does generally not allow for any form of altruism or kindness. Neither the environment nor the players interacting in it are evil per se, although the players themselves might be surprised as to how many players actually paid back what was given to them.

10
Conclusion

10.1 The findings

Being structured around the concepts of economically evil actions and evil social institutions, the purpose of this book was to fulfill goals on three different levels. *On the first level,* the goal was to complement the already existing body of literature on human behavior deviating from the simple and parsimonious model of economic man. However, whereas many bargaining gains in experimental economics center on altruism, fairness, and reciprocity, the focus of this book is on antisocial or evil actions, defined as intentionally harming another person materially. Evidence from the online computer game *EVE Online* shows that evil actions do in fact *exist.* Piracy (an egoistic action featuring a positive material payoff for the perpetrator), ransoming (a wanton action featuring neither loss nor gain), and suicide ganking (a malicious action featuring a negative payoff for the perpetrator) play an important role in this virtual environment. The extent of economic evil found in EVE furthermore suggests that such evil actions *matter* with respect to a society's economic performance. For example, more than 30 percent of the active population killed or fell prey to a kill in January. More than every fifth active member of the EVE society was directly involved in wars with casualties in January. A total of 3.3 percent of the population acted as pirates. More than 80,000 virtual rescue capsules were destroyed in January – each destruction being an example of a wanton action. Suicide ganks (a kamikaze tactic) bring evil even to the most secure areas of space. As such, their potential to destroy substantial parts of the capital stock of an economy make economically evil actions an important subject for further study.

Evil social institutions, defined as normative social rules that actively foster social conflict instead of promoting ways out of the struggle typical of the state of nature, *exist* and *matter* too. By relying on theories and evidence from philosophy, psychology, and New Institutional Economics, it was argued that one should also touch on natural evil (that is examine evil actions with a focus on the circumstances facilitating them) when explaining conflict and violence. Without recourse to some forms of natural evil, truly 'evil people' committing moral evil all day long are just not enough to explain the massive extent of economic evil. In EVE, there is for example an evil moral rule that guides ransoming behavior, inciting players to harm others although this negatively affects their short- and long-term interest for profit. Evil formal institutions, although publicly known for inciting violence and technically easily replaceable, allow for suicide ganking and wars in EVE.

To say that evil actions and evil rules exist and matter in *EVE Online*, in fact, is the most conservative statement that can be made regarding the significance of the findings. *On the second level*, the goals were more ambitious. Concerning evil actions, it was shown that a *'taste for harming'* seems to motivate EVE's evildoers. For piracy, ransoming, and suicide ganking alike, none of material self-interest in the short run, or in the long run, or theories of other-regarding preferences can explain the evidence at hand. This means that established economic theories on harming behavior cannot account for the evidence at hand. By looking at evil actions in EVE, one observes sudden outbursts of violence and perpetrators who care about the payoffs for their victims – provided they are negative. The presumption of *unconditional commitment to evil* can explain why players are willing to spend money to impair other peoples' income without appealing to feelings of envy or anger. Actors do evil for the sake of evil. The evidence presented, therefore, does not only add to the body of empirical data on human behavior in economics – from a new perspective and in a new environment – it also highlights a type of behavior not yet described in economics.

As for the second level goal concerning evil social institutions, having demonstrated their existence, it is even more surprising to discover their *rigidity*. Although there are no technical limitations as far as changes in the game mechanics are concerned, the evil rules governing ransoming, suicide ganking, and war (criticized from time to time and adapted a little bit since the publication of EVE) are still in place. They are publicly known for inciting social conflict and yet praised by the community of

EVE as being the factor that makes this particular game unique and valuable. There might be some people deciding to quit playing EVE because of these rules but in the eighth year of existence the population of this virtual world is still growing; this is outstanding for the computer game industry. Large parts of the population even consciously choose to live where the evil rules come to their full potential, in the more anarchic parts of the virtual universe. There is no guarantee that the evil social institutions of EVE will persist forever, but for now the outlook has to be fairly 'optimistic'. Given the general idea that institutions evolve in the direction of reducing social conflict and its destructive effects outlined in the theoretical part, it is stunning to see that evil rules, that actually foster social conflict, do so well in EVE.

Backed by all this 'negative' evidence on evil actions and evil rules in EVE, an online variant of a dictator game was conducted, in order to account for the online level of altruism and to show how more 'lifelike' experiments can be accomplished within virtual worlds. It is wrong to assume that EVE is a totally corrupted or corrupting environment, as it was shown that there is altruism in EVE and even that the level of altruism does not seem to decline with longer playing time. One cannot simply disqualify the findings by claiming that the research environment inappropriately favors economic evil per se. In fact, the mean allocations registered were about three times higher than those known from standard dictator games played offline. Nevertheless, admittedly, there is no perfect comparability between the online and offline experiments.

10.2 Gathering the findings

When considering the concrete findings just cited, it must be kept in mind that the way of gathering them also constitutes an important finding in itself for this book. *The third level goal* was to show that massively multiplayer online role-play games constitute a valid field of research for the social sciences. This book breaks new ground in examining the microeconomic data of one month of play by about 390,000 people from all over the world with all kinds of educational backgrounds interacting with each other in an economically structured environment.

It was argued that the main advantage of doing research in MMORPGs is to be able to do true fieldwork with huge sample sizes in a highly controllable environment. Furthermore, beyond mere interaction data, one can easily integrate social institutions shaping human behavior into the research. Since MMORPGs all are comparably young, all the contemporary witnesses of the society's formation are still alive and all the discussions around the establishment of the institutional framework are recorded in text-based form in Internet forums. In particular the subject of evil actions and evil rules lends itself to such research since one does not have to take into account ethical considerations of inciting people to harm each other as an experimenter – they already do it voluntarily and without external incentives.

There are obviously important limitations to drawing real-life conclusions from the behavior of players in MMORPGs. Firstly, people playing games might not always act in the same way as when they are doing 'serious business'. Although it was shown that play and economic behavior are related phenomena in many aspects, many players might, for example, be substantially less risk-averse in gaming contexts. Secondly, it does not go without saying that online behavior mirrors offline behavior and vice versa. The cited psychological evidence on the relatedness of online and offline behavior supports the idea that these are not two completely separate domains; however, the formal proof that online behavior can be used to easily predict offline actions has yet to be provided. Nevertheless, the demographic data shows that the sample is diverse: it not only consists of male teenagers who are socially isolated but of highly devoted and educated people who are not simply constructing a second identity to escape from real life. These people are playing the game for an average of 17 hours per week per character[1] and the average player has been active for more than two years. It is neither a case of dealing with 'somewhat strange people' nor of people that 'behave strangely online'. These are real people who make real decisions and execute real actions with real consequences. Even more important than that, examining actions in EVE means looking at people who act in an environment that is natural to them and that possesses its own developed social institutions, and not in an artificial laboratory situation. One does not have to ask people whether they behaved nicely or evilly (questions to which most of them will always give biased answers), one can simply *directly observe* what they are doing. This is paramount for research on human morality. Due to the huge sample size, even small but influential phenomena such as ransoming and suicide ganking can be identified. *Laboratory experiments and research in MMORPGs represent alternative ways of equal value to examine human behavior.* The latter approach – seemingly only 'descriptive' given the fact that the behavioral data is already available in a processible form – was not chosen because it appears to be easier to handle but because of its great potential. It always involves 'ethnographic' work in order to identify interactions of interest in a foreign society and the re-identification of these phenomena in huge amounts of data consisting of numbers in spreadsheets is demanding.

Many parallels could be identified between online behavior and patterns of evil behavior known from perpetrators and victims in the real world: they tend to tell different stories about what happened, there are sudden outbursts of violence, perpetrators justify their behavior with ideologies and changed semantics, and deindividuation raises the extent of evil, to name just a few. This should further the confidence in the validity of the data taken from EVE for many aspects. The world may be virtual, but the behavior and the people are real.

The practical example of this book examining evil actions and evil rules in EVE provides a good first impression about the possibilities of research in virtual worlds – and here the biggest unrecognized potential for future research is to be found. Based on an ever-growing amount of psychological literature examining the potential differences between online and offline behavior, all sorts of economic concepts and models can be put to the test in a complex, lifelike, and yet controllable environment. This book's underlying data was passively retrieved from an MMORPG and encompasses already existent day-to-day interactions of players in a given environment. The power of an extended cooperation between developers and researchers – with the former encoding scenarios the latter would like to have simulated (on a small scale without interrupting the daily business too much) – goes far beyond that.

10.3 Closing remarks

No real-life conclusions from the evidence from *EVE Online* other than the following shall be drawn: evil actions exist, matter, and are a phenomenon in their own right to be considered in economics. Furthermore, evil rules exist, matter, and might be more rigid than usually thought. One should not assume that in a state of nature everybody is interested in overturning the status quo. Some people may like it the way it is and may be able to institutionalize their preferences. In this respect, further real world research on evil actions and evil social institutions, notably in developing countries, has to be conducted. Economics should be concerned about evil.

Given the established philosophical and psychological findings, one should be more skeptical about the concepts of fairness and justice, even material self-interest, often being used too readily to explain harming behavior. Reconsidering the interpretation of such behavior is not a fundamental change in content but in emphasis – nevertheless an emphasis that might be advisable.

Notes

2 Introducing Moral Evil and Natural Evil

1. A form of natural *ill* then in Kant's terms, to be precise.
2. 'Mostly' is obviously a very ambiguous term. Although Schulte's view that this new type of natural evil 'by far exceeds the sphere of individual causation and responsibility' (1988, p. 350) might be true for certain instances of natural evil (for example the potentially harmful effects of decision-making relying on our physically built-in fast and frugal heuristics (Gigerenzer, 2008)) it may not be true for others (for example evil social rules). Social rules are something people usually take as given although they sometimes have the possibility to change them – or at least not to be part of situations that are governed contrary to their opinion about what good and fair rules are. After all, social institutions are man-made. How this affects the question of responsibility will be addressed shortly with respect to Doris' work in the following section, 'Evaluating evil'.

3 Defining Evil in an Economic Way

1. Although the APR curve seems to be pretty close to an income expansion path, that is the line that connects the optima of different indifference curves, they are not to be treated as analogs. First, because with respect to the actual shape of the APR curve, the income of *j* might decline as we move from west to east along it. Second, because the whole point about the argument is that *j*'s entire indifference curve map changes in dependence on *i*'s choice (Hirshleifer, 2001d, p. 210).
2. A typical public good game has the following structure (Camerer & Fehr, 2002; Ledyard, 1995): in a group of n players, each player is endowed with an amount of money y. Then each player has to decide how much of y to contribute to a public pot P. The individual contributions c_i $(0 < c_i < y)$ of each player i are added up and then P $(= \Sigma c_i)$ is split equally among the group. The individual payoff π_i thus equals to $y - c_i + P/n$.
3. The typical setup of an experimental ultimatum game is the following (Camerer, 2003; Fehr & Schmidt, 2006; Güth et al, 1982): two subjects, a proposer p and a responder r, are bargaining. The experimenter endows p with a certain sum of money S. Then, p decides how much of the money he wants to keep to himself, and how much of it he wants to give to r. In a second step, r decides if he wants to accept p's offer. If he accepts, then the payoff of p equals to $S - x$ (x é $[0, S]$ being the amount p gives to r) and the payoff of r equals to x. If he does not accept the offered amount x, then nobody gets anything. The responder is thus not any longer a passive recipient. He has the possibility to reject p's offer and to punish unfair behavior (by renouncing on his own payoff and, in this way, also destroying p's payoff).

4. The original design of a trust game comes from Berg, Dickhaut and McCabe (1995): two people, of which one is the *investor* (i) and one is the *trustee* (t), face each other. The investor is endowed with a sum of money S by the experimenter and then has to decide how much of S he wants to give to the trustee. The amount that the investor gives to the trustee (termed y, $y \in [0, S]$) is then tripled by the experimenter. In a second stage, the trustee decides how much of $3y$ he wants to give back to the investor. The trustee's payoff (π_t) equals to $3y - x$ ($x \in [0, 3y]$ being the amount that the trustee gives back to the investor). The investor's payoff (π_i) is $S - y + x$. In this setup, y measures trust and the amount returned, x, measures trustworthiness or reciprocity.
5. It appears that an 'evil' rule, then, is the exact opposite to what Mantzavinos defines as a moral rule. It will be argued below that one should rather consider 'evil' rules to be one specific instance of moral rules – the latter being defined mainly by the characteristics of informality and first-party enforcement.

4 Massively Multiplayer Online Role-Play Games as a Field of Research

1. When the developers or players of EVE post their opinion in the official EVE Forums, they use their in-game character name to sign it. These are the fictitious names of real people. Since there is no way of finding out the real name, this book will use the character names instead for referential purposes. Although an unsatisfactory solution overall, this facilitates the finding and verification of quotations. To distinguish real names from fictitious character names, each character name will end with an '*'.

   The same system will hold for developers from CCP Games, too. They generally post in forums using their developer names that always have a 'CCP' put in front of them (for example 'CCP Explorer*' or 'CCP Xhagen*'). This enables us to distinguish between player quotes and developer quotes in forums.
2. For alternative methodological approaches to game studies, compare Konzack (2002) and Aarseth (2003).
3. It is important to insert the word 'theoretically' in this sentence. The data examined here does not contain everything the players did, and even *CCP Games* do not possess this kind of data. It is in fact the case that not everything that happens on the EVE server is logged. This is mainly due to performance reasons (CSM & CCP Games, 2011, p. 6). The game would be much slower, if the computers had to write down everything the players do.
4. A *corporation* is a formal association of players who regularly play together.
5. An *alliance* is a formal association of corporations.
6. It is important to note, however, that compliance with the rules set by the developers is not perfect in all cases either, even if only in-game proceedings are considered. This has practical reasons. For example, it is forbidden to spam the in-game public chat channels. It would be possible to prevent this – for example by eliminating the public chat channels altogether – but the overall good of having such a chat channel in the game seems to be higher than the costs of having to deal with spammers. Also within the game, the developers are therefore sometimes forced to enact 'only' laws where natural laws would be theoretically possible.

7. More details on the emergence and functioning of this unique organization are presented by Óskarsson (2010).
8. The form of production in EVE that produces the least refined products.

5 *EVE Online*

1. For comparison, in the market-leading game 'World of Warcraft', all you lose when you get killed is some time, namely the time it takes to walk your 'ghost' from the nearest 'cemetery' back to where you have been killed. You keep all your possessions and skills.
2. One EVE-account can hold up to three characters. The number of characters per account remains fairly constant at around two over the years (Guðmundsson, 2007, p. 4, 2010f, p. 8).
3. Remark that we speak of the *'character'* if we are referring to the virtual representations of the *players*, that is the real world people.
4. ISK is also the international currency code for the Icelandic Crown – CCP Games being an Icelandic corporation. Wherever 'ISK' appears in this book, it always refers to the in-game currency of EVE rather than to the Icelandic Crown.
5. The main problems are that players who do RMT typically use macros (specialized little computer-programs) in order to control their characters. These macros put significant workload on the game server – which worsens the game performance for everybody. Also, RM-traders are not interested in the game itself but use it as a pure money-making tool. This runs counter to the spirit of the game and the gameplay experience for the community. Third, RMT often extends to credit card frauds, account hacking and other illegal behavior. (Guðmundsson, 2009a, p. 34).

   For a thorough description of CCP Games' effort against RMT, see the Quarterly Economic Newsletter of the 3rd quarter 2009, pp. 24–34 (Guðmundsson, 2009a).
6. Guðmundsson's definition of M1 being 'currency readily available for transactions' (2007, p. 7).
7. 'PvP' means player-versus-player combat, and thus the military aspect of EVE.
8. That is to say that not all items in EVE are traded via the public market system. Although most of them are, still, there are also the less formal *contract system* and individual *player-to-player transactions*. And this is also to say that there is no 'global' market across all 66 regions of EVE: whenever you look at the market window in-game, you will be perfectly informed about the prices in your region but do not know anything about the neighboring regions, which might be just one star gate away. There are, however, many ways of overcoming this lack of information, for example by using a different character in another region to check prices or by turning to out-of-the-game websites that list prices in different regions.
9. Half an hour per day, the EVE server is down and nobody is able to play. This is due to technical reasons; the time is needed by the developers mainly to 'clean up' the unnecessary data from the virtual universe.
10. There is also the possibility of bringing your security standing back up after you committed a crime. This generally means a lot of time and effort, however.

11. Including the newly introduced 'wormhole space'.
12. The argument that EVE might just be 'too young' (publication in 2003) for complex institutions like States to emerge and that the predictions of the models need some time to become operative should be weighed against the fact that – for a computer game – being seven years old means being as old as Methuselah.
13. In total, 521,592 humanly controlled characters were killed but this number is a combination of *NPC-kills* and *player kills*. The technical definition of an *NPC-kill* in contrast to a *player kill* is that, whereas the former involves *only NPCs as attackers*, the latter involves *at least one humanly controlled character acting as an aggressor.* This book is only interested in the latter form of kills.

    The number of 327,911 player kills encompasses *CONCORD-kills*. CONCORD-kills are kills by the virtual, computer-controlled police. These kills are included since in order to be killed by CONCORD, a player has to transgress well-known laws in hisec. Almost nobody gets killed by CONCORD for *accidentally* violating one of the virtual laws (for example not to attack innocent fellow players in hisec). However, many players let themselves be *intentionally* killed by CONCORD when they participate in a 'suicide gank'. This practice will be explained below (cf. Chapter 7). Getting killed by CONCORD is thus not due to inept play but rather to intentional transgression of the law.
14. The technical definition of a *war-kill* is that at least one of the attackers' corporations or alliances is at war with either the victim's corporation or alliance at the time of the kill.
15. The technical definition of a *factional warfare-kill* is that either the victim or at least one of the attackers is enrolled in a factional militia at the time of the kill, or that the kill happened in one of the officially contested solar systems, that is the typical fighting zones, at the frontiers between the four factions. This is an all-embracing definition for FW-kills that tends to consider more kills as FW-kills than is probably appropriate. However, taking into account the validity of the findings in this book, it is crucial not to underestimate the importance of FW.
16. The technical definition of a *CONCORD-kill* is that the character that fired the final shot that lead to the eventual destruction of the victim's ship was conducted by a police-NPC. This is a comparably narrow definition, since it does not consider kills in which CONCORD participated but did not lay the final blow as CONCORD-kills. The reasons for this narrow definition are analogous to the reasons for the broad definition of FW-kills (see preceding note).
17. The technical definition of an *intra-corporation kill* is that the victim character and the character that fired the final shot that lead to the eventual destruction of the victim's ship are in the same corporation at the time of the kill.
18. As for the technical definition of *erratic kills*: every *player kill* that cannot be attributed to either of the four typical categories of kills mentioned above (war, factional warfare, CONCORD-kill, intra-corporation kill) qualifies as an erratic kill.
19. The numbers do not add up to 327,911 kills (but to 332,331), since some kills may fall in more than one category and, notably, since many kills in factional warfare are actually effected by NPCs (namely the computer-controlled navies of the four empires).

6 Piracy

1. Nullsec kills will not be considered, since nullsec is controlled by the big player alliances. Many kills in these regions are kills made to protect the claimed territory, rather than piracy kills, although the involved parties may be not formally at war with each other.
2. The average value of salvage probably lies under 1 percent of the destroyed ship's worth and only few pirates actually salvage their victims' ships – because of the low profit, the considerable time investment, and more effective killing if the attacker's ship has not to be equipped with salvaging equipment, too (Precisionist* & RetardedNeuron*, 2011).
3. Doing so, items that were dropped by the victims but did not have any market value in January were ignored. Not having a market value means that these items were not traded publicly that month. These are either very rare items (and thus presumably very valuable ones), or items that only have a symbolic value in EVE (like for example the virtual insignias of NPC officers that are required by some NPC agents in certain missions as a sign of having effectively killed the required number of ships). The items with only symbolic value form the large majority of the neglected items, since the very rare and valuable items (like for example blueprints needed for space ship construction) are very rarely moved.

   Ignoring the worth of the items that do not possess any market value obviously underestimates the total value of the items considered; in this case it means underestimating the benefits of piracy. Since there is no easy and appropriate measure for these items, though, *this book will always only consider items that possessed a market value in January* in calculating the economic impact of the virtual killings.
4. All amounts given in EUR in the following are rounded amounts. Their purpose is to give a general idea of the amounts in real-world currency, not precise numbers.
5. This value is reached by dividing the online time since character creation by the total real time passed since character creation. Since the online time is only given in different classes rather than as precise number (see above), class means were used to calculate this value.
6. Measured by the amount of ISK in the wallet of each character at the end of January.
7. This might be an additional reason as to why there are so many acts of piracy conducted although no loot can be robbed eventually. The random process of loot destruction and persistence involves total uncertainty for the attackers. Still, it is very well possible to identify worthwhile targets of attack beforehand: every player in EVE can tell a shuttle from a transport ship and cheap from expensive ships. Furthermore, the ships of the pirates can be equipped with cargo scanners, able to detect what the cargo hold of the victim contains before actually attacking it.
8. As outlined above, one month in the EVE economy roughly translates into one year of real world economies.
9. It is very likely that these are so called *alt-chars*, that is secondary characters of players that are not used as often. Alt-char(acter)s are mainly used for economic reasons, more precisely to procure information about the prices of certain items in different regions. Remember that the EVE market is a regional

market, in which you can only directly see the prices for all items *in a specific region* but have no idea of the prices in the other 65 regions without recurring to additional information sources – like for example alt-chars. The single most important use of alt-chars is to stay in a station in a different region than the main character and make price queries for certain items from time to time. Switching between characters to check prices in the neighboring region (and thus being able to make a profitable interregional trade) is often the fastest and most accurate way of procuring the required information.

10. With respect to their share of total income and expenses.
11. Since the total login minutes are only given in different categories in *characters.csv* (see above), class means have been used to calculate this ratio.
12. Again, alt-chars are mainly used for quick price checks (takes only about 10 seconds per item) and thus have very low online times.
13. *PvP* means 'player versus player'. In this context, 'PvPers' simply are *pirates*, and 'PvP' translates to *piracy*.
14. Sometimes perpetrators claim that they shoot pods not because they personally benefit from it but because they know that they can harm the opposite party in a war this way (Elesentra* et al, 2009); the opposite faction incurs the costs of having to repurchase brain implants. This argumentation does not apply here, however, since all kills considered are those of non-warring parties. Therefore, one should picture victim and pirate as completely indifferent strangers aside from pure material self-interest.
15. Even if the mean ransom per pirate amounted to remarkable 24.2 million ISK (1.20 EUR) in January (median ransom: 6 million ISK), this seems appropriate given the fact that one decision to honor a ransom of one pirate probably does not change much the course of a universe of almost 800,000 characters and with more than 50,000 piracy kills per month. Furthermore, the money-making abilities of a character greatly increase over its lifetime, probably leading to high discount rates.
16. Total number of piracy kills with not more than five attackers: 49,187 (= 87 percent of all pirate kills). This limitation was chosen since encounters with more than five pirates further complicate the ransoming situation. It is difficult to coordinate so many players in such a tight situation, which means that these instances of ransoming are negligible.
17. Here and in the following, all tables presenting player citations stemming from Internet forums reproduce the posts literally, including potential orthographic or grammatical mistakes.
18. A solar system in lowsec
19. 'Tears', 'forum tears', or 'carebear tears' is what is 'created' when players complain in the official forums that EVE is too harsh. That is, they write a new forum entry complaining about what has happened to them – which is called 'whining'. Since they 'whine', there has to be somebody who collects the tears created in this process. These usually are the pirates who are always happy to hear somebody complaining about how cruel they are to others.
20. A technical device making it easier to prevent the pod from escaping (only functional in nullsec systems).
21. Noob = newb = newbie = n00b. Gamer slang for new player.

7 Suicide Ganks

1. 'Innocent' in this context means: you are not formally at war with the other character and he has not attacked and killed you in exactly the same fashion you attack him now in the last 30 days. Additionally, he is no 'outlaw' with a security status of -5.0 or below and thus free to be attacked by anybody.
2. If in the time span of two minutes before and one minute after the CONCORD kills additional characters get killed in the same system but by NPCs different from CONCORD (for example the faction navies), then these kills will be regarded as a part of the (attempted) suicide gank. This is because: first, it is not only CONCORD (that is the police) but also other NPCs around (the 'army') which prosecute crimes in EVE; second, because it is unlikely that NPC kills that are completely unrelated to the suicide gank take place at the same time in the same system; and third, because for successful suicide ganks it can be shown that the characters that get killed for example by the faction navies also participated in the initial player kill that started the whole process of the suicide gank.
3. Obviously, it is impossible to tell how many victims were attacked in the case the SG failed. If we assume only one victim per failed SG, we reach the total number of 647 attacked victims.
4. Gankers can insure their ships before committing an SG. Insurance in EVE is paid out even when the ship was willfully destroyed – which is obviously the case.
5. Setting up a suicide gank certainly takes at least one hour – therefore the comparisons of hourly wages is appropriate.
6. Worth of gankers' and victims' ships plus cargo destroyed during explosion.
7. To be sure, it is a different thing to allow for evil to happen or to actively incite players to commit evil. There is no game mechanic in place that forces players to attack other players in hisec even though that leads to individual losses. However, it is widely accepted that the omission to take action is also an action. In this sense, a rule that *is publicly known* for fostering evil may very well be called an *evil* rule.
8. PK = player killer, a person that regularly attacks other humanly-controlled characters.
9. POTW = picture of the week, a very good screenshot of an EVE space ship for example.
10. A reasonably powerful class of space ships.
11. Eliminating secondary and tertiary characters, that is characters that were created on an already existing account, the possibility still exists that seemingly new characters are controlled by experienced players who bought a secondary or even tertiary account, though.
12. Total login minutes divided by minutes since character creation.
13. This restriction was added in order to prevent some huge outliers with respect to total gains from blurring the picture. Most likely these characters were subsidized by more experienced characters of the same player.
14. For example *successful* multi-person SGs involved 394 victims and 1218 perpetrators. If we add additional 0.9249 *different* victims per *failed* SG (92.49 percent of the actual victim characters only get killed once), then

their number amounts to 204 (number of failed SGs (211) times 0.9249 = 204). Analogous calculations are used for the one-person SGs.
15. All numbers are combined numbers for multi-person and one-person SGs.

8 Wars – Other Forms of Natural Evil in EVE

1. NPC corporations, that is corporations not formally run by a human player are an exception to this rule. They cannot start wars against other corps or alliances, since the CEO (who is computer controlled) would have to agree to it. On the other hand, they cannot be the target of a war declaration by other corps either.
2. For the rest of this section, we will only be looking at war kills that happened in 'Empire space', that is hisec and lowsec combined, since only in this area can wars be said to be a tool to commit evil otherwise impossible or associated with much higher costs.
3. A 'nerf' is gamer slang for a change in the game mechanics that makes some tactic or tool *less powerful*. If for example the rules of chess were changed so as to limit the queen in its movement (for example only allowing it to move similarly to a rook), then the chess players could speak of *the queen nerf*. Nerfs are usually explained by the developers to be necessary for balancing reasons, that is to ensure that no single tactic becomes too dominant or even undefeatable in a game, thus making it boring to play.
4. Privateer Alliance
5. Ultima Online, a different MMORPG

9 Altruism in EVE – A Simple Experiment of Online 'Dictator Games'

1. In EVE, the message from the sender of the money to the recipient is, of course, a proof that the sender actually noticed his mistake, very unlike the pedestrian zone scenario. However, the key function of the EVE message is not to signal the *conscious* aspect of the action but the *erroneous* aspect. Whereas in real life nobody would doubt that you drop a 20 EUR bill *unwillingly*, in EVE this could be regarded as a random act of kindness: it happens that experienced players give away money to new players *for no reason* (Guðmundsson, 2010a). Furthermore, the additional message assures that the recipient of the money actually notices that he accidentally gained 50m ISK: experienced and wealthy players may not keep track of their wallet balance at all times.
2. Trial accounts for *EVE Online* are available for free and last for 14 days. Not everything you can do in EVE on a paying account is also possible on trial accounts. For example, you cannot directly transfer money to another player, you cannot trade privately with other players, and you cannot use the contract system.

10 Conclusion

1. Keep in mind that the average EVE player has *two* characters – that are sometimes logged in simultaneously, though.

Glossary of EVE Terms

Agent An agent is a special type of NPC character in EVE that provides the players with jobs. In every space station in EVE you can start a text-based conversation with an agent and he will give you a *mission*. A mission can be, for example, to bring item X from station A to station B (a *courier mission*), or to destroy particular NPC characters in system Y (a *combat mission*). After you have fulfilled the task, you can return to him and he will reward you with a sum of money or some items.

Alliance An alliance is a formal association of corporations in EVE, and thus the second level of organization (the first level being corporations). Alliances are the most important political actors in nullsec, in which CONCORD does not provide any protection from hostile players. The biggest alliances have thousands of member players.

CONCORD CONCORD ('Consolidated Cooperation and Relations Command') is the virtual, computer-controlled police force of EVE. In hisec, many crimes are harshly retaliated against by CONCORD – usually by destroying the ship of the aggressor. Every crime considered *punishable* by CONCORD interference will *always* be sanctioned: CONCORD always arrives, and always destroys the rule's transgressor. CONCORD-penalized crimes are, notably, to attack innocent players in hisec, to attack the property of the four empires (for example star gates), or to help outlaws (for example by repairing their ship). Every crime committed in Empire space will also lower the security status of the character.

Contract system The contract system is an alternative way to exchange in-game items in EVE. Unlike the market system, very rare or valuable items are normally traded via contracts, since you have the possibility to sell an item directly to another player without making the trade public.

Corporation A corporation ('corp' for short) is a formal association of players in EVE, and thus the first level of organization. Every player is always a member of a corporation at any time in EVE – be it a player-run corporation or an NPC corporation led by a computer-controlled character. Members of the same corporation are players that play together on a regular basis, that have a common purpose, and that might know each other in real life, too. Often, corporations are dedicated to one specific task in EVE, for example to mine asteroids (a *mining corp*), to attack other players (a *pirate corp*), or to offer protection for peaceful corps (a *mercenary corp*). Typically, players in the same corp communicate with each other using voice chat, which greatly facilitates real-time coordination of actions.

CSM The Council of Stellar Management (CSM) is a democratically-elected group of players that represents the views of the player base to CCP Games. Every EVE character has one vote to support his favorite CSM-candidate every six months. Normally, very experienced players that are usually associated to one of the big alliances in EVE get elected. However, there are also frequently candidates that claim to represent the views of the non-alliance players in their election campaign.

Dev blog Dev blogs (developer blogs) are a privileged way for the developers to interact with the community. In around 10 dev blogs per month, the developers publicly announce new developments or changes to the rules of the game. Although not everything said in dev blogs represents the official opinion of CCP Games, the content of dev blogs is taken very seriously by the player base.

Empire There are four main empires (also: factions) in EVE: the *Caldari State*, the *Gallente Federation*, the *Amarr Empire*, and the *Minmatar Republic*. Every character formally belongs to one empire but this membership does not have any relevant consequences for gameplay. Together, the four empires control the Empire space (comprising hisec and lowsec) in which no player-run alliance can claim territory. The virtual police force of CONCORD is maintained by all four empires and serves to guarantee law and order in Empire space.

Game master Game masters are employees of CCP Games whose job it is to settle conflicts between players in-game. They have the power to close down the accounts of players who violate the End User License Agreement or the Terms of Service of the game, for example by participating in real money trading. Unlike CONCORD, the response of the game masters to alleged crimes is not automated but every player can at any time contact a game master to report illegitimate behavior or to ask for help.

Hisec High security space (hisec) is the safest area of EVE. The computer-controlled police force of CONCORD directly retaliates against crimes committed in hisec only. All of the most important trade hubs in EVE lie in hisec space and many business-centered corporations have their headquarters here. Additionally, new players start to play the game in the relative safety of hisec.

Implant An implant is an in-game item. Plugged into the brain of a character, it raises this character's attributes, allowing, for example, for faster learning or for being a more efficient fighter by affecting the damage dealt by this character's weapons. Implants are comparably costly items that are tied to a specific character: after plugging them in once, they cannot be removed without being destroyed. Implants are also destroyed upon the death of the character – not when his ship is destroyed but if his pod (that is the rescue capsule the character finds himself in after ship destruction) gets destroyed as well.

Killboard Those players interested in PvP-combat typically announce their successes on killboards. The killboards list how many ships a character has destroyed, how much wealth he acquired by doing so, and so on; that is, a summary of how successful a player is in killing and robbing others.

Loot Loot is the in-game term for what can be retrieved from the wreck of another player's ship. The loot only designates what is left over after the explosion from the belongings the victim had in his cargo hold and the equipment that was fitted to his ship. In a second step, the wreck itself can also be *salvaged,* which generates some raw materials. Loot and salvage taken together constitute the gains of the kill for the attacker.

Lowsec Lowsecurityspace(lowsec)isanareaofmedium-security in EVE. Whereas CONCORD does not intervene for crimes committed here, the negative effect of a drop in individual security status is still applied for crimes that take place in lowsec. Lowsec is typically considered as the place where the pirates live.

Mission running This is one way to earn money in EVE, namely by talking to agents and asking for a job, rewarded with money and in-game items. Since mission running only involves fighting against computer-generated characters, it is the most important form for PvE activities in EVE.

Navy Besides CONCORD, the four empires have another group of computer-controlled characters that enforce their laws. Each faction has its own navy with the main function of patrolling the frontiers and securing the most important space stations. One notable task of the navies is to prevent players with a security status that is too low from entering Empire space by patrolling at the star gates. The navies, however, are not as powerful as CONCORD, which means that sometimes even outlaws can slip into hisec.

NPC A non-player character (NPC) is a character in EVE whose actions are controlled by the game-software itself in an automated way and not by a human player. Notable NPCs are agents, NPC pirates that regularly have to be killed when running a mission, and CONCORD.

NPC corporation An NPC corporation is a corporation led by an NPC. Every new player starts out as the member of such an NPC corporation when she plays EVE for the first time. NPC corporations are typically bigger than player-run corporations but also provide much less trust among the members who are often complete strangers to one another. One reason why many players stay in NPC corporations is that no war can be declared on NPC corporations; there is no more secure way of playing EVE than being the member of an NPC corporation and flying in hisec.

Noob A noob (also: newbie, newb, n00b, and so on) is a new player. In general, a noob is someone incapable of playing the game properly or of understanding what EVE is about. Calling somebody a noob may not necessarily refer to how long this character has actually been playing EVE. 'You're a noob!' is probably the most common badmouthing in EVE.

Nullsec Null security space (nullsec) is the most unsafe area in EVE and the one that comes closest to being a virtual representation of the natural state. There are no laws in nullsec except for alliance-internal rules. You can attack whomever you like in nullsec without having to fear any repercussions from CONCORD or any lowering of your security status. The only thing that separates nullsec from a perfect anarchy is that market exchange still works perfectly; it is not very vibrant, though.

Outlaw An outlaw is a player with a personal security status of -5.0 or lower. Anybody can attack an outlaw anywhere and anytime in EVE without having to fear a CONCORD intervention or a lowering of his security status.

Pirate Pirate is the rather general term for players that mostly earn their money by killing and robbing other players. It may also refer to players with an overall aggressive playing style.

Pod The pod is the rescue capsule a character finds herself in after the destruction of the ship she flew. When flying in a pod, you have no possibility of defending yourself (other than flying away as quickly as possible), let alone attacking other players. If in addition to the ship the player's pod is also destroyed, she will find herself reborn in a *clone* that was bought beforehand and waits to be activated in a pre-defined space station. If somebody gets 'pod-killed', this potentially has very severe consequences. Not only are valuable brain implants destroyed by having to use a clone to go on playing, but some skill points can also be lost.

PvE Player versus environment (PvE) refers to actions in which a humanly-controlled character plays against computer-controlled characters, notably when killing NPC pirates when running a mission. The player competes with the artificial intelligence of the software.

PvP Player versus player (PvP) refers to actions in which two or more humanly-controlled characters compete directly, for example by attacking each other with their space ships. In comparison to PvE, you match your abilities to play the game with other real human beings.

Real money trading Real money trading refers to exchanging in-game currency (ISK) for real world currency (for example USD). Real money trading is illegal yet happens to a significant extent. Some players choose to play EVE in order to make money and not for the sake of competing with other players.

Security rating Each solar system in EVE has an assigned security rating between 0.0 and 1.0. The solar systems with ratings between 1.0 and 0.5 form the area known as hisec. The solar systems with a rating between 0.4 and 0.1 form lowsec. And the systems with a security rating of 0.0 constitute nullsec space in EVE. The security rating of the solar system is not to be confused with the security status of an individual character.

Security status Each character has an individual security status between -10.0 and 10.0 that is raised whenever he does missions for NPC agents or kills NPC pirates, and gets lowered when he violates the laws of the virtual universe (for example by attacking an innocent player in hisec). The security status reduction for committed crimes varies for example with respect to the type of the crime, the security status of the victim, and the area where it was committed. If the security status of a player becomes too low, he may no longer be able to enter solar systems with a high security rating, thus limiting his travel opportunities. Players with a security status of -5.0 or lower are considered *outlaws*.

Skill A skill refers to what a character is able to do in EVE. For nearly every activity there is in EVE, there is also a skill that makes practicing this activity more efficient, for example by lowering the time it takes to mine an asteroid or by raising the amount of damage caused by your weapons. Skills are in-game items that can be bought on the market but that have to be trained in order to come into effect. Skill training takes place in real time. Once you have trained a skill, your character will possess that skill forever (unless pod-killed without having an up-to-date clone). The number of skill points a character has (every skill gives your character skill points when trained) is a very good approximation for the character age and power. The skill system overall fosters the division of labor: somebody very good at fighting is not usually very good at mining, unless he has already had the time to extensively train skills in both areas. To my knowledge, there is no character in EVE that has trained all the skills that exist to the maximum level.

War War is an affair of corporations and alliances in EVE, rather than of states. Every corporation and every alliance in EVE can declare war on any other corporation or alliance at any time (with the notable exception of NPC corporations, which never declare war but cannot have war declared on them either). The main effect of being at war with another corporation or alliance is that the respective members are now formally allowed to attack the members of the opposing party everywhere and every time in EVE. Even if two warring characters meet in hisec, CONCORD will not interfere with their battle. In order to declare war, the CEO of a corporation (or the executor corporation of an alliance) has to propose a vote to the members. The majority of the shareholders of the corporation (or the alliance, respectively) must vote in favor of going to war. The CEO can then start the war by paying a war fee to CONCORD. Additional war costs will be charged as the war continues. If a corporation is 'wardecced' ('to wardec' is EVE-slang for declaring war on a corporation), all members will be informed immediately and the war will only come into effect 24 hours after this notice.

Bibliography

The raw, digital data on EVE provided by CCP Games and the interviews conducted with developers are subject to a nondisclosure agreement between the author and CCP Games. The extent and structure of the data are outlined in Section 4.3.1.

Aarseth, E. (2003). Playing Research: Methodological Approaches to Game Analysis. Presented at the DAC Conference, Melbourne.

Aas, B. G., Meyerbrö ker, K., & Emmelkamp, P. M. G. (2010). Who Am i – And If So, Where? a Study on Personality in Virtual Realities. *Journal of Virtual Worlds Research, 2*(5). Retrieved from https://journals.tdl.org/jvwr/article/view/776/708

Agamben, G. (1998/2003). *Was von Auschwitz bleibt. Das Archiv und der Zeuge.* Frankfurt am Main: Suhrkamp.

Allison, S. E., von Wahlde, L., Shockley, T., & Gabbard, G. O. (2006). The Development of the Self in the Era of the Internet and Role-Playing Fantasy Games. *American Journal of Psychiatry, 163*(3), 381–385.

Alucard Strat*. (2011, March 15). EstFleet (Khanid HiSec / LowSec). *Alliance and Corporation Recruitment Center.* Retrieved June 21, 2011, from http://www.eveonline.com/ingameboard.asp?a=topic&threadID=1482502

Anderson, C. A., & Carnagey, N. L. (2005). Violent Evil and the General Aggression Model. In A. G. Miller (Ed.), *The Social Psychology of Good and Evil* (pp. 168–192). New York: The Guilford Press.

Andreoni, J. (1988). Why Free Ride? Strategies and Learning in Public Goods Experiments. *Journal of Public Economics, 37,* 291–304.

Andreoni, J., & Miller, J. (1993). Rational Cooperation in the Finitely Repeated Prisoners' Dilemma: Experimental Evidence. *Economic Journal, 103,* 570–585.

Andreoni, J., & Miller, J. (2002). Giving According to garp: An Experimental Test of the Rationality of Altruism. *Econometrica, 70,* 737–753.

Anscombe, E. (1957/2000). *Intention.* Cambridge, MA: Harvard University Press.

Aquinas, T. (n.d.). *Scriptum super Sententiis.* Retrieved from http://www.corpusthomisticum.org/iopera.html

are34*. (2011, March 25). Tempest Legion, highsec Wardecs/Lowsec PewPew. *Alliance and Corporation Recruitment Center.* Retrieved June 21, 2011, from http://www.eveonline.com/ingameboard.asp?a=topic&threadID=1487054

Arendt, H. (1951/1973). *The Origins of Totalitarianism.* New York: Harcourt Brace.

Arendt, H. (1989). *Nach Auschwitz – Essays & Kommentare 1.* (E. Geisel & Bittermann, Eds). Berlin: Edition Tiamat.

Arendt, H. (1965/2007a). *Über das Böse: Eine Vorlesung zu Fragen der Ethik* (2nd edn). München: Piper.

Arendt, H. (1963/2007b). *Eichmann in Jerusalem* (2nd edn). München: Piper.

Aronson, E., Wilson, T., & Akert, R. M. (2008). *Sozialpsychologie* (6th edn). München: Pearson Education.

Atima* et al. (March 28, 2011). Hourly Wages for Mining, Mission Running and Station Trading. Retrieved March 28, 2011, from http://www.eveonline.com/ingameboard.asp?a=topic&threadID=1487196&page=1

Atlas, S. A. (2008). Inductive Metanomics: Economic Experiments in Virtual Worlds. *Journal of Virtual Worlds Research, 1*(1), 1–15.

Aupers, S. (2007). a Second Job? the Emergence of Institutions in Online Computer Games. Presented at the 2007 Annual Meeting: American Sociological Association.

Azael Lightshade*. (2011, May 14). [V i L e] – Recruiting Pirates and Scum! *Alliance and Corporation Recruitment Center.* Retrieved June 21, 2011, from http://www.eveonline.com/ingameboard.asp?a=topic&threadID=1510630

Azhpol* et al. (2011, May 18). Ransoming a Pod. *Crime and Punishment.* Retrieved June 21, 2011, from http://www.eveonline.com/ingameboard.asp?a=topic&threadID=1512917

Bailenson, J., & Yee, N. (2005). Digital Chameleons: Automatic Assimilation of Nonverbal Gestures in Immersive Virtual Environments. *Psychological Science, 16*, 814–819.

Balicer, R. (2005). Modeling Infectious Diseases Dissemination Through Online Role-Playing Games. *Epidemiology, 18*(2), 260–261.

Bandura, A., & Reich, W. (1990). Mechanisms of Moral Disengagement. In W. Reich (Ed.), *Origins of Terrorism: Psychologies, Ideologies, Theologies, States of Mind* (pp. 161–191). New York: Cambridge University Press.

Bandura, A., Underwood, B., & Fromson, M. E. (1975). Disinhibition of Aggression through Diffusion of Responsibility and Dehumanization of Victims. *Journal of Personality and Social Psychology, 9*, 253–269.

Banks, J., Plott, C., & Porter, D. (1988). An Experimental Analysis of Unanimity in Public Goods Provision Mechanisms. *Review of Economic Studies, 55*(182), 301–322.

Bargh, J. A., McKenna, K. Y. A., & Fitzsimons, G. M. (2002). Can You See the Real Me? Activation and Expression of the 'True Self' on the Internet. *Journal of Social Issues, 58*(1), 33–48.

Bartle, R. (1996). Hearts, Clubs, Diamonds, Spades: Players Who Suit Muds. *Journal of Online Environments, 1*(1), Retrieved from http://www.mud.co.uk/richard/hcds.htm

Bartle, R. (2004). *Designing Virtual Worlds.* Berkeley: New Riders Publishers.

BattleClinic. (2011, May 6). Killboards – EVE Online – BattleClinic. *BattleClinic.* Retrieved May 6, 2011, from http://eve.battleclinic.com/killboard/index.php

Baumeister, R. F. (1997). *Evil: Inside Human Violence and Cruelty.* New York: Freeman.

Baumeister, R. F., & Vohs, K. D. (2005). Four Roots of Evil. In A. G. Miller (Ed.), *The Social Psychology of Good and Evil* (pp. 85–101). New York: The Guilford Press.

Becker, G. S. (1962). Irrational Behavior and Economic Theory. *Journal of Political Economy, 70*(1), 1–13.

Becker, G. S. (1968). Crime and Punishment: An Economic Approach. *Journal of Political Economy, 76*(2), 169–217.

Becker, G. S. (1973). A Theory of Marriage: Part I. *Journal of Political Economy, 81*(4), 813–846.

Becker, G. S. (1976). *The Economic Approach to Human Behavior.* Chicago: University of Chicago Press.

Berg, J., Dickhaut, J., & McCabe, K. (1995). Trust, Reciprocity and Social History. *Games and Economic Behavior, 10*, 122–142.
Berkowitz, L. (1993). *Aggression: Its Causes, Consequences, and Control*. New York: McGraw-Hill.
Berkowitz, L. (1999). Evil Is More Than Banal: Situationism and the Concept of Evil. *Personality and Social Psychology Review, 3*, 246–253.
Bessi è re, K., Seay, A. F., & Kiesler, S. (2007). The Ideal Elf: Identity Exploration in World of Warcraft. *CyberPsychology & Behavior, 10*, 530–535.
Blasterella*. (2009, September 19). Question on War Dec Limit. *Warfare & Tactics*. Retrieved June 28, 2011, from http://www.eveonline.com/ingameboard.asp?a=topic&threadID=1180667
Bodholdt, R. H., Richards, H. R., & Gacono, C. B. (2000). Assessing Psychopathy in Adults: The Psychopathy Checklist-Revised and Screening Version. In C. B. Gacono (Ed.), *The Clinical and Forensic Assessment of Psychopathy: a Practitioner's Guide* (pp. 55–86). Mahwah: Erlbaum.
Bohnet, I., & Frey, B. (1999a). The Sound of Silence in Prisoner's Dilemma and Dictator Games. *Journal of Economic Behavior and Organization, 38*, 43–57.
Bohnet, I., & Frey, B. (1999b). Social Distance and Other-regarding Behavior in Dictator Games: Comment. *The American Economic Review, 89*(1), 335–339.
Bolton, G. E., & Ockenfels, A. (2000). a Theory of Equity, Reciprocity and Competition. *American Economic Review, 100*, 166–193.
Brown-Kruse, J., & Hummels, D. (1993). Gender Effects in Laboratory Public Goods Contributions: Do Individuals Put Their Money Where Their Mouth Is? *Journal of Economic Behavior and Organization, 22*, 255–267.
Buchanan, J. M. (1975/2000). *The Limits of Liberty: Between Anarchy and Leviathan*. Indianapolis: Liberty Fund.
Camerer, C. F. (2003). *Behavioral Game Theory: Experiments in Strategic Interaction*. Princeton: Princeton University Press.
Camerer, C. F., & Fehr, E. (2002). Measuring Social Norms and Preferences Using Experimental Games: a Guide for Social Scientists. Working paper No. 97. Zürich: Institute for Empirical Research in Economics, University of Zurich.
Castronova, E. (2001). Virtual Worlds: A First Hand Account of Market and Society on the Cyberian Frontier. *CESifo Working Paper, 618*, 1–41.
Castronova, E. (2003). On Virtual Economies. *Game Studies: The International Journal of Computer Game Research, 2*(3). Retrieved from http://gamestudies.org/0302/castronova/
Castronova, E. (2008). a Test of the Law of Demand in Virtual World: Exploring the Petri-Dish Approach to Social Sciences. *CESifo Working Paper, 2355*, 1–23.
CCP Atlas*. (2007, April 17). Loot'n Toot'n Freighters. *EVE Online | EVE Insider | Dev Blog*. Retrieved June 28, 2011, from http://www.eveonline.com/devblog.asp?a=blog&bid=446
CCP Chronotis*. (2010, March 30). The Circle of Life. *EVE Online | EVE Insider | Dev Blog*. Retrieved June 22, 2011, from http://www.eveonline.com/devblog.asp?a=blog&bid=746
CCP Explorer*. (2011, January 23). New PCU Record (63,170). *EVE General Discussion*. Retrieved March 22, 2011, from http://www.eveonline.com/ingameboard.asp?a=topic&threadID=1454845&page=2

CCP Fallout* et al. (2010, March 30). New Dev Blog: The Circle of Life. *EVE Online | EVE Insider | Forums*. Retrieved June 22, 2011, from http://www.eveonline.com/ingameboard.asp?a=topic&threadID=1293612

CCP Fear*. (2008, August 6). Serious Security. *EVE Online | EVE Insider | Dev Blog*. Retrieved June 22, 2011, from http://www.eveonline.com/devblog.asp?a=blog&bid=577

CCP Games. (2011a). End User License Agreement. *EVE Online | Rules & Policies | End User License Agreement*. Retrieved June 20, 2011, from http://www.eveonline.com/pnp/eula.asp

CCP Games. (2011b). Terms of Service. *EVE Online | Rules & Policies | Terms of Service*. Retrieved June 20, 2011, from http://www.eveonline.com/pnp/terms.asp

CCP Games. (2011c). Chat Channels: Rules of Conduct. *EVE Online | Rules & Policies | Chat Channels: Rules of Conduct*. Retrieved June 20, 2011, from http://www.eveonline.com/pnp/chatrules.asp

CCP Games. (2011d). User and Character Name Policy. *EVE Online | Rules & Policies | User And Character Name Policy*. Retrieved June 20, 2011, from http://www.eveonline.com/pnp/namepolicy.asp

CCP Games. (2011e). Reimbursement Policy. *EVE Online* | Rules & Policies | Reimbursement Policy,. Retrieved June 20, 2011, from http://www.eveonline.com/pnp/reimbursment.asp

CCP Games. (2011f). Suspension and Ban Policy. *EVE Online | Rules & Policies | Suspension And Ban Policy*. Retrieved June 20, 2011, from http://www.eveonline.com/pnp/banning.asp

CCP Games. (2011g). Alliance and Corporation Recruitment Center. *EVE Online | EVE Insider | Forums*. Retrieved April 5, 2011, from http://www.eveonline.com/ingameboard.asp?a=channel&channelID=109585

CCP Hellmar* et al. (2003a, June 8). Guns at the Gate. *EVE Online | EVE Insider | Dev Blog*. Retrieved June 22, 2011, a from http://www.eveonline.com/devblog.asp?a=blog&bid=16

CCP Hellmar* et al. (2003b, June 7). CONCORD Deploys Special Ops. *EVE Online | EVE Insider | Dev Blog*. Retrieved June 22, 2011, b from http://www.eveonline.com/devblog.asp?a=blog&bid=15

CCP kieron* et al. (2006, July 3). Bricks, & Brutality, Contracts & Code, and Milestones, Oveur's Blog. *EVE Online | EVE Insider | Forums*. Retrieved June 21, 2011, from http://www.eveonline.com/ingameboard.asp?a=topic&threadID=359879

CCP kieron* et al. (2007, April 17). Freighters, War Costs and Corp Love, A New Dev Blog. *EVE Online | EVE Insider | Forums*. Retrieved June 28, 2011, from http://www.eveonline.com/ingameboard.asp?a=topic&threadID=507760

CCP LeKjart* et al. (2003, June 3). Pks in Secure Areas. *EVE Online | EVE Insider | Dev Blog*. Retrieved June 22, 2011, from http://www.eveonline.com/devblog.asp?a=blog&bid=5

CCP Oveur*. (2006, June 29). Nothing Endures But Change. *EVE Online | EVE Insider | Dev Blog*. Retrieved June 21, 2011, from http://www.eveonline.com/devblog.asp?a=blog&bid=350

CCP Prism X*. (2008, September 26). Icon ID. *EVE Technology Lab*. Retrieved April 15, 2011, from http://www.eve-search.com/thread/882659

CCP Taera* et al. (2008, August 6). New Dev Blog: Serious Security. *EVE Online | EVE Insider | Forums*. Retrieved June 22, 2011, from http://www.eveonline.com/ingameboard.asp?a=topic&threadID=840506

CCP TomB* et al. (2004a, January 15). Alliances and Warfare. *EVE Online | EVE Insider | Dev Blog*. Retrieved March 28, 2011, a from http://www.eveonline.com/devblog.asp?a=blog&bid=114

CCP TomB* et al. (2004b, January 21). Alliances and Warfare Pt. 2. *EVE Online | EVE Insider | Dev Blog*. Retrieved June 20, 2011, b from http://www.eveonline.com/devblog.asp?a=blog&bid=116

Charness, G., & Rabin, M. (2002). Understanding Social Preferences with Simple Tests. *Quarterly Journal of Economics, 117*, 817–869.

Chesney, T., Chuah, S., & Hoffmann, R. (2007). Virtual World Experimentation: A Exploratory Study. *Working Paper, Nottingham University Business School*.

Cole, H., & Griffiths, M. D. (2007). Social Interactions in Massively Multiplayer Online Role-Playing Games. *CyberPsychology & Behavior, 10*(4), 575–583.

Colpe, C., & Schmidt- Biggemann, W. (Eds). (1993). *Das Böse. Eine historische Phänomenologie des Unerklärlichen*. Suhrkamp.

CSM. (2008, May 31). CSM meeting 02–31st May 2008. Retrieved from http://www.eveonline.com/council/transcripts/2008/CSM_Meeting_31_05_2008.pdf

CSM Ankhesentapemkah*. (2008, December 18). Suicide Ganking Part 2. *Suicide Ganking Part 2 – CSMWiki*. Retrieved June 22, 2011, from http://evajobse.net/csmwiki/index.php/Suicide_Ganking_Part_2

CSM, & CCP. (2008, June 23). CSM–CCP Meetings 01–20–23 of June 2008. Retrieved from http://www.eveonline.com/council/transcripts/2008/CSM_CCP_Meetings_20–23_06_2008.pdf

CSM, & CCP Games. (2010, February 20). CSM Meeting with CCP, February 18th to 20th, 2010 Iceland. Retrieved from http://www.eveonline.com/council/transcripts/2010/CSM_CCP_Meetings_18–20_02_2010.pdf

CSM, & CCP Games. (2011, January 13). csm Meeting Minutes – December 2010 Summit. Retrieved from http://www.eveonline.com/council/transcripts/2010/CSM_CCP_Meetings_15–17_12_2010.pdf

Darley, J. M., & Batson, C. D. (1973). From Jerusalem to Jericho: A Study of Situational and Dispositional Variables in Helping Behavior. *Journal of Personality and Social Psychology, 27*, 100–108.

Davidson, D. (1980). *Essays on Actions and Events*. Oxford: Oxford University Press.

de Quervain, D. J. F., Fischbacher, U., Treyer, V., Schelthammer, M., Schnyder, U., Buck, A., & Fehr, E. (2004). The Neural Basis of Altruistic Punishment. *Science, 305*, 1254–1258.

Del ReyII*. (2007, May 31). FRIST T3 DESIGN ... CALDARI. *EVE General Discussion*. Retrieved March 23, 2011, from http://www.eveonline.com/ingameboard.asp?a=topic&threadID=529319&page=1

Denzau, A. T., & North, D. C. (1994). Shared Mental Models: Ideologies and Institutions. *Kyklos, 47*(2), 3–31.

Destiny Corrupted*. (2011, May 21). Suicide Ganking: Solutions? *Crime and Punishment*. Retrieved July 19, 2011, from http://www.eveonline.com/ingameboard.asp?a=topic&threadID=1513761

Diener, E., Fraser, S. C., Beaman, A. L., & Kelem, R. T. (1976). Effects of Deindividuation: Variables on Stealing Among Halloween Trick-or-Treaters. *Journal of Personality and Social Psychology, 33*(2), 178–183.

Doris, J. M. (2002). *Lack of Character: Personality and Moral Behavior.* Cambridge: Cambridge University Press.

Downing, S. (2009). Attitudinal and Behavioral Pathways of Deviance in Online Gaming. *Deviant Behavior, 30,* 293–320.

Downing, L. L., & Johnson, R. D. (1979). Deindividuation and Valence of Cues: Effects on Prosocial and Antisocial Behavior. *Journal of Personality and Social Psychology, 37,* 1532–1538.

Duntley, J. D., & Buss, D. M. (2005). The Evolution of Evil. In A. G. Miller (Ed.), *The Social Psychology of Good and Evil* (pp. 102–123). New York: The Guilford Press.

Eagleton, T. (2010). *On Evil.* New Haven: Yale University Press.

Egenfeldt-Nielsen, S., Smith, J. H., & Tosca, S. P. (2008). *Understanding Video Games: The Essential Introduction.* New York: Routledge.

Elesentra* et al. (2009, May 12). Why Do Pirates Podkill? *Warfare & Tactics.* Retrieved May 17, 2011, from http://www.eve-search.com/thread/1070465/page/1

Elster, J. (1998). Emotions and Economic Theory. *Journal of Economic Literature, 36,* 47–74.

Engelmann, D., & Fischbacher, U. (2002). Indirect Reciprocity and Strategic Reputation Building in An Experimental Helping Game. Working Paper No. 132. Zürich: Institute for Empirical Research in Economics, University of Zurich.

Eriksen, C. (2011, August 9). EVE and the CSM. Interview.

European Central Bank. (2011a, March 15). The ecb's Definition of Euro Area Monetary Aggregates. *ECB: Monetary Aggregates.* Retrieved July 24, 2011, a from http://www.ecb.int/stats/money/aggregates/aggr/html/hist.en.html

European Central Bank. (2011b, March 15). Monetary Aggregates. *ECB: Monetary Aggregates.* Retrieved July 24, 2011, b from http://www.ecb.int/stats/money/aggregates/aggr/html/index.en.html

EVE-history.net. (2007, November 17). Privateer Alliance. *Privateer Alliance – EVE History.* Retrieved June 28, 2011, from http://eve-history.net/wiki/index.php/Privateer_Alliance

EVElopedia. (2011a). About EVE Online. *About EVE Online – EVElopedia – The EVE Online Wiki.* Retrieved March 22, 2011, a from http://wiki.eveonline.com/en/wiki/About_EVE_Online

EVElopedia. (2011b). Piracy Guide. *Piracy Guide – EVElopedia – The EVE Online Wiki.* Retrieved May 17, 2011, b from http://wiki.eveonline.com/en/wiki/Piracy_guide#Ransoming

EVElopedia. (2011c). Ransoming. *Ransoming – EVElopedia – The EVE Online Wiki.* Retrieved May 17, 2011, c from http://wiki.eveonline.com/en/wiki/Ransoming

Falk, A. E., & Fischbacher, U. (2006). a Theory of Reciprocity. *Games and Economic Behavior, 54,* 293–315.

Fehr, E., & Fischbacher, U. (2004). Third Party Punishment and Social Norms. *Evolution and Human Behavior, 25,* 63–87.

Fehr, E., & Gä chter, S. (2000). Cooperation and Punishment in Public Goods Experiments. *American Economic Review, 90*, 980–994.

Fehr, E., & Schmidt, K. M. (1999). a Theory of Fairness, Competition and Co-Operation. *Quarterly Journal of Economics, 114*, 817–868.

Fehr, E., & Schmidt, K. M. (2006). The Economics of Fairness, Reciprocity and Altruism – Experimental Evidence and New Theories. In S. C. Kolm & J. M. Ythier (Eds), *Handbook of the Economics of Giving, Altruism and Reciprocity* (Vol. 1). Amsterdam: Elsevier Science and Technology.

Fliessbach, K., Weber, B., Trautner, P., Dohmen, T., Sunde, U., Elger, E., & Falk, A. E. (2007). Social Comparison Affects Reward-Related Brain Activity in the Human Ventral Striatum. *Science, 318*(5854), 1305–1308.

Foo, C. Y., & Koivisto, E. M. I. (2004). Defining Grief Play in MMORPGs: Player and Developer Perceptions. Presented at the International Conference on Advances in Computer Entertainment Technology ACE, Singapore.

Forsythe, R., Horowitz, J. L., Savin, N. E., & Sefton, M. (1994). Fairness in Simple Bargaining Experiments. *Games and Economic Behavior, 6*, 347–369.

Foucault, M. (1975/1995). *Discipline & Punish: The Birth of the Prison*. (A. Sheridan, Trans.) (2nd edn). New York: Vintage Books.

Frank, R. (1988). *Passions within Reason: The Strategic Role of Emotions*. New York: W. W. Norton & Co.

Frankfurt, H. (1978). The Problem of Action. *American Philosophical Quarterly, 15*, 157–162.

Freud, S. (1930/1994). *Das Unbehagen in der Kultur, und andere kulturtheoretische Schriften* (10th edn). Frankfurt: Fischer.

Frohlich, N., & Oppenheimer, J. (2001). Some Doubts about Measuring Self-Interest Using Dictator Experiments: The Costs of Anonymity. *Journal of Economic Behavior and Organization, 46*, 271–290.

Funder, D. C., & Ozer, D. J. (1983). Behavior as a Function of the Situation. *Journal of Personality and Social Psychology, 44*, 107–112.

Gächter, S., & Falk, A. E. (2002). Reputation and Reciprocity: Consequences for the Labour Relation. *Scandinavian Journal of Economics, 104*, 1–26.

gamerDNA. (2008). Bartle Test of Gamer Psychology. *Bartle Test of Gamer Psychology | gamerDNA*. Retrieved November 27, 2008, from http://www.gamerdna.com/quizzes/bartle-test-of-gamer-psychology

Gigerenzer, G. (2008). Moral Intuition = Fast and Frugal Heuristics? In W. Sinnott-Armstrong (Ed.), *Moral Psychology: The Cognitive Science of Morality: Intuition and Diversity* (Vol. 2). Cambridge, MA: MIT Press.

Gigerenzer, G., Todd, P. M., & The ABC Research Group. (1999). *Simple Heuristics That Make Us Smart*. New York: Oxford University Press.

Greygal*. (2009, December 31). Paid Ransom to Lord Carvin [ID10T], But He Destroyed Me Anyway. *Crime and Punishment*. Retrieved June 21, 2011, from http://www.eveonline.com/ingameboard.asp?a=topic&threadID=1242602

Griffiths, M. D., Davies, M. N. O., & Chappell, D. (2004). Demographic Factors and Playing Variables in Online Computer Gaming. *CyberPsychology & Behavior, 7*(4), 479–487.

Guðmundsson, E. (2007, November 12). Quarterly Economic Newsletter – EVE Online 3rd Quarter 2007. Retrieved from http://www.eveonline.com/devblog.asp?a=blog&bid=518

Guðmundsson, E. (2008a, February 20). Quarterly Economic Newsletter – EVE Online 4th Quarter 2007. Retrieved from http://www.eveonline.com/devblog.asp?a=blog&bid=542

Guðmundsson, E. (2008b, October 16). Quarterly Economic Newsletter – EVE Online 1st Quarter 2008. Retrieved from http://www.eveonline.com/devblog.asp?a=blog&bid=594

Guðmundsson, E. (2009a, November 9). Quarterly Economic Newsletter – EVE Online 3rd Quarter 2009. Retrieved from http://www.eveonline.com/devblog.asp?a=blog&bid=707

Guðmundsson, E. (2009b, June 4). Quarterly Economic Newsletter – EVE Online 1st Quarter 2009. Retrieved from http://www.eveonline.com/devblog.asp?a=blog&bid=665

Guðmundsson, E. (2009c, August 18). Quarterly Economic Newsletter – EVE Online 2nd Quarter 2009. Retrieved from http://www.eveonline.com/devblog.asp?a=blog&bid=686

Guðmundsson, E. (2010a, August 13). The Economics of EVE. Interview.

Guðmundsson, E. (2010b, November 12). War Is the Engine That Drives the Universe. *EVE Online | EVE Insider | Dev Blog*. Retrieved March 24, 2011, b from http://www.eveonline.com/devblog.asp?a=blog&bid=822

Guðmundsson, E. (2010c, February 23). Quarterly Economic Newsletter – EVE Online 4th Quarter 2009. Retrieved from http://www.eveonline.com/devblog.asp?a=blog&bid=734

Guðmundsson, E. (2010d, June 10). Quarterly Economic Newsletter – EVE Online 1st Quarter 2010. Retrieved from http://www.eveonline.com/devblog.asp?a=blog&bid=767

Guðmundsson, E. (2010e, August 10). Quarterly Economic Newsletter – EVE Online 2nd Quarter 2010. Retrieved from http://www.eveonline.com/devblog.asp?a=blog&bid=780

Guðmundsson, E. (2010f, November 12). Quarterly Economic Newsletter – EVE Online 3rd Quarter 2010. Retrieved from http://www.eveonline.com/devblog.asp?a=blog&bid=822

Guðmundsson, E. (2011, April 4). Quarterly Economic Newsletter – EVE Online 4th Quarter 2010. Retrieved from http://www.eveonline.com/devblog.asp?a=blog&bid=892

Güth, W., Schmittberger, R., & Schwarze, B. (1982). An Experimental Analysis of Ultimatum Bargaining. *Journal of Economic Behavior and Organization, 3*, 367–388.

Hare, R. D. (1991). *The Hare Psychopathy Checklist-Revised*. Toronto: Multi-Health Systems.

Hare, R. D. (1999). *Without Conscience: The Disturbing World of the Psychopaths Among Us*. New York: Guilford Press.

HeliosGal*. (2011, January 28). Unnerf the privateer nerf. *EVE General Discussion*. Retrieved June 28, 2011, from http://www.eveonline.com/ingameboard.asp?a=topic&threadID=1458064

Henrich, J., & Smith, N. (2004). Comparative Experimental Evidence From Machiguenga, Mapuche, Huinca, and American Populations. In J. Henrich, R. Boyd, S. Bowles, C. F. Camerer, E. Fehr, & H. Gintis (Eds), *Foundations of human society*. Oxford: Oxford University Press.

Henrich, J., Boyd, R., Camerer, C. F., Fehr, E., & Gintis, H. (2001). In Search of Homo Oeconomicus: Behavioral Experiments in 15 Small-Scale Societies. *American Economic Review, 91*(2), 73–78.

Hinrichsen, H. (2011, August 13). On Darkness and Harshness. Interview.

Hirshleifer, J. (1995). Anarchy and Its Breakdown. *Journal of Political Economy, 103*(1), 26–52.

Hirshleifer, J. (2001a). The Expanding Domain of Economics. In J. Hirshleifer (Ed.), *The Dark Side of the Force: Economic Foundations of Conflict Theory* (pp. 306–341). Cambridge: Cambridge University Press.

Hirshleifer, J. (2001b). *The Dark Side of the Force: Economic Foundations of Conflict Theory*. Cambridge: Cambridge University Press.

Hirshleifer, J. (2001c). The Bioeconomic Causes of War. In J. Hirshleifer (Ed.), *The Dark Side of the Force: Economic Foundations of Conflict Theory* (pp. 25–42). Cambridge: Cambridge University Press.

Hirshleifer, J. (2001d). On the Emotions as Guarantors of Threats and Promises. In J. Hirshleifer (Ed.), *The Dark Side of the Force: Economic Foundations of Conflict Theory* (pp. 198–219). Cambridge: Cambridge University Press.

Hirshleifer, J., & Osborne, E. (2001). Truth, Effort, and the Legal Battle. In J. Hirshleifer (Ed.), *The Dark Side of the Force: Economic Foundations of Conflict Theory* (pp. 131–163). Cambridge: Cambridge University Press.

Hobbes, T. (1651/1998). *Leviathan*. Oxford: Oxford University Press.

Hoffman, E., McCabe, K., & Smith, V. (1996). On Expectations and Monetary Stakes in Ultimatum Games. *International Journal of Game Theory, 25*, 289–301.

Hoffman, E., McCabe, K., Shachat, K., & Smith, V. (1994). Preferences, Property Rights and Anonymity in Bargaining Games. *Games and Economic Behavior, 7*, 346–380.

Holler, M. J., & Illing, G. (2006). *Einführung in die Spieltheorie* (6th edn). Berlin: Springer.

Hreiðarsson, E. S. (2011, August 12). Game Masters in EVE. Interview.

Huggins, M., Haritos- Fatouros, M., & Zimbardo, P. G. (2002). *Violence Workers: Police Torturers and Murderers Reconstruct Brazilian Atrocities*. Berkeley: University of California Press.

Huizinga, J. (1955). *Homo Ludens: A Study of the Play-Element in Culture*. Boston: Beacon Press.

Humphreys, S. (2009). Norrath: New Forms, Old Institutions. *Game Studies: The International Journal of Computer Game Research, 9*(1). Retrieved from http://gamestudies.org/0901/articles/humphreys

Hussain, Z., & Griffiths, M. D. (2008). Gender Swapping and Socializing in Cyberspace: An Exploratory Study. *CyberPsychology & Behavior, 11*(1), 47–53.

Isaac, R. M., & Walker, J. (1987). Success and Failure of the Voluntary Contribution Process: Some Evidence from Experimental Economics. Discussion paper 87–1. Tucson: University of Arizona.

Juul, J. (2003). The Game, the Player, the World: Looking for a Heart of Gameness. In M. Copier & Raessens (Eds), *Level Up: Digital Games Research Conference Proceedings* (pp. 30–45). Utrecht: Utrecht University.

Juul, J. (2005). *Half-Real: Video Games Between Real Rules and Fictional Worlds*. Cambridge, MA: MIT Press.

Kagel, J. H., & Roth, A. E. (Eds). (1995). *The Handbook of Experimental Economics*. Princeton: Princeton University Press.

Kant, I. (1972). *Gesammelte Schriften. Abt. IV: Vorlesungen, Bd. 5, 2. Hälfte, Teilbd. 2. Vorlesungen über Metaphysik und Rationaltheologie*. (Vol. 28). Berlin: Walter de Gruyter.

Kant, I. (1788/1974). *Kritik der praktischen Vernunft. Grundlegung zur Metaphysik der Sitten*. Werkausgabe (Vol. 7). Frankfurt am Main: Suhrkamp.

Kant, I. (1781/2000a). *Kritik der reinen Vernunft 1*. Werkausgabe (14th edn, Vol. 3). Frankfurt am Main: Suhrkamp.

Kant, I. (1781/2000b). *Kritik der reinen Vernunft 2*. Werkausgabe (14th edn, Vol. 4). Frankfurt am Main: Suhrkamp.

Kant, I. (1793/2009). *Religion within the Bounds of Bare Reason*. (W. S. Pluhar, Trans.). Indianapolis: Hackett Publishing.

Kant, I. (1795/2010). *Perpetual Peace: A Philosophical Essay*. New York: Cosimo, Inc.

Kennedy Lincoln*. (2008, October 13). Err....Ok Then. Don't Punk Me. *Crime and Punishment*. Retrieved June 21, 2011, from http://www.eveonline.com/ingameboard.asp?a=topic&threadID=895570

Kjarval, S. J. (2011, August 11). On Cooperation and Conflict In EVE. Interview.

Klink. (2009). World Of Warcraft Player Claims A Bounty On His Head In And Out Of Video Game. *World Of Warcraft Player Claims A Bounty On His Head In And Out Of Video Game | Fun Tech Talk*. Retrieved November 24, 2010, from http://www.funtechtalk.com/world-of-warcraft-player-claims-a-bounty-on-his-head-in-and-out-of-game/

Kolo, C., & Baur, T. (2004). Living a Virtual Life: Social Dynamics of Online Gaming. *Game Studies: The International Journal of Computer Game Research*, *4*(1). Retrieved from http://www.gamestudies.org/0401/kolo/

Konzack, L., & Mayra, F. (2002). Computer Game Criticism: a Method for Computer Game Analysis. *CGDC Conference Proceedings* (pp. 89–100). Tampere University Press. Retrieved from htp://imv.au.dk/~konzack/tampere2002.pdf

Kreps, D. M., & Wilson, R. (1982). Reputation and Imperfect Information. *Journal of Economic Theory, 27*, 253–279.

Lastowka, F. G., & Hunter, D. (2004). The Laws of Virtual Worlds. *California Law Review, 92*(1), 3–73.

Lazear, E. P. (2000). Economic Imperialism. *Quarterly Journal of Economics, 115*(1), 99–146.

Ledyard, J. O. (1995). Public Goods: A Survey of Experimental Research. In J. H. Kagel & A. E. Roth (Eds), *The Handbook of Experimental Economics* (pp. 111–194). Princeton: Princeton University Press.

Lehdonvirta, V. (2010). Virtual Worlds Don't Exist: Questioning the Dichotomous Approach in MMO Studies. *Game Studies: The International Journal of Computer Game Research, 10*(1). Retrieved from http://gamestudies.org/1001/articles/lehdonvirta

Leibniz, G. W. (1710/1996). *Die Theodizee* (5th edn). Suhrkamp Verlag.

Levi, P. (1986/1993). *Die Untergegangenen und die Geretteten*. (M. Kahn, Trans.). München: Deutscher Taschenbuch Verlag.

Levine, D. (1998). Modeling Altruism and Spitefulness in Experiments. *Review of Economic Dynamics, 1*, 593–622.

Lin, H., Sun, C. T., & Tinn, H. H. (2003). Exploring Clan Culture: Social Enclaves and Cooperation in Online Games. *Proceedings of DiGRA 2007*. Presented at the DiGRA Conference 2007, Utrecht: Utrecht University. Retrieved from http://www.digra.org/dl/db/07312.38207.pdf

List, J. A., & Cherry, T. L. (2000). Learning to Accept in Ultimatum Games: Evidence from An Experimental Design That Generates Low Offers. *Experimental Economics, 3*, 11–31.

Locke, J. (1690/1988). The Second Treatise of Civil Government. *Two Treatises of Government* (student edition., pp. 265–428). Cambridge: Cambridge University Press.

Lofgren, E. T., & Fefferman, N. H. (2007). The Untapped Potential of Virtual Game Worlds to Shed Light on Real World Epidemics. *The Lancet Infectious Diseases, 7*, 625–629.

Lona Lwyd*. (2008, April 26). Payed Ransom But Got Killed. *Crime and Punishment*. Retrieved June 21, 2011, from http://www.eveonline.com/ingameboard.asp?a=topic&threadID=758456

Lorenz, K. (1963/1998). *Das sogenannte Böse: Zur Naturgeschichte der Aggression* (26th edn). München: Deutscher Taschenbuch Verlag.

Luminus Mallus*. (2010, July 1). [Proposal] Acceleration Gates and Bookmarks in Pve – Exploration. *Assembly Hall*. Retrieved March 23, 2011, from http://www.eveonline.com/ingameboard.asp?a=topic&threadID=1345967

Mackie, J. (1985). *Persons and Values*. Oxford: Oxford University Press.

Mantzavinos, C. (2001). *Individuals, Institutions, and Markets*. Cambridge University Press.

Mantzavinos, C., North, D. C., & Shariq, S. (2004). Learning, Institutions, and Economic Performance. *Perspectives on Politics, 2*(1), 75–84.

Marshall, A. (1890/2009). *Principles of Economics* (8th edn). New York: Cosimo, Inc.

McKenna, K. Y. A., & Bargh, J. A. (2000). Plan 9 From Cyberspace: The Implications of the Internet for Personality and Social Psychology. *Personality and Social Psychology Review, 4*(1), 57–75.

Meredith, A., Hussain, Z., & Griffiths, M. D. (2009). Online Gaming: A Scoping Study of Massively Multi-Player Online Role Playing Games. *Electronic Commerce Research, 9*(1–2), 3–26.

Merriam-Webster. (2005). Evil. *The Merriam-Webster Dictionary*. Merriam Webster Inc.

Messinger, P. R., Ge, X., Stroulia, E., Lyons, K., Smirnov, K., & Bone, M. (2008). On the Relationship between My Avatar and Myself. *Journal of Virtual Worlds Research, 1*(2). Retrieved from https://journals.tdl.org/jvwr/article/view/352/263

Milgram, S. (1974). *Obedience to Authority*. New York: Harper & Row.

Miller, A. G. (Ed.). (2005). *The Social Psychology of Good and Evil*. New York: The Guilford Press.

Miller, A. G., Gordon, A. K., & Buddie, A. M. (1999). Accounting for Evil and Cruelty: Is to Explain to Condone? *Personality and Social Psychology Review, 3*, 254–268.

MMO Data. (2010a). MMOG Subscriptions with a Peak between 1.000.000 and 12.000.000. *MMO Data*. Retrieved November 11, 2010, a from http://mmodata.net/

MMO Data. (2010b). MMOG Subscriptions with a Peak between 150.000 and 1.000.000. *MMO Data*. Retrieved November 11, 2010, b from http://mmodata.net/

Morningstar, C., & Farmer, F. R. (1991). The Lessons from Lucasfilm's Habitat. In M. Benedikt (Ed.), *Cyberspace: First Steps*. Cambridge, MA: MIT Press.

Murray, M. (2008). Leibniz on the Problem of Evil. (E. N. Zalta, Ed.)*The Stanford Encyclopedia of Philosophy (Fall 2008 Edition)*. Retrieved from http://plato.stanford.edu/archives/fall2008/entries/leibniz-evil/

Nash, J., & Schneyer, E. (2004). Virtual Economies: An In-Depth Look at the Virtual World of Final Fantasy XI: Online. Retrieved from http://lgst.wharton.upenn.edu/hunterd/VirtualEconomies.pdf

Neiman, S. (2004). *Evil in Modern Thought: An Alternative History of Philosophy*. Princeton University Press.

Newman, L. S. (2002). What Is a 'Social-Psychological' Account of Perpetrator Behavior? The Person versus the Situation in Goldhagen's 'Hitler's Willing Executioners.' In L. S. Newman & R. Erber (Eds), *Understanding Genocide: The Social Psychology of the Holocaust* (pp. 43–67). New York: Oxford University Press.

North, D. C. (1990). *Institutions, Institutional Change and Economic Performance*. Cambridge: Cambridge University Press.

North, D. C. (2005). *Understanding the Process of Economic Change*. Princeton: Princeton University Press.

Óskarsson, P. J. (2010). Democracy and the Internet – The Theoretical Foundations and Practical Applications. University of Iceland, Master's thesis.

Precisionist*, & RetardedNeuron*. (2011, May 4). Salvaging as a Pirate. *Crime and Punishment*. Retrieved May 5, 2011, from http://www.eveonline.com/ingameboard.asp?a=topic&threadID=1506292

Rabin, M. (1993). Incorporating Fairness into Game Theory and Economics. *American Economic Review, 83*(5), 1281–1300.

Rabin, M. (1998). Psychology and Economics. *Journal of Economic Literature, 36*, 11–46.

Ross, L. (1977). The Intuitive Psychologist and His Shortcomings. In L. Berkowitz (Ed.), *Advances in Experimental Social Psychology* (Vol. 10, pp. 173–220). New York: Academic Press.

Roth, A. E., & Erev, I. (1995). Learning in Extensive-Form Games: Experimental Data and Simple Dynamic Models in the Intermediate Term. *Games and Economic Behavior, 8*, 164–212.

Roth, A. E., Prasnikar, V., Okuno- Fujiwara, M., & Zamir, S. (1991). Bargaining and Market Behavior in Jerusalem, Ljubljana, Pittsburgh and Tokyo: An Experimental Study. *American Economic Review, 81*, 1068–1095.

Sabini, J., Siepmann, M., & Stein, J. (2001). The Really Fundamental Attribution Error in Social Psychological Research. *Psychological Inquiry, 12*, 1–15.

Salen, K., & Zimmerman, E. (2004). *Rules of Play: Game Design Fundamentals*. Cambridge, MA: MIT Press.

Schelling, T. C. (1960). *The Strategy of Conflict*. London: Oxford University Press.

Schelling, T. C. (1978). Altruism, Meanness, and Other Potentially Strategic Behaviors. *American Economic Review, 68*(2), 229–230.

Schulte, C. (1988). *radikal böse – Die Karriere des Bösen von Kant bis Nietzsche*. München: Wilhelm Fink Verlag.

Schultheiss, D. (2007). Long-Term Motivations to Play Mmogs: a Longitudinal Study on Motivations, Experience and Behavior. *Situated Play, Proceedings of DiGRA 2007 Conference*. Presented at the DiGRA 2007 Conference.

Seinen, I., & Schram, A. (2006). Social Status and Group Norms: Indirect Reciprocity in a Helping Experiment. *European Economic Review, 50*, 581–602.

SkwisgaarSkwigelf*. (2011, April 10). [SKULD] Is Recruiting Players of Any Age Interested In pvp. *Alliance and Corporation Recruitment Center.* Retrieved June 21, 2011, from http://www.eveonline.com/ingameboard.asp?a=topic&threadID=1494450

Slater, M., Antley, A., Davison, A., Swapp, D., Guger, C., Barker, C., Pistrang, N., et al. (2006). A Virtual Reprise of the Stanley Milgram Obedience Experiments. *PLoS ONE, 1*(1), e39. doi:10.1371/journal.pone.0000039

Slonim, R. L., & Roth, A. E. (1998). Learning in High Stakes Ultimatum Games: An Experiment in the Slovak Republic. *Economics of Governance, 66*, 569–596.

Smith, A. (1776/1999). *The Wealth of Nations Books IV–V.* London: Penguin Classics.

Smith, J. H. (2006a). The Games Economists Play – Implications of Economic Game Theory for the Study of Computer Games. *Game Studies: The International Journal of Computer Game Research, 6*(1). Retrieved from http://gamestudies.org/0601/articles/heide_smith

Smith, J. H. (2006b). Tragedies of the Ludic Commons: Understanding Cooperation in Multiplayer Games. *Game Studies: The International Journal of Computer Game Research, 7*(1). Retrieved from http://gamestudies.org/0701/articles/smith

SOFOGA. (2010a). GameStat 2010/I: Repräsentativstudie zu Computer- und Konoslenspielen. *Gamestat: The Social Fabric of Virtual Life.* Retrieved November 16, 2010, a from https://sofoga.uni-hohenheim.de/83372.html

SOFOGA. (2010b). Wie sieht der "typische" Computer- und Videospieler aus? *Die Spieler: The Social Fabric of Virtual Life.* Retrieved November 16, 2010, b from https://sofoga.uni-hohenheim.de/83384.html

SOFOGA. (2010c). Computer- und Videospielen: Ein "soziales" Hobby? *Soziales Spielen: The Social Fabric of Virtual Life.* Retrieved November 16, 2010, c from https://sofoga.uni-hohenheim.de/83382.html

Sosa, E. (2009). Situations against Virtues: The Situationist Attack on Virtue Theory. In C. Mantzavinos (Ed.), *Philosophy of the Social Sciences: Philosophical Theory and Scientific Practice.* Cambridge: Cambridge University Press.

Staub, E. (1999). The Roots of Evil: Personality, Social Conditions, Culture, and Basic Human Needs. *Personality and Social Psychology Review, 3*, 179–192.

Staub, E. (2005). Basic Human Needs, Altruism, and Aggression. In A. G. Miller (Ed.), *The Social Psychology of Good and Evil* (pp. 51–84). New York: The Guilford Press.

Stringham, E. (Ed.). (2005). *Anarchy, State and Public Choice.* Cheltenham: Edward Elgar.

Surreptitious*. (2006, November 25). Privateers & Privateer Alliance. *Alliance and Corporation Recruitement Center.* Retrieved June 28, 2011, from http://www.eveonline.com/ingameboard.asp?a=topic&threadID=431525&page=1

Tangney, J. P., & Stuewig, J. (2005). A Moral-Emotional Perspective on Evil Persons and Evil Deeds. In A. G. Miller (Ed.), *The Social Psychology of Good and Evil* (pp. 327–355). New York: The Guilford Press.

Tooley, M. (2010). The Problem of Evil. (E. N. Zalta, Ed.)*The Stanford Encyclopedia of Philosophy (Spring 2010 Edition)*. Retrieved from http://plato.stanford.edu/archives/spr2010/entries/evil/

Tulathimutte, T. (2010). Trust, Cooperation, and Reputation in Massively Multiplayer Online Games. *Game Research – The Art, Business, and Science of Video Games » Trust, Cooperation, and Reputation in Massively Multiplayer Online Games*. Retrieved November 11, 2010, from http://game-research.com/index.php/articles/trust-cooperation-and-reputation-in-massively-multiplayer-online-games/

Tullock, G. (Ed.). (1972). *Explorations in the Theory of Anarchy*. Blacksburg: Center for Study of Public Choice.

Tullock, G. (Ed.). (1974). *Further Explorations in the Theory of Anarchy*. Blacksburg: Center for Study of Public Choice.

Turbefield, J., & Ó skarsson, P. J. (2011, August 14). The development of EVE. Interview.

Unvisibility*. (2007, October 28). Whats the One Nerf You Wish Never Happened. *EVE General Discussion*. Retrieved June 28, 2011, from http://www.eveonline.com/ingameboard.asp?a=topic&threadID=623701

Verone*. (2007). EVE Guide Making ISK as a Pirate. *EVE Guide Making ISK as a pirate :: Wiki :: EVE Online :: ZAM*. Retrieved May 17, 2011, from http://eve.allakhazam.com/wiki/EVE_Guide_Making_ISK_as_a_pirate

Walther, J. B. (1996). Computer-Mediated Communication: Impersonal, Interpersonal, and Hyperpersonal Interaction. *Communication Research, 23*(1), 3–43.

Wang, C. K. J., Khoo, A., Liu, W. C., & Divaharan, S. (2008). Passion and Intrinsic Motivation in Digital Gaming. *CyberPsychology & Behavior, 11*(1), 39–45.

Welner, M. (1998). Defining Evil: a Depravity Scale for Today's Courts. *Forensic Echo, 2*(6), 4–12.

Wilson, G. (2009). Action. (E. N. Zalta, Ed.)*The Stanford Encyclopedia of Philosophy (Fall 2009) Edition)*. Retrieved from http://plato.stanford.edu/archives/fall2009/entries/action

The World Bank. (2011). *World Development Report 2011. Conflict, Security, and Development*. Washington DC. Retrieved from http://wdr2011.worldbank.org/fulltext

Woodward, J. (2009). Why Do People Cooperate as Much as They Do? In C. Mantzavinos (Ed.), *Philosophy of the Social Sciences: Philosophical Theory and Scientific Practice*. Cambridge: Cambridge University Press.

Yee, N. (2006). The Demographics, Motivations, and Derived Experiences of Users of Massively Multi-User Online Graphical Environments. *Presence: Teleoperators and Virtual Environments, 15*, 309–329.

Yee, N. (2009). Befriending Ogres and Wood-Elves: Relationship Formation and the Social Architecture of Norrath. *Game Studies: The International Journal of Computer Game Research, 9*(1). Retrieved from http://gamestudies.org/0901/articles/yee

Yee, N., & Bailenson, J. (2007). The Proteus Effect: The Effect of Transformed Self-Representation on Behavior. *Human Communication Research, 33*(3), 271–290.

Yee, N., Bailenson, J., Urbanek, M., Chang, F., & Merget, D. (2007). The Unbearable Likeness of Being Digital: The Persistence of Nonverbal Social Norms in Online Virtual Environments. *CyberPsychology & Behavior, 10*(1), 115–121.

Yi, M. (2004, December 18). They Got Game. *SFGate*. San Francisco. Retrieved from http://www.sfgate.com/cgi-bin/article.cgi?f=/chronicle/archive/2004/12/18/MNGUOAE36I1.DTL

yopparai*. (2011, May 17). ASTARTES CORP – NPC Null-Sec Small Gang pvp Corp now Hiring Interns. *Alliance and Corporation Recruitment Center.* Retrieved June 21, 2011, from http://www.eveonline.com/ingameboard.asp?a=topic&threadID=1512438

Zimbardo, P. G. (1976). Making Sense of Senseless Vandalism. In E. P. Hollander & R. G. Hunt (Eds), *Current perspectives in social psychology* (4th edn, pp. 129–134). Oxford: Oxford University Press.

Zimbardo, P. G. (1992). *Quiet rage: The Stanford Prison Experiment.* Academic distribution by Stanford University.

Zimbardo, P. G. (2005). A Situationist Perspective on the Psychology of Evil – Understanding How Good People Are Transformed into Perpetrators. In A. G. Miller (Ed.), *The Social Psychology of Good and Evil* (pp. 21–50). New York: The Guilford Press.

Index

Note: References in **bold** print are used for principal pages, ordinary type for the rest.

The manufacturer's authorised representative in the EU is Springer Nature Customer Service Centre GmbH, Europaplatz 3, 69115 Heidelberg, Germany. If you have any concerns regarding our products, please contact ProductSafety@springernature.com

Printed and bound by CPI Group (UK) Ltd, Croydon, CR0 4YY
14/10/2026
02233138-0008